Image Formation
and Psychotherapy

Image Formation and Psychotherapy

Revised Edition of
Image Formation
and Cognition

Mardi Jon Horowitz, M.D.

Jason Aronson, Inc.
New York and London

Credits

Portions of Chapter 10 were published in the paper "Visual Imagery on Brain Stimulation," coauthored with John E. Adams, M.D., and Burton Rutkin, Arch Gen Psychiat 19:469, 1968. The research work was supported by research grants from the US Public Health Service (VRA: RD-2211-P and RD-1225-M).

Portions of Chapter 11 were published in Amer J Psychiat 126:565, 1969, copyright 1969 by the American Psychiatric Association, and are reproduced by permission.

Portions of Chapter 12 were published in Amer J Psychiat 123:789, 1975, copyright 1975 by the American Psychiatric Association, and are reproduced by permission.

Library of Congress Cataloging in Publication Data

Horowitz, Mardi Jon, 1934-
  Image formation and psychotherapy.

  Rev. ed. of: Image formation and cognition.
2nd ed. c1978.
  Bibliography.
  Includes indexes.
  1. Imagery (Psychology) 2. Cognition.
3. Imagery (Psychology)—Therapeutic use.
4. Art therapy. I. Title.
BF367.H67 1983   153.3'2   83-2597
ISBN 0-87668-636-6

Manufactured in the United States of America.

*To Nancy
with love*

CONTENTS

PREFACE

The nature of image formation is relevant to any study of thinking and emotion, and so to the conduct of psychotherapy. A short example can illustrate the important issues. A man chased by a lion will retain an image of the lion rather than looking over his shoulder to remind himself why he is running. The image has information derived from perception, which in turn motivates continued action for escape. Much later, after this frightening event, the man might relive his experience as an intrusive image. If he misinterpreted the intrusive image as a perception, he might once again run in terror. This time the image would be maladaptive: others seeing his strange action would regard his behavior as deviant. This simple instance contains the three classic issues of image formation: when are images useful, how do we differentiate internal images from perceptions, and how do we control image formation? In psychotherapy, images are sometimes useful to full expression of ideas and feelings, to forming new and creative solutions to conflicts, and to altering the balance of controls in the direction of greater personal freedom.

While image formation was a major topic of research in both academic psychology and psychoanalysis at the turn of the century, the field was virtually deserted after World War I. During the next decades, experimental cognitive research was carried out by sparse numbers of investigators who generally worked in isolation, and whose papers met with little interest. In psychoanalysis and dynamic psychotherapy there was a growing interest in the functions of the ego, with special emphasis on the defensive aspects of thought processes, perception, and the regulation of emotion. Even in psychoanalytic theory, however, there was less interest in dream thinking and comparatively greater emphasis on thought in words as it emerged in the course of free associations during a session.

In the last twenty years there has been an upsurge of interest in cognitive studies. Paradoxically, we discovered how little we know about thought and how incomplete our theories are.

My own studies of image formation began in 1959 at the Langley Porter Neuropsychiatric Institute when I was confronted with the problem every clinician faces: how to communicate verbally with withdrawn and mute psychotic patients. Realizing that communication need not necessarily be verbal, and bringing into play an interest in painting, I began using "art therapy." But instead of analyzing what the patient drew, I decided to be a participant-observer, to enter into the processes of graphic communication; in effect, to send messages as well as receive them. Often I saw how a patient would struggle, both with and against his image experiences, and I was confronted by a problem central to image formation: self-control over thoughts.

Later, as a psychotherapist and psychoanalyst I was again impressed by this formidable phenomenon: deep motives, early and repressed memories, and new ideas or feelings emerged not only in dreams and fantasies but in spontaneous or even intrusive images emerging "on the spot" during my patient's free associations. Once again, these images sometimes seemed strange, alien, even meaningless to the very person who generated their formation; they were like "messages from the unconscious" which were often in symbolic code, and not always easy to decipher.

The book is organized into four sections. The first part is designed to introduce a working vocabulary, and to describe the wide range of image experiences, and the circumstances that are likely to increase such experiences. Since the focus of this book is the subjective experience of images, this beginning with phenomenology is appropriate.

The second part deals with psychodynamic influences on image formation, and begins with a review of early concepts of the role of the image in thought. Then I present a model of how images relate to other aspects of thought representation. A brief review of the psychodynamic view of image formation and the problem of control over image formation follows. Three case histories explain unbidden images and illustrate in some detail the psychodynamic meaning of image experiences presented elsewhere through short vignettes.

The third section of the book concerns neurobiologic influences over image formation and directs attention to the physical factors that change conscious experience.

The fourth and final section of the book is on the therapeutic uses of images.

ACKNOWLEDGMENTS

I am grateful for the opportunity to conduct research provided by the Research Career Award Program of the National Institute of Mental Health. The encouragement and support of everyone associated with that program, especially Bert Boothe, was of lasting value to me. I am also very thankful for specific research project grants from the National Institute of Mental Health, the Office of Naval Research, Mount Zion Hospital and Medical Center, the Chapman Research Fund, and the research fund of the American Psychoanalytic Association. I thank the staff of Oakland Naval Hospital, Mount Zion Medical Center, and the Langley Porter Psychiatric Institute of the University of California for offering support and facilities.

My debts to individuals are numerous and include many more than the few I mention. I must cite Jurgen Ruesch, Enoch Callaway, Edward Weinshel, Harold Sampson, Emanuel Windholz, Robert Wallerstein, Jerome Singer, Sydney Segal, Jack Arlow, Morton Reiser, George Mahl, Jack Block, Leo Goldberger, Ernest Haggard, and George Klein who have all helped me with provocative discussion and advice.

In addition I want to thank those who carefully read all or part of the manuscript: Leo Goldberger for a complete and critical reading; Adrienne Applegarth and Daniel Greenson for suggestions on the chapters concerning clinical theory; Robert Byrne and Nancy Wilner for editorial advice as well as the personal encouragement of a friend, and Stephanie Scharf Becker, whose concern for clarity forced me to rethink relevant problems. For excellent secretarial work I thank Marilyn Jones and

Phyllis Cameron, who with good humor typed illegible drafts. Jordan Horowitz, Leigh Lachman, and Peter Armetta helped to compile the references found at the end of each chapter.

I also wish to thank my patients and friends who over the years shared with me their innermost thoughts and feelings. To sufficiently thank my wife, Nancy, for her constant encouragement, comments, and faith is indeed difficult, and by dedicating this work to her, I hope to express at least a part of my deep gratitude. Finally, I thank my children Ariana, Jordan, and Joshua for cheering me on.

Part I

Phenomenology of Image Formation

1

IMAGES AND IMAGE FORMATION

Any thought representation that has a sensory quality we call an image. Images can involve the senses of seeing, hearing, smell, taste, touch, and movement; but since my focus is on visual images, I use the word "image" for mental contents that have a *visual* sensory quality (unless otherwise indicated). While "image" refers to a specific experience, "imagery" refers to different types of image experience collectively.

A person can describe an image in many ways, including information about contents, vividness, clarity, color, shading, shapes, movement, foreground and background characteristics, and other spatial relationships. Furthermore a person can often tell how the image entered his awareness, its duration, associated emotions, the relationship of the image to objects in the external world, efforts to change or dispel it, and the sequential or simultaneous arrangement of a series of images.

While people can describe image *contents*, they are usually unaware of all the underlying processes or motives which go into image *formation*. Neurobiologic and psychologic explanations can elaborate how and why a given image appears, in a particular person, at a particular time. While neurobiologists focus on the anatomic and physiologic substrates as causes, psychologists focus on the cognitive use, psychodynamic meaning, and motivational aspects of image formation. These two approaches interrelate but in a complicated and ambiguous manner since the two bodies of theory developed from extremely different types of observations and methods. At present, neither approach alone or in combination will fully explain an image experience. But it is useful to retain the conceptual distinctions between "image" and "image formation" and the need for both psychologic and biologic explantions.

DOES ONE "SEE" AN IMAGE?

Philosophers, faced with the logical problem of seeing something that is not there and not seeing something that is there, have labored over conceptual models of what constitutes "seeing" and how seeing relates to belief and knowledge.[4] By definition, to see is to perceive with the eye. Unfortunately the verb "to see" is commonly used to describe both external perceptions and internal visual representations; what often results is confusion about both events and their relationship to each other.[1,3] People can agree that they see a tree in the yard or a car on the road, but they agree much less on whether they all see a mirage, an illusion, or a hallucination. To avoid ambiguity, and the questionable application of "to see," I shall use a less misleading vocabulary. When I mean an image is produced within the psychic system, I shall use the verb "to form" as in, "he formed an image of a vase." When I mean an image is derived directly from external visual stimuli, I shall use the verb "to perceive" as in "he perceived a vase." When I use "to see," as in quoting a patient's report, I shall try to do so in a clear context by describing the degree of vividness, the sense of localization, the sense of reality, and the presence or absence of corresponding external objects.

The word "image" is also problematic because, in its root meaning, it means "replica."[2] It is important to remember that images are not merely imitations, but memory fragments, reconstructions, reinterpretations, and symbols that stand for objects, feelings, or ideas. To avoid confusion, the word "image" in this text will never refer to external replicas but only to mental representations.

REFERENCES

1. Sarbin TR: The concept of hallucination. J Pers 35:359, 1967
2. ———, Juhasz JB: Toward a theory of imagination. J Pers 38(1):52, 1970
3. ———, Juhasz JB: The social context of hallucinations. In Siegel RK, West LJ (eds): Hallucinations: Behavior, Experience, and Theory. New York, Wiley, 1975
4. Soltis JF: Seeing, Knowing and Believing: A Study of the Language of Visual Perception. Reading, Mass, Addison-Wesley, 1966

2

TYPES OF IMAGES

In order to approach the psychology of image formation with a meaningful grasp on a variety of experiences, I have grouped the different types of images into four categories (Table 2-1). The categories stem from four different approaches to an image experience. That is, one can emphasize an image's vividness, its context, the influence of perception on the internal image, or image contents, depending on what he thinks is the most relevant aspect of the image experience. Relevance depends on the interpretation one makes of the image for that person at that time. While later chapters will discuss the theory and reasons for how we choose to label an image, (ie, how an observer determines what part of the image he wishes to emphasize), this chapter will define and explain clinical terminology, as well as provide a brief overview of the issues related to the general categories.

The clinician should be familiar with the following classification and phenomenology of images because an understanding of the variety of image experiences is important in inquiry about complaints and worries that patients report in evaluation and psychotherapy sessions. Image episodes are often kept private rather than reported in social circumstances and so are hard to describe in words. Individuals may think a relatively common experience is unique to them, and possibly the first sign of impending madness or at least loss of control over mental functions.

Appropriate recognition and labeling of such episodes, including sensitive questioning that leads to clarification of the experience, is in and of itself a quite supportive technique in psychotherapy. The clinician's ability

5

Table 2-1
Categories and Types of Images

Images Categorized by Vividness
1. Hallucination
2. Pseudohallucination
3. Thought image
4. Unconscious image

Images Categorized by Context
1. Hypnagogic or hypnopompic image
2. Dream image; nightmare
3. Psychedelic image
4. Flashback
5. Flickering image

Images Categorized by Interaction with Perceptions
1. Illusion
2. Perceptual distortion
3. Synesthesia
4. Déjà vu
5. Negative hallucination
6. After-image

Images Categorized by Content
1. Memory image; eidetic image
2. Imaginary image
3. Entoptic image
4. Body image; body schema experience
5. Phantom limb
6. Paranormal hallucination
7. Imaginary companion
8. Number and diagram forms

to distinguish reality from fantasy beliefs about the image experienced reduces secondary anxiety which may be a pronounced portion of the syndrome picture. It also gives the patient confidence that he is being treated by a person who expertly understands psychologic experiences. Inquiry may usefully include questions about the state of mind in which the image experience is contained, with careful attention to trigger contexts and degree of reflective self-control (volition) over onset and continuation of images.

IMAGES CATEGORIZED BY VIVIDNESS

Man dwells in fantasy as well as in reality, and the problem is knowing the difference between the two realms. Sometimes images are mistaken for perceptions, sometimes perceptions seem imaginary. The correct separation of the two sources of information depends to a large extent on the degree of vividness of the experience. As internal images become more vivid, they are more likely to be localized as external and appraised as real. Because such errors are frequent among persons in states of psycho-pathology, the vividness of an image is a central clinical issue. The descriptions below range from most to least vivid.

Hallucinations

A hallucination is an image of internal origin that seems as real, vivid, and external as the perception of an object.* The episode is almost invariably regarded as an involuntary experience rather than a thought process. Hallucinations occur in any sensory modality. Schizophrenics, for example, report auditory hallucinations more frequently than visual hallucinations. Not all hallucinations are unpleasant, and some persons derive great comfort from, even respond ecstatically to, their visions. Hallucinations occur in any state of consciousness, including full wakefulness.

"Hallucination" is a slippery term and, as Sarbin[22] points out, subject to misapplication. One problem is that there are few words or phrases which distinguish perceptions of external objects from images that exist only in the mind. A person who states, "I saw my mother," does not clearly indicate whether he (1) perceived his mother, (2) mistook a woman on the street for his mother, (3) conjured up an internal image of his mother, or (4) hallucinated his mother. In ordinary communication we escape difficulty by adding descriptive statements or asking questions. Unfortunately, persons with psychiatric disturbances frequently have such disordered communication that it may be impossible for a patient to elaborate on a statement like, "I saw my mother."[21]

Descriptive difficulties also occur in psychiatric diagnoses. The common association of hallucinatory symptoms with psychotic episodes, especially schizophrenia and toxic psychosis, leads to some erroneous conclusions. Persons who hallucinate tend to be diagnosed as having a psychosis, although normal persons can also have hallucinations. Bereaved persons, for example, sometimes hallucinate the deceased as part of a grief reaction that is not psychotic. On the other hand, persons who appear psychotic and report *images* may be misdescribed as having

---

* By the strict definition proposed by Esquirol in 1838[30] an experience is hallucinatory only when it appears to be real without any immediate contribution from external perception. If there is a real perceptual contribution, even if it is very distorted in the image formation process, then the experience is labeled illusion rather than hallucination. In actual practice, however, a person who has extreme illusions, especially if the distortions persist, is often said to be hallucinating.

hallucinations. Proper assessment of hallucinations can be made only after extended and clear descriptions.

Pseudohallucination

The distinction between pseudohallucinations and hallucinations, on the one hand, and between pseudohallucinations and thought images, on the other hand, is attributed to Kandinski[15] and was reexamined by Sedman.[26] Frequently, there is a clinical "in-between" type of phenomenon in which images are very vivid yet lack the sense of reality found in hallucinations. Some patients may oscillate between hallucinations and pseudohallucinations or between pseudohallucinations and thought images. While not subjectively localized in the external environment or, if projected externally, not possessing a sense of reality, pseudohallucinations have a more intense and compelling quality than thought images. Perhaps a useful criterion is the reaction of the subject: even though the person does not believe what he images is real, and even though the images differ in quality from an actual perception, he nonetheless reacts to them emotionally as if they were real. Perhaps this emotional reaction is closely related to the common quality of pseudohallucinations: they seem to occur contrary to the actions of the will and do not dissipate at once in spite of efforts to dispel them.[13] A pseudohallucination might be described like this:

> I get this fantastic image of my mother with a green snake coiled around her neck. It's choking her. So lifelike and in color; I know it is just in my mind, but I get terrified. I get it every night now; I wish I could make it go away. I can get myself to think of it now, but it's not the same as at night. Now it's scary but not so bright or frightening.

Thought Image

A thought image is an ordinary ingredient of mental life. Vividness may range from relatively weak to very clear, but by definition thought images are always localized internally. Content ranges from fantasy to visualizations of logical problems in geometry. Poetry, for example, frequently calls forth a succession of vivid thought images.

Memory of images is sometimes inaccurate. An episode of image experience may be appraised as a "thought image" when it occurs, but the memory of the episode, reviewed later, may be appraised as if the image derived from perception. This could be a "retrospective hallucination" or simply an error in memory. In some states of consciousness, memory is so impaired that such errors of retrospective appraisal are frequent.

Unconscious Image

For the sake of completeness, I include a term that the reader may come across in psychoanalytic literature, the unconscious image. This seems to be a contradiction in terms: if an image is unconscious, how is it experienced as an image? Psychoanalytic theory assumes that an unconscious image was once conscious but, because of its involvement in psychologic conflict, is deliberately "forgotten" through the process known as repression.[7] Though the unconscious image (perhaps expressive of a fantasy) may be inhibited from awareness, we assume that it may nonetheless influence thought and behavior.

These four types of imagery, contrasted above by degree of vividness, are also distinguished by other factors as illustrated in Table 2-2. The

Table 2-2
Distinguishing Hallucination, Pseudohallucination,
Thought Image, and Unconscious Image by Several Criteria

Event	Usual Vividness	Usual Subjective Localization	Objective Localization	Sense of Reality
Hallucination	great	extrapsychic	intrapsychic	seems real
Pseudo-hallucination	great to moderate	extra-or intrapsychic	intrapsychic	seems unreal (but may behave "as if" real)
Thought image	moderate to dim	intrapsychic	intrapsychic	seems like memory or imagination
Unconscious image	none	none	repressed memory storage	presence is denied

table presents only generalizations, and a specific experience may oscillate from moment to moment on any factor.

IMAGES CATEGORIZED BY CONTEXT

The context in which one forms an image is another important issue in explanations of psychodynamics and psychopathology. Suppose a person reports what we determine to be a hallucination. We would be alarmed if that person were a surgeon who experienced the event during an operation, or a jet pilot during a landing approach, or a carpenter at his lathe. If, on the other hand, the person hallucinated while falling asleep, or while on a drug, we might more readily accept the report as within the realm of normal experience. The various labels defined below attempt to make an image experience understandable by describing the context of occurrence.

Hypnagogic or Hypnopompic Images

A hypnagogic image is one that occurs in the twilight state between wakefulness and sleep; hypnopompic images are exactly the same but occur while waking up. Because these experiences can be extremely vivid and seem real, they are sometimes called hypnagogic hallucinations. On the other hand, the experiences may also be pseudohallucinations or thought images. Hypnagogic images are characterized by a sense of nonvolitional control over contents and tend to progress from logical thought to fantasy. Figures 2-1 through 2-3 are drawings by an artist of his flow of nonhallucinatory hypnagogic images.

Here is an example of a verbal report:

Customarily as I drift off to sleep I find a succession of visual experiences. When I close my eyes I see darkness but then it lightens to gray. Next I see colored lights and sometimes very complex geometric forms that dance, rotate, or sparkle about. Soon a succession of images of people and scenes parades before me. I find these quite interesting and often go to sleep while watching them. At times, however, I get vivid hallucinations which may frighten me awake. For instance, once all of a sudden I saw a spider on my pillow; another time a crab. They were ugly and scary and caused me to start up in bed thinking they were real. Within seconds I knew them to be hallucinations—still, I had to wait several long seconds after waking up for them to fade.

The Isakower[10] phenomenon is a particular type of hypnagogic image which is a visual sensation of large approaching masses. Isakower suggests that the image contents may be memory images of the mother's breasts or face.*

Dream Images; Nightmares

Nightly dreams are largely visual experiences. Recent sleep research has demonstrated that most persons dream about five times a night during cycles of rapid eye movement sleep (REMS). REMS means a state of activated brain activity as manifested by the electroencephalogram and rapid eye movements during the sleeping period. If persons are awakened during REMS, they are very likely to report a dream-like experience, an experience of visual quality. If they are awakened out of non-REM sleep, they may report thoughts but these are less frequently in visual form.[2]

Example of a dream report from a REM awakening:

> I was riding with a guy on the back of a motorcycle. I was in my new blue dress, he was dressed all in black. Then suddenly we were sitting in my back yard eating a lot of stuff spread out on a blanket. In the next scene there were a bunch of letters on a sign or something but I couldn't see them well enough to know what it said.

Example of a report from a non-REM awakening:

> Thinking of going on a picnic tomorrow. What food to buy. That's all.

Nightmares are a special form of dream. Ordinarily we define a nightmare as a dream which is very unpleasant. There is, however, a relatively common cluster of experiences that constitute the classic nightmare. The three elements, as described by Jones,[14] are: (1) frightening visual images, (2) associated feelings of paralysis, and (3) smothering sensations. A typical nightmare:

> A terrible devil sat on my chest and glowered at me with burning red eyes. I couldn't get the strength to stir, my hands couldn't clench, and I felt like I

---

* Lewin[16-18] suggests that memory images of the white (brown, or yellow) expanse of the mother's face or breasts might be revived as sleep approaches because of the similarity of the state to falling asleep while sucking. The images then serve as a "dream screen" onto which other images are projected.

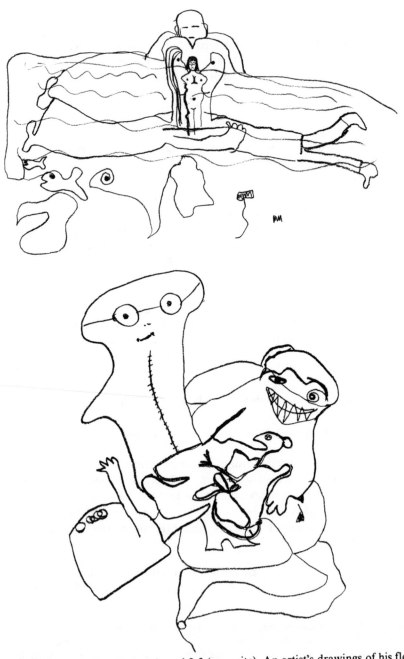

Figs. 2-1 (above), 2-2 (below), and 2-3 (opposite). An artist's drawings of his flow of hypnagogic images.

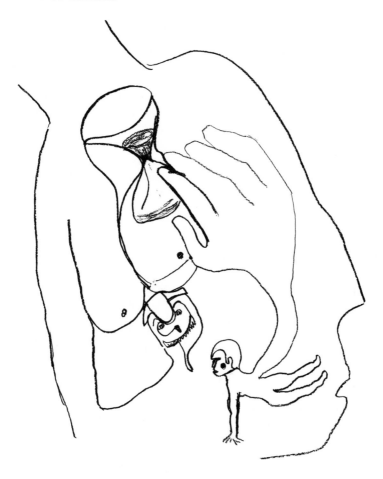

couldn't breathe. Next I was being pursued by the devil, I was running as if through molasses—so slow but I just couldn't move any faster although I was desperate. I awoke just before he got me, sobbing with fright, still with the feeling of being unable to get my breath, and with my heart throbbing.

The resemblance of dreaming to the waking experience of hallucinations has led to various versions of a release hypothesis. According to such hypotheses, hallucinations are dreams released in the daytime due to some pathologic processes.

Psychedelic Images

Hallucinogenic drugs (such as LSD) frequently produce a kind of image, often of hallucinatory quality, that is rare in the ordinary experience of most persons. A psychedelic image experience often begins with unusual perceptions such as fluorescent colors or scintillating effects, and progresses on to development of intense visual thought images, illusions, pseudohallucinations, or true hallucinations.[27] The content often seems novel, weird, and compelling—accompanied not infrequently by a sense of uncanny and even mystical meaningfulness. Sometimes a visionary sense of "knowing" or symbolic synthesis remains after the drug has worn off, although the actual images experienced may be forgotten.[6] The contents and form are not unique to drug hallucinations since similar phenomena are reported during delirium caused by fever, starvation, or trances.

Example of a psychedelic image:

> First I was disappointed, the cube (LSD) wasn't going to give me any effect. Then I noticed a particular halo of light surrounding the dark head of my trip guide. I shut my eyes and saw a kaleidoscope of scintillating colors streaming endlessly in fantastically complex and reduplicated shapes. I was startled, opened my eyes and saw the pattern, ever changing on the wall. Then there was a parade of images and images within images, a whole world of pictures which I can scarcely recall. I do remember one where everyone was garbed in color with black dots like a butterfly. We were perched on the edge of a hill, by a tree, overlooking a deep blue valley. We had butterfly wings and were proud beings from the unknown future. I knew I could fly upwards and upwards with the greatest of confidence.

Flashback

Images formed during a drug-induced state may be reexperienced repeatedly after the drug has worn off. The terms flashback, flashing, and throwback are "hippie" slang and refer to the subjective sensation of unbidden returns of visual images first formed during the drug intoxication but later repeated long after the drugs have worn off. A secondary meaning is that the image is a repetition of a perception long past.

> A man with bat wings, swooping down onto me. I just get it anytime now—over and over again. Maybe a little more when I'm high on pot. It happened as part of my acid trip—that bat man really scared me too. And it was with

a whole bunch of other things. Now it just comes into my mind anytime, the flashback. It scared me at first; now I'm used to it, but I can't make it happen and I can't make it stop.

Flickering Images

The experience known as flickering images consists of a rapid succession of images which intrude upon awareness and are difficult to remember. Physical stress usually precedes the experience, which may occur in a state of fatigue but not necessarily drowsiness. Consciousness takes on a dreamlike state but without disruption of ongoing emotion or behavior. Forbes[5] coined the term, "dream scintillations," and postulated the cause to be transient, local circulatory disturbances. Saul[23] noted that both his own experiences and those reported by Forbes immediately followed strenuous physical activity. I have suggested revising the term to "flickering images" since the person is not asleep and hence not dreaming, and also because the event could be a transient change in consciousness due to a minor variant of temporal lobe epilepsy or migraine.[9]

Here is a detailed account of a single episode of flickering images.

I was walking quietly, thinking nothing in particular, about half an hour after a strenuous swim in unusually cold water. I noticed the gradual development of a bilateral, right-sided blurring of vision. Form could not be distinguished clearly although there was only a mild diminution in illumination. Next I began to have the sensation of a rapid succession of visual images in my mind's eye, but I could not retain or recapture them. I was anxious about the visual impairment but had undiminished volitional control over my actions. I was unable either to block out these images or to decipher their meaning. It seemed that these flickering images caused me to feel queasy and vaguely nauseated. They lasted about one half hour. I was able to "think around them" in verbal thought but only with effort and with a very short concentration span.

The images were sometimes colored. They did not resemble delayed after-images, as might have occurred from light reflections off wave forms in the water. At times they were images of recognizable objects such as faces, fragments of landscape, et cetera. Even when I recognized what the brief images were, however, they seemed to have no relationship to those that immediately preceded or followed them. These images were located in my mind. I never had the feeling that they were real. Although I was anxious, the images did not have affective charge other than the queasy feeling.

IMAGES CATEGORIZED BY
INTERACTION WITH PERCEPTION

The third important feature for persons assessing image reports, in addition to degree of vividness and context, is concern for an interaction of the image contents with perception, and the possible motives for such contamination. For example, if a person reports an illusionary image, we are concerned with how closely his subjective experience resembled the objects perceived. We infer that psychologic motives are different when a person mistakes a nearby policeman in uniform for his father and when he mistakes a distant bird for an airplane.

Illusion

An illusion occurs when a perceiver transforms stimuli until they resemble something other than the external object. The experience is subjective, often vivid, localization is external, and usually there is at least a brief sense of reality.

Illusions are common in everyday life and more common in certain mental states such as fear or anticipation. Inattentiveness, boredom, and fatigue increase the incidence, but in such cases the illusion is quickly dispelled by heightened or focused attentiveness. Many illusions apply a learned schemata; for example when proofreading a manuscript the reader may see words spelled correctly when there is an error. Illusions are not always experienced as a surprise. Many children (and adults) spend hours deliberately making images out of clouds, cracks in the ceiling, or the wandering patterns of wood grain.

Does the above definition of "illusion" include mirages? Since several persons may consensually validate seeing a mirage, this might disqualify it as an illusion. But a mirage may or may not be an illusion, depending upon how distant the subjective experience is from the shared optical sensations. On a desert or ocean, for example, certain atmospheric conditions may lead to strange shapes of light and form that can actually be photographed—seeing these "mirages" is an actual perception. If, however, the person believes that he sees "the minarets of the lost city of Atlantis," then this experience may be labeled an illusion.

Perceptual Distortions

Perceptual distortions include changes in shape, size, shimmerings, apparent bendings of actual straight lines, and altered color experiences.

Sometimes vertical objects appear tilted or even inverted; stationary objects may have apparent movement. These may appear during auras of persons with epilepsy or migraine headache, during drug intoxications, and as flashbacks after prolonged or repeated use of hallucinogens.* In states of fatigue, people commonly experience perceptual distortion. Here are two examples:

> I didn't drop any acid (take LSD) for a week after the twelfth trip (LSD experience). But things went on—like I'd see blue as a fantastic electrical radiance. And sometimes I'd be looking at a seam or a line between walls and the line would kinda vibrate or collapse, bend in on itself.

> During the preliminary phase before my migraines I know they are inevitable because everything appears very tiny and far away (*micropsia*). The shapes are quite distinct, not any dimmer; everything just shrinks up.

Distortions in perception are often present as part of a syndrome of image events in psychiatric or neurologic patients. That is, a patient may, during an acute phase of illness, describe various events that are categorized separately as hallucinations, illusions, pseudohallucinations, and perceptual distortions. Sometimes a disintegrative episode begins with perceptual distortions and, as the condition deteriorates, advances to hallucinations.

Synesthesias

Synesthesias are blends of images from more than one mode of representation. For example, images from one sense are translated into images from another sense giving an unusual quality to immediate experience. Synesthesia is most commonly reported as "color hearing." That is, auditory stimuli are imaged in both auditory and in visual form, usually as a sensation of changing colors. The movie *Fantasia* and light shows with rock music give an external version of this internal phenomenon. Some persons always experience their thoughts synesthetically or invariably translate perceptions in one sense into images of another sense. Usually, however, the synesthetic experience is episodic rather than constant and persons who are not used to it may become startled when they experience a synesthesia.

---

*Visual perceptual distortions, such as changes in contour, size, tilt, color, or movement, are called metamorphosias by neurologists. For a detailed description of the variety of this phenomenon, see Willinger and Klee.[29]

An example of a constant type of synesthesia:

Everything I hear has a color—nouns, music, and numbers especially. For example, whenever I hear the name "Marsha" I see a green blob on the left of my mind and a yellow blob on the right, the edges are ragged. Marsha is always green and yellow. Also, when I hear music I think I get about the same color patterns every time I hear the record. Every number has its own color, always the same, and when you tell me the numbers, I hear you but see the colors too, the colors help me remember.

Déjà Vu Experiences

Mention of this type of experience seems desirable although the experience is perhaps more one of mood or interpretation than images. A déjà vu experience consists of seeing a new situation as one that repeats a past experience when actually this is not true. The déjà vu experience is not restricted to visual perception but, when it does involve perception, it is a particular kind of illusion: an illusion of familiarity rather than misinterpretation of form.

As I entered the hospital room I had the uncanny sensation that I had seen all these things before, that I had this entire same experience at some previous time. Yet I had never before set foot in this particular hospital. Seeing the bed and the hanging curtains seemed especially meaningful in terms of this sensation of memory. For a moment I felt as if I were unreal and transformed into some other time dimension.

Déjà vu phenomena, like many of the visual experiences described in this chapter, may occur in full wakefulness in healthy persons. It occurs more frequently during stress, altered states of consciousness, psychedelic experiences, and the auras of epileptic seizures.

Other special feeling tones that may accompany visual perceptions include *depersonalization* or *derealization*. Depersonalization occurs when perception of the physical self is dislocated from the concept of personal identity. An example occurs when a person believes a part of his body belongs to someone else. Children at times delight in playful mimicry of this experience as when the hands are crossed and fingers move in apparently strange ways. Derealization occurs when current experience seems in some way no longer real. In terms of perceptual experience, there may be illusions of distance, graying, diminishing of visual intensity, or loss of three-dimensional quality. There may be confusion of image and perception, self and other, reality and fantasy. An extreme and very special form of derealization is the negative hallucination.

Negative Hallucinations

Negative hallucinations might have been considered under vividness along with hallucinations proper. Instead they are considered under this, the perceptual dimension, because negative hallucinations consist of not seeing something which is within the field of vision. This is a rarely reported phenomenon, because clinical interviewers are unfamiliar with the experience, seldom ask about it, and because patients would find this type of experience most difficult to notice or describe.

Sometimes very mild versions of negative hallucinations occur in everyday life. For example, one may be looking for some object, look right at it, but yet not consciously see it. Some positive hallucinations and illusions involve an aspect of negative hallucination: the real stimuli of perception are omitted from conscious representation and replaced by internal images. Relatively discrete negative hallucinations can apparently be produced in hypnotic trances and through the use of posthypnotic suggestion as illustrated by the following example:

> During a hypnotic trance the subject was told firmly that he would be unable to see Dr. Jones, an observer, even after being awakened from the hypnotic trance. If he looked directly at Dr. Jones, the suggestion continued, he would see right through him. In order to end the posthypnotic effect, the subject was told that this "not seeing" would end after he counted to ten.
> The subject was then awakened and chatted normally with the hypnotist. When asked if he could see Dr. Jones, he said he could not. When asked what he saw on the chair Dr. Jones occupied, the subject insisted the chair was empty. The hypnotist then asked the subject, since the chair was empty, would he please go sit on it. The subject got up to comply but then walked around the room. He was asked why he refused to sit on the chair. The subject replied, "It looks too uncomfortable." Next, the suggestion was terminated by asking the subject to count to 10. He then reacted in a startled manner saying Dr. Jones was now in the chair and must have entered unobserved. When asked about his discomfort about the instruction to sit in the chair, the subject claimed he could not see Dr. Jones during the previous period but had a very anxious feeling that he must avoid the apparently empty chair.

One problem with hypnosis is how to interpret the subjective and introspective reports of the person in the trance. There is no situation where compliance is more of a problem. Is the hypnotic subject merely complying with the expectations of the hypnotist, or can hypnosis change perception? Whatever the answer, many skeptical subjects have reported the experience of negative hallucinations, and such reports are also found in persons unfamiliar with the term and the theory. Therefore, the phenomenon does appear to exist in subjective experience.

Such extremes of perceptual inhibition are not restricted to hypnosis. Certain forms of psychopathology, particularly conversion reactions, may lead to strategic nonperception. For example, one woman patient reported that she saw men from the waist up but was blind to them below the waist. Her selective negative hallucination did not apply to women. Other patients may report the symptom of *tunnel vision* in which only the center of the visual field is seen, as if one were looking through a long tunnel. The wider field of vision is blotted out. These inhibitions of perception occur without any evidence of neurologic pathology and are reversible with psychotherapy.

After-Images

An after-image is a residue that persists after removal of an external signal. The reader may have experienced both "negative" and "positive" after-images, terms borrowed from photography. For example, if for several seconds you look at a red object and then glance at a white wall you may "see" projected onto the wall the color green, opposite to red on the color wheel—this is a *negative after-image*. A *positive after-image*—a residue of the reddish impression—may also occur. Richardson[20] gives a review of the relevant research literature.

Usually after-images last only a few seconds after the stimulus leaves the visual field. Sometimes the images persist for a long time or recur after a latency period,[8] and are of special interest because of their uncontrolled and unexplained entry into awareness.

Paliopsia is a rare and weird after-image that is noted in certain types of organic lesions of the brain[3] and under the influence of some hallucinogenic drugs. In paliopsia an image continues after the gaze is deflected. For instance, if you were to look at a person's profile and then move your gaze away toward a nearby lampshade you might see the profile or a single eye on the lampshade. You might even see a chain of profiles as illustrated in Figure 2-4.

IMAGES CATEGORIZED BY CONTENT

The remaining types of images described in this chapter receive their names from their characteristic content. Their vividness may range from hallucination or pseudohallucination, down to the status of "unconscious" images. As for context, they may occur in any of the various states described earlier. And, to a greater or lesser extent, their presence may result from perceptual interactions.

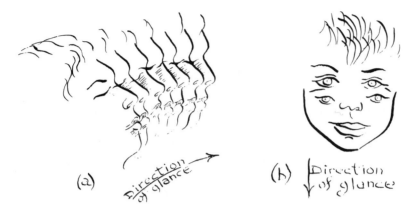

Fig. 2-4. An example of paliopsia. The subject had taken hashish and noted this type of after-image. When he shifted his gaze across the features of his companion, he noted a chain of images (a). When he moved his gaze up and down, a single feature, the eyes, was reduplicated (b).

Memory Image

A memory image is a reconstruction or resurrection of a past perception. Often people use memory images to recollect forgotten details.

Memory images may be quite dim, almost nonsensory in nature, or they may be extremely distinct, even projected onto blank spaces such as walls or paper in an effort to localize them externally. When memory images are especially vivid they are called *eidetic images* and persons with eidetic capacity are sometimes said to have photographic memory. *Eidetic images* are more common in children, as the capacity is often lost at the onset of adolescence. Some adults, however, retain this capacity. For example, the famous psychologist Titchener reportedly had the ability to remember the books he had read with distinct and accurate revisualization of the pages.[19]

Jaensch[11] performed a classic study of young persons with eidetic images. He typologized his subjects as basedowoid or tetanoid by the vividness and sense of localization of their reported experiences. The "basedowoid type" experienced eidetic images as vivid and externally localized, like perceptual images. Jaensch's terms are seldom used, however.

Persons with vivid memory images may find good use for their trait. More than one medical student has found an answer during a practicum by "reprojecting" an illustration from his anatomy text and finding from his image the information he needs. Architects, mathematicians, dancers, artists, and spies would probably also benefit to the degree that they could retain vivid memory images.

Imaginary Images

An imaginary image contains contents that have never been perceived with that particular organization. The component parts of an imaginary image are derived from images of past perceptions and recombined to form new concepts and fantasies. Sometimes people use imaginary images to invent creative solutions, such as the architect who forms an image of a new idea for a drainage system. People also use imaginary images to daydream. Usually, a stream of thought or a daydream will be partly composed of memory images and partly composed of imaginary images that are new constructions of memory components. Often a person will confuse the imaginary and memory images, that is, he may think his image is historically correct when aspects of it are fictive, or he may believe he only imagines something that he really once saw.

The phrase "imaginary image" can be confusing because it is used in two ways. One way, as above, differentiates content, which is either perceptual memories or a recombination of precepts. The other use of this term distinguishes the sources of image content, which are intrapsychic ("imaginary") and extrapsychic.*

Entoptic Images

Entoptic images, experienced as intrapsychic, relate to perception, since they arise from stimulation of optic structures within the eye or in some portion of the optic neural circuits as they travel to high brain centers. "Seeing stars" on blows to the eye or head is an entoptic experience (Fig. 2-5). Ophthalmologic researchers were at one time disconcerted by this phenomenon. They would go to great lengths to seal off all visual perceptions using complex blindfolds, only to hear subjects report little dancing lights, geometric figures, sparklers, or vague luminescent shapes. Such reports were sometimes blamed on the "ideoretinal light"—excitations of optic neurones arising from within the retina without benefit of light from the external world.

Entoptic events may also occur secondary to the physical properties of the eye itself. For example, the shadows cast upon the light sensitive

---

* Some investigators use the term "nonobject bound" to refer to images whose derivation is entirely intrapsychic and "object-bound" for images based on external sources.[1,24]

Fig. 2-5. An entoptic image.

receptors of the retina by blood vessels or "floaters" may lead to entoptic images. (Floaters are debris or residues of embryonic development that may still float uselessly in the aqueous or vitreous fluids that balloon out the eye. They are technically termed *muscae volitantes*.)

Example of entoptic images:

A physician was in the hospital suffering from leukemia. He knew his diagnosis and wanted to keep track of the count of his white blood cells as he was treated with antileukemic drugs. Although this information was withheld from him, he made relatively close approximations by an unusual method. By staring off at blank spaces of the ceiling and moving his face from side to side, he could see the shadows of cells moving in the capillaries of the retina. He could tell if the blood cells were densely or loosely packed in the vessels. (This is made possible by the orbital anatomic arrangement: the capillaries of the retina stand between the source of light, the pupil, and the nerve cells.)

Body Image; Body Image Experiences

The body image is a hypothetic construct of usually unconscious images that operates as a specialized, internal, analog data-center for information about the body and its environment.[4,25] It is in constant transactional relationship with current perception, memory, emotions, drives, thoughts, and actions. The body image includes information about the shape, appearance, position, and organization of the body and its immediate surroundings. Theoretically, there may be a series of body images: the most current one being stacked upon and developed out of a series of body images and concepts of personal space extending backwards in time to the earliest body images of childhood.[9] Some of these body images may be preconscious, in a psychoanalytic sense: they can be raised into consciousness with volitional effort. Other body images are unconscious, cannot be deliberately raised to conscious representation, and emerge only under unusual circumstances.

When body image experiences gain consciousness, the degree of vividness will determine whether the image is a thought image, a pseudohallucination, or a hallucination. Thought images of the body commonly occur when a person anticipates performing an unusual, nonautomatic physical act. Pseudohallucinatory body image experiences may occur in states of unusual body sensations or when injuries change the physical structure of the body. For example, after a disfiguring facial burn or plastic surgery, some patients experience vivid images of the body as it was and as it is. In altered states of consciousness, whether induced by drugs or other processes, strange body experiences are common. These may include a feeling of leaving the body, of seeing it from a distance, of shrinkage or expansion, or specific changes in a given body part.

One of the most intriguing body image experiences is the *autoscopic phenomenon*—a visualization of the self, perhaps with hallucinatory vividness, depicted as if seen from some external point. The autoscopic phenomenon, also known as "the double," may occur during fatigue, anxiety, toxic states, or in organic pathology of the brain.[28]

Phantom Limb

This is a version of body image disturbance which is so discrete that it has received a separate clinical label. The phantom limb experience occurs following amputation or loss of a body part. For example, about one quarter of the women who have had a breast removed surgically report phantom breast sensations.[12] In the postamputation period the person continues to have "sensations" in the missing part just as if it were still present. Clinical study suggests that these sensations can be considered in both neurophysiologic and psychologic terms. Subjectively the experience can be realistic and even painful.

Paranormal Hallucination or Vision

The mystic, religious, extraterrestrial, or supernatural nature of the content gives this special variety of hallucination or pseudohallucination its title. Religious visions, ghosts, goblins, demons, fairies, guardian angels, and other apparitions fall into this category.

Imaginary Companions

Children sometimes insist that an imaginary playmate, human or animal, is always with them. Situation comedies on television have made use of this fact: "Oh, oh, don't sit on Herman, he's sitting there." Sometimes imaginary companions can achieve great vividness, and children will "actually see," that is, hallucinate, the imagined person or pet. But most will say they are only imagining the companion in their minds. In both instances complete descriptions of color, form, shape, size, texture, and movement are given with such clarity that some form of visual image of the imagined object must be present.

Number Forms and Diagram Forms

A number form is a characteristic schema that a person uses to form visual images of numbers. People who use number forms for all arithmetic calculations are often surprised to learn not everyone shares this type of mental representation. And people without number forms are sometimes surprised and incredulous to hear of them. Some persons with number forms have very idiosyncratic visuo-spatial patterns as in the following example:

Whenever I have to do any calculation with numbers, I visualize the numbers as a kind of ladder. It starts at the bottom of the left leg with one and goes up—two, three, four, each equidistant and written out in my handwriting until it gets to 13, then it jogs over to 14 and goes up on that leg of the ladder to 21, then it curves back to the left on 22. Then it goes to 30, rungs over for 31 to 40, then back for 41 and on to 100. After one hundred I don't seem to get the number form except for the last two digits. When I multiply two numbers like 12 × 23, then I see all of the numbers in the ladder but 12 and 23 are kind of lit up brighter than the others. I also see the days of the week but probably this is pretty conventional. Each day goes from left to right starting with Sunday in a kind of revolving drum so that a new level of the drum or spiral is started each Sunday. Whenever I make an appointment I mark it visually at the proper place on the drum. Today always stands out brighter on my visual image; "yesterday" and "tomorrow" are a little brighter than the other days but less bright than "today."

REFERENCES

1. Caston J: Completion effects and attention in hallucinatory and nonhallucinatory patients and normal subjects. J Nerv Ment Dis 148:147, 1967
2. Dement W, Kleitman N: The relation of eye movements during sleep to dream activity. J Exp Psychol 53:339, 1957
3. Feldman M, Bender M: Visual illusions and hallucinations in parieto-occipital lesions of the brain. In Keup W (ed): Origin and Mechanisms of Hallucinations. New York, Plenum, 1970
4. Fisher S, Cleveland SE: Body Image and Personality. Princeton, NJ, Van Nostrand, 1958
5. Forbes A: Dream scintillations. Psychosom Med 11:160, 1949
6. Freedman DX: On the use and abuse of LSD. Arch Gen Psychiat 18:330, 1968
7. Freud S: Hysterical phantasies and their relation to bi-sexuality. Stand Ed 9, 1959
8. Hanawalt NG: Recurrent images: new instances and a summary of the older ones. Amer J Psychol 67:170, 1954
9. Horowitz MJ: Body image. Arch Gen Psychiat 14:456, 1966
10. Isakower OA: A contribution to the patho-psychology of phenomena associated with falling asleep. Int J Psychoanal 19:331, 1938
11. Jaensch ER: Eidetic Imagery and Typological Methods of Investigation. London, Kegan, Paul, 1930
12. Jarvis JH: Post mastectomy breast phantoms. J Nerv Ment Dis 144(4):266, 1967
13. Jaspers K: General Psychopathology. Manchester, Manchester Univ Press, 1962
14. Jones E: Papers on psychoanalysis, 5th ed. Baltimore, Williams & Wilkins, 1948
15. Kandinski V: Zur lehre von jen halluzinationen. Arch Psychiat 11:453, 1880
16. Lewin BD: Inferences from the dream screen. Int J Psychoanal 29:224, 1948a
17. ———: Reconsideration of the dream screen. Psychoanal Q 22:174, 1948b
18. ———: Sleep, the mouth and the dream screen. Psychoanal Q 15:419, 1946
19. McKellar P: Imagination and Thinking. New York, Basic, 1957
20. Richardson A: Mental Imagery. New York, Springer, 1969
21. Ruesch J: Disturbed Communication, the Clinical Assessment of Normal and Pathological Communicative Behavior. New York, Norton, 1957
22. Sarbin TR: The concept of hallucination. J Pers 35:359, 1967
23. Saul L: Dream scintillations. Psychosom Med 27:286, 1965
24. Scheibel M, Scheibel A: Hallucinations and brain stem reticular core. In West LJ (ed): Hallucinations. New York, Grune & Stratton, 1962
25. Schilder P: The Image and Appearance of the Human Body: Studies in the Constructive Energies of the Psyche. New York, International Univ Press, 1950

26. Sedman G: A comparative study of pseudohallucinations, imagery and true hallucinations. Brit J Psychiat 112:9, 1966
27. Siegel RK, Jarvik ME: Drug induced hallucinations in animals and man. In Siegel RK, West LJ (eds): Hallucinations: Behavior, Experience, and Theory. New York, Wiley, 1975
28. Todd J, Denhurst K: The double: its psychopathology and psychophysiology. J Nerv Ment Dis 122:47, 1955
29. Willinger R, Klee A: Metamorphosia and other visual disturbances with latency occurring in patients with diffuse cerebral lesions. Acta Neurol Scand 42:1, 1966
30. Zilboorg G: A History of Medical Psychology. New York, Norton, 1941

3

THE CIRCUMSTANCES THAT
INCREASE IMAGE FORMATION

Certain mental states encourage image formation. As with any psychologic phenomenon, paradoxic effects occasionally occur, and a few persons may experience decreased image formation under circumstances that increase image formation in most persons. These paradoxic effects occur because image formation is influenced not only by internal and external stimuli and motives but also is regulated by defensive or controlling motives. For example, most persons in conditions of perceptual deprivation report an increase in the frequency of vividness of imagery; a few persons, however, report a decrease in image formation, presumably because their controlling or defensive processes increase at a sharper rate than their impulsive processes.

Although individuals vary, generalizations can be made about the likelihood of image experiences under various circumstances. These generalizations help the clinician to evaluate a given image report in terms of the "expectability" of that occurrence. As emphasized in Chapter 2, the average person may hallucinate in some circumstances, but the same hallucination in another context may suggest the presence of some abnormality. This chapter describes generalizations about image formation in several states ranging from normal wakefulness to dreaming sleep. These generalizations are derived from clinical observations and experimental studies. In the last 35 years, many investigators studied the effects of sensory, sleep, or dream deprivation and accumulated evidence about what circumstances change image formation.

NORMAL WAKEFULNESS

Most persons form images at some time during their normal waking mental life, though they differ in frequency of images. Some persons think largely in a flow of visual images, others rarely experience a visual image and think mostly in words.

Whatever the habitual style in problem-oriented or reality-oriented thinking, most people (about 95 percent) can form a visual image in full wakefulness when given a specific, instruction.[11,80,105,106] For example, when asked to form an image of a Christmas tree, most people will have at least a dim quasi-visual representation, some will have a technicolor tree with glowing lights, and only a very few will be unable to form any image. To form *visual* images is easier for more persons than to form images in any other sensory mode. For example, Brower[18] found that on specific instruction, 97 percent of his subjects formed a visual image, 59 percent could form an auditory image, and 39 percent could form an image of smell. Sheehan[105] also found that subjects could form more vivid visual images than images in other sense modes. A conflicting finding is reported by Lindauer;[72] he found that tactile and gustatory-type words aroused more vivid images than visual type words.

Daydreaming or fantasizing while awake tends to further increase the visual quality of thought. Singer[112] has studied daydreaming extensively and finds that about 96 percent of his adult subjects report at least some daydreaming activity every day although they differ widely in their frequency of fantasy. Most of these daydreams take the form of visual images of people, objects, or events. Singer reports variations based on sex, age, intelligence, social class, and other variables. For example, persons between 18 and 29 years of age reported more frequent daydreams than persons 30 to 39. Persons 40 to 49 reported the least daydreaming activity of his three age subgroups.

Images may also increase when planning decreases and persons enter a state of directionless thought, as in the use of free association technique in psychotherapy. In such a technique, patients are asked to reduce attention to external stimuli, or efforts to remember or solve a particular problem, or efforts to rehearse future events. They are asked to report whatever comes to mind, including a parade of images which may occur in some patients.[65] At other times, a reduction in planning may be involuntary— sometimes a train of problem-solving thought reaches an impasse, and persons report an increase of images when baffled.

Images may also occur when a person expects certain external stimuli, when there is an unrewarded straining toward perception. In situations of boring perceptual search, unusually vivid internal images may occur, especially when the search leads to fatigue or a kind of trance-like state. This can be an occupational hazard of lookouts, aircraft spotters, radar operators, and jet pilots. For example, pilots flying at high altitudes, especially if the ground is concealed by clouds and they have little to do, may experience the "breakoff phenomenon," a state of detachment and confusion into which unbidden but vivid images may intrude.[19]

CHILDHOOD

There is a general impression that imagery experiences of all types are more frequent in childhood and diminish by the time of adolescence. Eidetic images, imaginary companions, hallucinations, and night terrors are included in the types of experience more common in children. Daydreaming is also probably more commonplace, and children apparently spend more time in dreaming sleep. Children also think in simpler, more concrete, and more iconic forms than they will during later adolescence and adulthood.

Night terrors may start in a child at age 5, continue for several years, and then remit spontaneously at, for example, age 10. They may also continue into adulthood or occur there for the first time. They do occur more frequently in children.[68] Intensive studies have been conducted on eidetic experiences in children. Haber[54,55] and Haber and Haber[56] examined 151 elementary school pupils and found that 55 percent of them could retain mental images after viewing pictorial stimuli. But only 12, or 8 percent could reproduce detailed information from inner examination of their images, so the eidetic capacity was not related to age: older subjects had this ability about as frequently as younger subjects. Richardson[95] has offered an excellent review of eidetic imagery and notes that figures quite comparable to those of Haber and Haber have been found in cross-cultural studies of children and adults. In his cross-cultural studies, Doob[28] did not find any correlation between eidetic ability and the abstract ability or cognitive complexity of a society.

Hallucinations are also thought to appear more frequently or at least more "easily" in children. That is, hallucinatory experiences, or intrusive imaginings that are labeled by others as hallucinatory experiences, are found in children who are not presently psychotic but rather caught up in reactions to traumas or psychologic conflicts.[22,103] Eisenberg has described the problems of communication, language, and of differentiating the vivid image, or pseudohallucination, that may terrify a child although the child "knows" it is unreal, from the hallucination which is experienced with perceptual reality. Children have not learned to differentiate their own experiences with the subtlety and security they will attain at a later age. Also, when the experiences reported by schizophrenic persons are considered in isolation from reports from nonschizophrenic persons, hallucinations appear to be less prominent in the infantile childhood schizophrenic than the late developing or adult schizophrenic.[32] For example, of 40 children of mixed diagnosis, aged 5 to 15, on an inpatient psychiatric unit, only two (5 percent) had hallucinations, and one of these was diagnosed as a nonpsychotic behavioral disorder.[31] The same authors found that 81 percent of 33 other patients had hallucinations and this group all had a diagnosis of childhood psychosis of *late onset*. In contrast, none of 47 children with an *infantile* onset of psychosis was found to have unequivocal hallucinations.

Overall, these findings suggest that a preoccupation with imagery and a relatively lower level of control may characterize the era of mid-childhood.

REVERIES AND HYPNAGOGIC STATES

Image formation changes in quality and quantity as alertness wanes. At first the speed of thinking slows and the inclination to daydream increases. Images become more frequent and more vivid. Persons experience the contents and arrangement of the images as less controlled. In the deepest hypnagogic states, hallucinations may occur and suddenly activate the person to full wakefulness.

One of the earliest studies of reverie and hypnagogic states is a paper by Silberer[111] in which he reported the use of hypnagogic reverie for the investigation of symbolism and hallucination formation (see Rapaport's translation and annotated version[93]). Silberer found that two conditions, drowsiness and the "antagonistic" active or forced effort to think, led to an "autosymbolic" phenomenon. This autosymbolic experience is quasi-hallucinatory: a visual symbol or metaphor comes forth automatically and represents a previously verbal thought. For example, Silberer was drowsy and yet forcing himself to think through how to correct an awkward phrase in an essay he was writing. He then experienced a visual image of smoothing a piece of wood with a plane: a metaphor for the goal of his thoughts.

Rapaport[92] attempted to train himself to write automatically during periods of altered consciousness so that he could review the records later when fully awake. He collected records of his thoughts at various levels of alertness from waking to sleeping. The reports include daydreams, reveries, hypnagogic hallucinations, and dreams. During this progression, Rapaport noted that his reflective self-awareness decreased, the ability to exert effort decreased, logical thinking decreased, and visual images increased in frequency and vividness.

Rapaport observed the same cognitive motif treated quite differently at different levels of awareness as had also been observed by Varendonck[121] and Freud.[47] The motif concerned his wish to remain conscious and record his thoughts in spite of his urge to sleep. In full wakefulness he could conceptualize this as an antithesis: I must—I cannot. The next phase was a hypnagogic visual image of two waves that he was trying to bring together. He also saw somebody trying frantically to approach a door that slowly shut. He then fell asleep and dreamt he was on the way to an examination and was afraid he would be late. Then he "fell off," as if into deeper sleep. He then dreamt "a father in a monastery, painting, saying to his son, 'I am so glad you got in before they shut the door.'" Each of the four treatments of the motif becomes more concrete, more symbolic or metaphoric, and more visual. The final treatment seems like a wish-fulfillment. Note also the increased penetration of the current conceptual theme, "I must—I cannot" into other personal life issues and childhood memories as he entered dreaming sleep.

Stoyva[118] has indicated five conditions which foster entry into a hypnagogic reverie. These are reduction in the level of sensory stimuli, maintenance of a level of arousal sufficient to provide some self-awareness, reduction of a proprioceptive input, an ability and use of the ability to shift into a state of "passive volition," and a shift from dominance of the sympathetic to the parasympathetic nervous system. Monotony in a state of relaxation, combined with a setting aside of problem-solving thought has increased such experiences, especially if a diffuse kind of sensory stimulation is used to maintain arousal.[48,64] Fortuitously, in studies designed to examine the use of biofeedback techniques, deep relaxation has been induced with a resultant increase in hypnagogic phenomena such as imagery.[118] The images, especially faces, that appear in the hypnagogic state can have a vividness, detail, and novelty quite unlike that possible during alert image formation.[80] In contrast to dreams, it appears that slow eye movements (SEMs) are more likely to accompany image experiences in this altered state of consciousness.[26] While some hypnagogic experiences elaborate upon a nidus provided by some real sensation, Holt[63] has found no correlation between awareness of entoptic phenomena such as phosphenes and the occurrence of hypnagogic phenomena. A recent comprehensive review by Schacter[101] of all hypnagogic experiences emphasized their "snapshot" quality and affective flatness as compared to dreams, although bizarre and fantastic qualities characterize both. Personality trait correlations are relatively unremarkable.[8]

DREAMS

Like hallucinations, dreams are an extremely vivid form of imagery. Unlike hallucinations, all people experience dreams on a regular basis: each time a person sleeps, he or she dreams. People vary in dream recollection, however, so that dream interpretation becomes variably useful in psychotherapy.

Dreams are a series of images, chiefly visual, although auditory, tactile, kinesthetic, and other forms of images and words may also occur. During a dream, ideas and feelings that are unfamiliar to waking life may emerge: raw hostility, strange erotic fantasies, new ideas, prophetic statements, and forgotten memories are commonplace in dreams. In psychotherapy, a patient may gain increased conviction about the personal importance of usually unconscious themes because of the penetration of such concepts into dreaming experiences.

Until recently we were dependent for dream reports on daytime recollection. Based on this source of introspective data, many clinicians believed, as did laymen, that people differ in how much they dream each night. Apparently this is not true. Recent studies of rapid eye movement sleep have given researchers the opportunity to wake people at various times throughout the night. Even people who do not remember dreams in the daytime and do not report having any dreams will report visual image events of fantasy-like quality during such procedures. Dreams reported in the daytime, as in psychotherapy, have a more cohesive story line than those reported on awakenings immediately after conclusion of a rapid eye movement period. Some dream researchers also find that laboratory dream narratives tend to be long and incoherent, less intense than the tightly organized and more drive-laden reports from dreams experienced at home.[27,57]

There are between three and five discrete dreams each night in almost every sleeper[23] and the several dreams of the night often have some kind of continuity and theme.[84] Early in the evening the dreams tend to revolve around residues of the day's events.[47] As the night progresses, the dreams tend to center more on childhood and past events.[122] Dreams can incorporate internal or external stimuli or they may be impervious to such stimuli. Sometimes stimuli not consciously perceived but subliminally received during waking life surface while asleep.[35,36,41,91] Dream investigators have stimulated volunteers during dreaming sleep with lights, sounds, or temperature changes. The stimulus was clearly incorporated in 20 to 60 percent of dreams in one study of Dement and Wolpert.[25] When an external stimulus is incorporated into a dream, it is often changed symbolically and incorporated into the ongoing dream fantasy. Similar transformations occur during the processing of subliminal perceptions, even during waking life, as such stimuli enter into formation of consciously experienced visual images.[1,29,30,43,107-109]

While dreaming, people enter various types of emotional states. Psychoanalytic studies of dream formation indicate that latent thoughts are more readily disguised than emotions. Thus, the ideas represented in the image contents may be accompanied by feelings that appear incongruent. Pleasant image contents may be associated with anxiety or anger. On the other hand, the person may have very pleasant or erotic feelings while having image contents that are of destructive or frightening themes. Such incongruities lead many people to regard dreams as "crazy" or meaningless. Plato accepted dreams as a normal form of madness and suggested that psychotics were persons who continued the bizarre mental life of the dream into wakefulness.

Studies of the manifest content of dreams across groups of persons reduce some of the mystery of the individual dream experience. They show dreaming to be a variety of thought carried out in hallucinatory images and guided by primitive (as well as sophisticated) roles and regulations. Thus starving men report an increase in dreams of food and less dreams of sex; young children between ages 5 and 6 dream of magical happenings and ghosts; children aged 11 to 12 dream of play and travel; and aged persons have, as frequent dream contents, images reflecting feelings of helplessness and weakness as well as lost resources (for a review of manifest dream content in normal and pathological states see Kramer[70]).

RAPID EYE MOVEMENT SLEEP AND ITS ASSOCIATION WITH DREAM THINKING

The ability to sample dream states increased markedly when the psychologic experience of dreaming was related to neurophysiologic indices. Aserinski and Kleitman[3] noted that during the night there were periodic cycles of a brain wave recording characteristics of "alertness" and rapid eye movements (REMs). Dement and Kleitman[24] found that subjects awakened from this "Stage 1" REM sleep reported dreams relatively frequently (about 80 percent of the time). When subjects were awakened from non-REM sleep, they reported mental contents suggestive of dreams only infrequently (20 percent or less of reports in most subjects).

Many studies have been conducted in multiple sleep laboratories since these initial discoveries. Some kind of thinking seems to go on during every stage of sleep. The four to five REM periods that most subjects have in an average night seem to be accompanied by visual images of hallucinatory vividness. These images are often arranged in some kind of story line organized by primary process principles. Reports of subjects on awakenings from non-REM sleep contain conspicuously fewer visual images. The thoughts are experienced more as words or simple ideas with less admixture of primary process thinking.[94] Of interest, Fiss et al[43] have found that persons awakened from REM sleep show more primary process responses on projective psychologic tests (such as inkblot interpretation) than persons wakened from non-REM sleep.

The presence of hallucinatory visual images during REM sleep led to efforts to find linkages between neurophysiologic events and these subjective experiences. During REM sleep various areas of the brain associated with vision enter an excitation state as shown by depth electrode studies in animals. So far nothing can be said with certainty, but some evidence suggests that the optical receptive areas of the brain are excited before the associative, cortical, or "thinking" areas.[21] Were this so, cyclic, optical-type excitations (either peripheral or central) might provide raw sensory material out of which the psychologically meaningful dream is constructed.

That some sensory stimuli, of endogenous origin, provide a nidus for dream formation is an interesting but still speculative notion. Only milliseconds are required for transmission of impulses along nerve tracts, and the sequence of excitation of structures is difficult to measure. Once measured, the significance of recordings is hard to determine, or, and even if an area appears to be activated "first," we are unsure what this means. The highly interactional relationship of images, perception, eye movements, and schemata for tracking and matching visual stimuli with head movement and position may make any "which comes first" question hard to answer, or even inappropriate.

There are some data that relate the subjectively experienced images of the dream with neurophysiologic or behavioral events that can be objectively recorded. While there have been conflicting reports, some investigators have found the direction of eye movements, as recorded with the electrooculogram or electromyogram of eye muscles, may correspond at times with the reported dream contents on subsequent awakening.[25] For example, Roffwarg et al[96] found that vertical eye movements might be associated with a dream report such as climbing stairs while horizontal eye movements might be associated with reports such as watching a tennis match.

An added perspective to the relationship between REMs and visual images involved studies of persons with brain lesions and the congenitally blind. Greenberg[51] found that persons with brain damage in visual association areas had diminished or absent eye movements toward the impaired visual field. In congenitally blind subjects investigators did not, at first, find rapid eye movements during sleep, although the characteristic brain wave pattern was present.[10,85] New methods of measuring eye movements, however, demonstrated that the congenitally blind do have rapid eye movements, even though they do not dream in visual images.[2,53] Thus, rapid eye movements may be a part of the neurophysiology of Stage 1 REM sleep regardless of the presence of visual images in the subjective dream. Perhaps this is one example of physiologic functions which precede and are then coordinated with psychic processes. In the case of REMs, optic excitations which are controlled by the lower brain on a physiologic and automatic level may provide the material which is later given subjective meaning on a psychic level.

NIGHTMARES

Nightmares are a form of dreaming in which a usually warded-off mental content enters awareness as hallucinatory imagery and leads to painful emotional responses.[75] Patients in psychotherapy are motivated to report nightmares. Repressed traumatic memories may have their first conscious recollection as a result of first emerging as a nightmare.

The gradual alteration of state of consciousness from wakefulness, through hypnagogic reverie, to dreaming is associated with an increase in the relative proportion of image thinking as compared to verbal thinking. When the vivid image thinking evokes the fear responses that characterize a nightmare, the person appears to defensively alter state of consciousness in the direction of wakefulness, to interrupt the free flow of pictorialization. Thus, during nightmares, some persons are aware of self-reflection about the dreaming process—while they are still asleep they realize they are dreaming, and strive to wake themselves to stop dreaming. The sudden awakening from the nightmare is often composed of both general excitation from response to the hallucinatory images and the defensive intent to stop the images.

Keith[68] has pointed out that the term nightmare often labels rather different phenomena of sleep. Night terrors and anxiety dreams are both subsumed under this term, yet have different experiential and behavioral qualities. Night terrors are more like the classic nightmare of Jones, described in Chapter 2, while anxiety dreams are what are commonly called simply bad dreams. Verbalizations, screaming, thrashing, sitting up, and somnambulism are more frequent in night terrors; relaxation during the anxiety dream is often maintained. The mental content is often simpler but violently aggressive and/or terrifying in the night terror, while anxiety dreams may be complex and also more disguised in terms of meaning. Waking from a night terror often leads to a confused, disoriented, and even unresponsive state, while waking from an anxiety dream leads to a period of relative lucidity, orientation, and clear memory for the dream experience. The night terror is more frequent in children but also occurs later in life. Recent sleep studies have indicated that the night terror experience occurs as an eruption from "Stage 4" sleep, usually associated with nondreaming mentation, while the anxiety dream occurs in the context of REM sleep.[38-40]

While the form is different, the basic contents of the imagery experience during these altered states of consciousness are not very different. Like the anxiety dream, albeit in more direct and terrifying form, the night terror often contains fears of being crushed, enclosed, abandoned, choked, dying, falling, or destroying others. The mental contents are sometimes traumatic experience, and often traumatic experience derived from reality with later fantasy elaborations.[41,68] In addition, a night terror may be like a daytime panic attack, an experience of high somatic responsivity in fear systems, that is later given a psychologic meaning structure.

DREAM DEPRIVATION

Dream deprivation is a selective form of sleep deprivation. Whenever a person enters Stage 1 of rapid eye movement sleep, he is awakened. The first night may require five such awakenings and the person may lose about 80 percent of his normal amount of dream time. On subsequent nights the sleeper enters Stage 1 REM sleep more frequently so that eventually 12 or more awakenings may be necessary. If allowed to sleep, the person shows a rebound effect; instead of "dreaming" for 20 to 25 percent of his sleep time, he may "dream" 50 to 60 percent of the time. Early dream research findings were thought to indicate a possible need for dreaming.[37] It was reasoned that a dream-deprived person might "dream," that is, hallucinate, while he was awake during the day. Studies by Fisher and Dement[37] yielded supportive results: subjects were thought to have a latent hallucinatory propensity during the dream-deprived state. Pivik and Foulkes[90] found that dream deprivation led to intensified dream content on subsequent REM awakenings. Other studies yield less supportive data and the question of the waking effects of dream deprivation, at present, is undecided.[42] Greenberg et al[52] reported an increase in primary process thinking as shown only on responses to Rorschach tests given during the day. Sampson[98] reported that objective psychologic tests showed no significant changes after dream deprivation but that the behavior of subjects shifted: some subjects developed oral cravings, childish behavior, and an increase in aggressive themes in their reported dream fragments. My own studies suggested an increase in fantasy images, but awakening control subjects in non-REM sleep led to similar increases in fantasy. The apparent increase in primary process or imagery seemed due to the emotional effects of the experiment: multiple awakenings, close contact with the investigators for many nights, and so forth, rather than dream deprivation per se.

Past studies have found that total sleep deprivation increases visual imagery experiences, even to the point of hallucinations. The presence of other disturbances in reality-relatedness has led some investigators to consider sleep deprivation as a means of producing a transient "model psychosis" in normal persons.[16,69,74,124] Again, there is often a progression from entoptic-type images and perceptual distortions to hallucinations suggesting a release phenomenon. There is, however, a tremendous amount of individual variation. Disc jockeys on marathons and high school students engaged in feats of sleeplessness may go many days and not report hallucinations.

NEUROSES AND PSYCHOSES

Increased image formation may occur as a person loses the subjective sense of volitional control over mental processes. In neurotic states enhanced image formation seldom reaches hallucinatory intensity during waking life; in the psychoses hallucinations and pseudohallucinations occur more frequently.

There are few rules about what kinds of neurotic disorders may lead to increased image formation. Individuals vary too widely and the diagnostic categories now in use do not correlate with the presence or absence of any specific type of image experience. Patients with phobic or panic disorders may image themselves as helplessly losing bodily control,[25] vomiting, urinating, defecating, fainting, or dying of a heart attack in the situation believed to be threatening. Patients with obsessional disorders may report recurrent intrusive images of sadistic scenes, often without emotional accompaniment. Also patients with compulsive personality disorders tend to use isolation and to compartmentalize certain concepts in images by denying these images' translation into words.[9] Patients with histrionic or hysterical personality disorders may have images of sexual danger or disaster accompanied by a feeling of guilty fearfulness.

Some generalizations can be applied to increased image formation as seen in psychosis. Hallucinations are notoriously, perhaps too notoriously, common in schizophrenic episodes and are more frequent in acute flare-ups.[13] But no hard and fast rule is applicable: persons with involutional psychosis, hysterical psychosis, transient psychotic regressions in borderline personality, or organic brain syndromes also may hallucinate. The diagnosis of schizophrenia should never be based on the presence of hallucinations alone.[100]

Visual hallucinations are less frequent than auditory hallucinations in the group of schizophrenic syndromes. Jansson[67] reviewed the admission records of 293 young schizophrenic patients and found that 84 had evidence of hallucinations. Of these 84, 87 percent had auditory hallucinations and 44 percent had visual hallucinations. Some patients had both auditory and visual, a few had hallucinations of smell, touch, or taste. Small et al[114] found a similar, but smaller visual percentage: 30 percent of schizophrenic subjects reported visual hallucinations. Jansson found a slight but not statistically significant trend toward a more favorable course in patients with visual hallucinations only. He found no association between the mode of hallucination, auditory or visual, and premorbid personality. Schizophrenic patients may continue to hallucinate as they pass from the acute to chronic phase of their syndromes. Malitz et al[78] found that 50 percent of 100 chronic schizophrenics had auditory hallucinations; only 9 percent reported visual hallucinations. Havens[58] also notes the comparative reduction of visual hallucinations in chronic schizophrenics while auditory hallucinations appear to be common. Clinically, the more disoriented, excited, and confused the patient is, the more likely he is to have visual hallucinations.

An unusually careful study of hallucinations in psychiatric disorders was conducted by Goodwin, Alderson, and Rosenthal.[50] They examined the hospital chart of every new admission into a large psychiatric inpatient service in a teaching hospital over a 3-month period. If the patient had experienced hallucinations as part of the present illness he was selected for a special research interview. The first part of this interview focused on the psychiatric disorder, the second was a detailed inventory of the hallucinatory experience.

There were 117 patients interviewed, and every patient could be included in one of the following categories: affective disorder, chronic schizophrenia, acute schizophrenia, alcoholism, organic brain syndrome, or hysteria (Briquet's syndrome). In every diagnostic category except organic brain syndrome, auditory hallucinations of voices were the most frequent modality. For organic brain syndromes, visual hallucinations were the most frequent, occurring in 89 percent of the nine subjects with this diagnosis compared with 44 percent with voices and 33 percent with other auditory hallucinations. Auditory and visual hallucinations were each present in 85 percent of patients with alcoholism. Visual hallucinations were prominent but less frequent than auditory hallucinations in the other diagnostic categories, being present in 72 percent of the 28 patients with affective disorder, compared to 82 percent with auditory voices and 25 percent with tactile hallucinations. For the 32 chronic schizophrenic patients, voices again were present in most cases (92 percent) and visual modality hallucinations were also prominent (72 percent) with tactile (53 percent), olfactory (19 percent), and gustatory (6 percent) sensations being reported less frequently. Fewer acute schizophrenics had visual hallucinations as compared with chronic schizophrenic patients (46 percent compared with 72 percent). In summary, about three-fourths of patients with affective disorder and schizophrenia had experienced visual hallucinations. Yet textbooks have often contained the statement that visual hallucinations are common in organic syndromes and rare in the functional psychoses.[15] This view apparently underestimates this relatively high frequency of visual hallucinations in the functional psychoses. Visual hallucinations cannot be regarded as a sign specific to any diagnosis.

Visual hallucinations were always in color with only one exception in the 117 patients. The majority of the contents were people, in normal size and shape. As frequently reported, the alcoholic patients tended to see animals.[17] Such reports were present in 70 percent of the 27 patients with alcoholism who reported some type of hallucination. Otherwise, these authors found no useful diagnostic differences in contents of hallucinatory experience.

During a psychotic episode there may be both an increase in imagery and a decrease in the ability to discriminate the components of imagery that come from internal and external sources. Both factors can contribute to hallucinatory experience. Mintz and Alpert,[83] for example, contrasted the auditory imagery after external stimulation in 20 hallucinating schizophrenic patients to that in 20 nonhallucinating schizophrenic patients and 20 nonpsychotic control patients. These subjects were all asked to imagine listening to a recording of "White Christmas." Then they heard sentences read to them at various levels of intelligibility, achieved by auditory filter systems. They were scored for accuracy of report and also gave self-ratings for their confidence in the accuracy of their reports. As a group, the hallucinatory subjects reported significantly higher vividness of imagery than the other groups, and were the least accurate in deciding if they had internal contributions to interpretation of the spoken sentences. That is, they were the least accurate in discriminating internal and external sources of information.

The contents of hallucinatory or pseudohallucinatory images vary widely with the current internal motives of the patient and should not be ignored in rehabilitative or maintenance psychotherapy. Persons who feel that they are losing mental control may project this feeling into bodily sensation and into images of bodily disintegration—volcanoes erupting, or persons or things coming apart, or scenes of world destruction. Those who feel totally neglected and alienated may form images that show hollowness, emptiness, or objects being eaten away. Such image contents depict feelings and impulses in a concrete, displaced, or symbolic form. Other common hallucinations may provide an explanation for the sense of disintegration: the images may be of machines or persons who are emitting controlling rays or influences. Still other image contents that commonly are reported provide something that is needed or restorative. Just as the starving man may hallucinate food, a schizophrenic patient may hallucinate people who are praising him, telling him how to behave, or condemning him for his impulses. These figures may range from relatives to cosmic religious figures. The person who fears he has destroyed the world may envision complicated metaphysical structures to restore it.

There will be differences in hallucinations according to social, sexual, and age factors since these influence internal motives. Forgus and Dewolfe[44] attempted a content analysis of themes in schizophrenic hallucinations. In their small sample of 18 men and 12 women, they found that 67 percent of the women reported hallucinations containing themes of conscience disturbance ("repent") while this theme was found in only 7 percent of men. Men were more likely to hallucinate themes such as compensatory grandiosity ("You are God") or coping with problems ("Do your job").

Researchers have also studied the manifest content of dreams of schizophrenic patients. While never diagnostic, some dream contents apparently occur or are reported more frequently in groups of schizophrenic persons. For example, hostility may be blatant and self-directed; scary dreams may occur with frequent change of scenes, or banality of content; or an isolated actionless person may be pictured surrounded by open spaces or strangers.[70] By and large, however, many dream reports of schizophrenic persons are just like those of normal persons, and nonschizophrenic persons experience, at times, dreams such as those described above.

Persons with depressive psychosis also may have an increased incidence of certain dream contents when the reports of groups are compared. Hostility is present about one-half the time and divided equally between the dreamer and some other dream character; the dreams often include family members and themes of escape.[70]

NEUROBIOLOGIC CHANGES
IN THE EYE OR BRAIN

Any type of electrophysiologic, biochemical, or physical change involving the eye, the optic tracts, or the brain may lead to increased imagery experiences. In fact, visual hallucinations may be a major presenting symptom in toxic delirium. The imagery experiences range from perceptual distortions, through elementary sensations, to full hallucinations.

INCREASES IN IMAGE FORMATION
INDUCED EXPERIMENTALLY

Much recent research has involved image formation in one way or another: that is why the topic of imagery is once again important in contemporary psychology and psychiatry.[61,62] The research aims to create experimental extensions of unusual but natural occurrences that tend to evoke hallucinations in some people. One reason for excitement was the hope of learning more about hallucinations and what kinds of circumstances foster this type of break with reality. Many investigators hoped to discover a kind of artificial psychosis or laboratory equivalent of psychosis so that the pressing problem of mental illness could be solved. Unfortunately, the syllogism is not necessarily accurate: schizophrenics may hallucinate, but making people hallucinate may not reveal the cause of schizophrenia. However, the research has revealed the lack of clarity about how to define different types of imagery and has indicated the need to differentiate clearly two types of loss of control over image formation: loss of control over contents, and loss of control over vividness and other formal properties.

SENSORY DEPRIVATION

A person may be deprived of one sensation, say vision, of more than one, or of all sensations. Natural occurrences include variations ranging from social isolation to specific deprivations of sensation. Persons trapped in mine disasters, on liferafts or lifeboats, or confined to isolation and nonmotility after heart surgery, or to darkness after cataract removal operations may share one sensation in common: they may experience vivid and unbidden images of hallucinatory intensity.[82,115]

The first experimental studies on perceptual deprivation were done early in the 1950s at McGill University.[12] The investigators put subjects alone in a blank room and had them listen to a meaningless hum of "white" noise (a sound like a radio between stations). In this state of strangely reduced perception and isolation, subjects reported increased visual imagery, loss of control over thought contents, and hallucinations.

In sensory deprivation, image experiences often emerge progressively. At first the normal level of visual images in thought intensifies. Then sensations of geometric figures, lights, or colors may emerge (entoptic images). Volitional control—the ability to direct a sequence of thought or images—diminishes and hallucinations occur in some subjects.[46,123,125,127] Experimenters noted that in certain individuals the "hallucinations" might occur as soon as the first hour and subsequently diminish. This led to the hypothesis that the early hallucinations were the result of an attempt to obtain stimulation from the external world and that this wish to cling to the external world might be subsequently relinquished.[130]

Such observations led to more studies, and repeated experimentation demonstrated that hallucinations could occur without prolonged exposure to sensory deprivation. Within a ten-minute period after the placement of the eye patches, binocularly eye-patched subjects reported imagery similar to that of persons subjected to prolonged sensory deprivation.[126] Also the kinds of images reported and the extent to which subjects reported imagery after deprivation varied with suggestion[81,97] but could not be accounted for merely by suggestion.[128]

Goldberger and Holt[49] correlated the occurrence of imagery during sensory deprivation-isolation conditions with measures from an extensive assessment including a battery of objective tests, qualitative data from projective techniques, interviews, and autobiography. It was difficult to find any special correlation of other measures such as personality traits to the process of forming images. The authors interpreted the correlations that did occur in a general way: subjects who were emotionally free, intellectually flexible, and wished to cooperate had some tendency to report more images than those who were relatively more emotionally constricted, intellectually rigid, and less motivated to be a "good subject."

These studies led to two theories which are not necessarily antagonistic. One maintains that wakeful consciousness requires continued incoming stimuli to maintain alertness. To preserve this level of stimulus nutriment, internal images may be facilitated when external signals are not available. The second theory posits that image formation increases because a person enters an altered state of consciousness. The relative reduction in reality-oriented (secondary process) thought leads to an increase of primitive thought forms (primary process).[49] Both theories suggest that there is an ever-available internal source of images and that these images are released or facilitated under appropriate circumstances.

Persons who have a general tendency to "loosened" thinking or who have a limited capacity to volitionally regulate their thought processes may have a tendency to more disruptive imagery experiences during even mild sensory deprivation[59] even though they may be less inclined or less capable than other persons to give detailed and frank introspection reports.

A tremendous effort went into sensory deprivation research, but many energetic investigators feel that the field still lacks defining principles and organized theory.[71] Two serious problems confounded the work. One is that the various investigators never agreed upon a set of definitions to differentiate image experiences. Some called almost all image reports "hallucinations"; others used far more stringent definitions.[119,126,129] The second problem was the tremendous variability between subjects in terms of what was experienced during isolation, sensory depatterning, sensory restriction, or sensory deprivation.[49,82] Partly this variation in subjects was due to variances in thought styles, which will be discussed in the next two chapters, and partly it was due to the unreliability and variability of introspective reports.

The problem of introspective reports haunts every research study on image formation and is worth considering briefly at this point. Visual thought images are essentially private: no one but the subject can know of them except through some form of description. These descriptions of intraspychic events have long been suspect as an instrument of science.[4] Why? The answer can be summarized under the headings of false positive and false negative reports.

False Positives, Miscommunications, and Semantic Confusions

Language is loaded with words that refer to vision[99] and these words seem to be "primed" in any communication about thought. When a person says, "I see," he may be referring to a wide range of psychic phenomena from hallucinations to perception to a vague word representation. Moreover, patients or research subjects vary greatly in their reports. One person may describe a moderately vivid thought image as if it were a hallucination; another person may give a bland description of a hallucination. The observer must modify descriptions by other observations of the style of the patient in order to get to the phenomenologic "facts."[104] The descriptions of very disturbed patients are often labeled as hallucination when the patient may have vivid visual thought images that are *not* actually experienced as occurring in the external environment. The therapist and his patients, the investigator and his subjects, rarely are found to share spontaneous definitions and labels of cognitive events. This variable is compounded by a further source of error: the tremendous susceptibility of image formation to suggestion based on the demand characteristic of a therapy context or an experiment.[86,87]

False Negatives

1. When reporting images, individuals often neglect sensations with minor or mild intensity since they expect an image to be vivid and durable.
2. Attentiveness and memory for visual images are variable. Some people do not include their peripheral awareness of visual thought images as part of "what is (has been) on the mind." Even after repeated instruction and reinstruction, some subjects give additional responses at a later time, eg, "Oh, did you want me to tell that, too?" Fleeting images are easily forgotten. Intrusive images may be ignored.
3. Some persons find it hard to translate visual images into words and either do not do so or else give distorted verbal reports of their subjective experience.
4. Certain individuals have a thought style in which personal, intimate, affect, and impulse-loaded ideas are presented predominantly in im-

agery. Some such subjects are reticent about telling their imagery content on the grounds that it would betray too much or be like "reading their minds," although they are willing to describe their "real thoughts" (by which they mean thoughts in word representation).

While there is always the possibility of false negatives and false positives, introspective reports remain our only source of information about the internal subjective experiences of another person. As theoretical psychologists like Bakan[4] and Maher[77] have pointed out, the *knowing* of the *meaning* of a report is acceptable in the framework of clinical psychology and psychiatry and must eventually find its place in our scientific method. The problem with this use of "knowing," through rapport or empathy, through construction within oneself of another's experience, is that bias and distortion readily occur.

DRUGS AS ENHANCERS OF IMAGE FORMATION

After taking psychedelic drugs such as LSD, psilocybin, mescaline, and peyote, some people report remarkable increases of image formation and a variety of other altered experiences.[60] One theory to explain this increase is that the drugs alter the regulation of optic pathways by inhibition and facilitation.[45] This is the release theory of hallucinations and is often credited to Hughlings Jackson.[66] Jackson assumes that thought images, hallucinations, and perceptions may to some extent share the same neural substrates, a view shared by Freud[47] and restated by Evarts.[34] Ordinarily, excitation by internal images is inhibited before it activates perceptual neural structures.* In altered states of consciousness, such as those induced by drugs, inhibition decreases and internal imagination or memory images may gain access to the perceptual neural substrates. What results is hallucination.

Support for this view is gained in such experiments as those of Marrazzi,[79] who showed that LSD may lower the threshold for the occurrence of experimentally induced illusions. Another support for the release theory is the progression of image experiences observed as the drugs take effect. The first sign of drug effect is usually some kind of perceptual distortion; then entoptic-type images and illusions commonly appear.[60] Thought images become more vivid and less controlled. Finally

---

*Cohen[20] has reviewed the contrasting view of de Clerambault, Kandinsky, and Baillarger that hallucinations and thought images arise from separate mechanisms.

they advance toward hallucinations in terms of vividness and external projection.[76] This progression is similar to that experienced on falling asleep, entering a delirium from a high fever or alcoholism, or sensory deprivation.

While some drugs seem to have a primary effect on the visual representation system, drugs also create other effects that contribute to enhanced image formation. Loss of concentration, loss of short-term memory, and loss of ability to sequence thoughts in a meaningful train of associations are such factors.[88] Other drug effects that probably increase image formation include loss of capacity to exert volitional control, passivity, feelings of elation, body image changes, and turning toward primitive types of thought organization.[73] Thus, psychologic factors are important in addition to whatever specific neurobiologic changes in the visual system are induced by drugs. For example, Slater et al[113] found that subjects who were alone taking LSD averaged 1.8 severe hallucinatory or illusion experiences, while subjects taking LSD in a group averaged only 0.8 experiences.

Many drugs other than the psychedelic agents increase image experiences. Indeed, visual hallucinations are sometimes a clinical clue that a toxic drug-induced delirium is the cause of a patient's psychotic episode. Bromide psychosis is one example. Also, excessive use of amphetamine type drugs (dexedrine, benzedrine, "speed," and so forth) may induce hallucinatory psychosis, although visual images are not remarkably enhanced on a single ingestion.* Ellinwood[33] found auditory and visual hallucinations in one-half of patients treated in a psychiatric hospital for amphetamine psychosis. Most patients with auditory hallucinations also had visual hallucinations. Fear and suspiciousness were prominently associated with the hallucinations, and the patients reported a heightened awareness of faces and eyes. Chapter 11 will dwell on delayed drug effects.

HYPNOSIS

The word hypnosis customarily refers to an induction procedure performed by a hypnotist, to a state of consciousness called a "trance," and to several effects which can be achieved in this state. In the trance state, persons can be instructed to form visual images, to dream, or even to hallucinate. Their descriptions of the experience which ensues may re-

---

*For a review of hallucinogens see Hoffer and Osmond,[60] Schultes,[102] and Siegel.[110]

semble the descriptions of persons who spontaneously dream or hallucinate. Apparently the factors of suggestion, the role of being hypnotized, and the regressed state of consciousness of the trance all contribute to enhanced image formation.

How many of the reported image effects are specific to hypnotic procedures and the hypnotic state? Starker[117] finds that visual imagery is enhanced by suggestion, but that this is not an effect limited to induction. Barber[5,6,7] has done extensive systematic research work with hypnosis. He contends that the hypnotic state is a superfluous construct which does not add to our understanding because it involves circular reasoning: because the hypnotic state is used to account for high levels of response (eg, increased image formation), subjects who manifest high responses to suggestions are said to be in a hypnotic state. On the other hand, Orne[87] suggests that under hypnosis there is a relatively specific change in the subjective experience of hypnotized individuals. Both contentions have merit: the hypnotic experience is a distinct one, for those who have experienced it; the experiences under hypnosis, however, can be effected without trance induction. For example, Spanos and Barber[116] set out to contrast the image experiences, on specific instructions, of subjects hypnotized and subjects not hypnotized. They found that one-third of a group of 102 student nurses reported that they clearly experienced a strongly suggested visual hallucination (seeing a cat in their laps) even though they were not induced into a hypnotic state. Subjects who were hypnotized had an increase of such visual reports beyond this baseline level, but the degree of increase was not remarkable in comparison with this high level of response in nonhypnotized subjects. The operational definition of hallucination in this study seems to have a low threshold for positive categorization. I would prefer the term pseudohallucination since I doubt that one-third of the student nurses lost their reality testing capacity. But the study does show how powerful suggestion alone can be without the addition of specific efforts to alter the state of consciousness.

Sometimes, in a hypnotic trance, subjects are instructed to form positive or negative hallucinations: to "see" something that is not there, or not to see something that is there. Many subjects report complete compliance with the suggestions. The question is, are the positive hallucinations really as vivid to the subject as a perception? If evidence were found that the hallucinations replicated perceptual experience, then this would show that psychologic motivation can lead internal images into entry of the perceptual substrates. Some ingenious experimental psychologists have attempted to answer this question.

Brady and Levitt[14] showed subjects a rotating drum marked with vertical stripes. As the drum turns, the stripes move across the subject's visual field; these moving stripes cause a reflex movement of the eyes that is called nystagmus. Nystagmus is involuntary, and subjects asked merely to imagine the drum, after it had been removed, did not develop nystagmus types of eye movements. Brady and Levitt then hypnotized subjects and asked them to hallucinate the rotating drum: in the trance state many subjects did develop the same kind of nystagmus eye movements that they showed while watching the drum in reality. Underwood[120] tried a similar method using optical geometrical illusions and telling subjects to see or not to see various aspects of the geometric figure. He found evidence for positive but not negative hallucinations. In spite of these findings, however, some investigators remain uncertain as to the apparent perceptual reality of hypnotic hallucinations, and the reader may wish to withhold judgment until further research is published.

CONCLUSION

Any situation that induces an altered state of consciousness will change image experiences. While this statement sums up a great many clinical and experimental observations, it also is a tautology: altered states of consciousness are defined by the contents of consciousness, the organization of these conscious contents, and the precursors and residues of the awareness of these contents. Thus, altered states of consciousness are partially defined by the presence or absence, vividness, content, and volitional control of images. While there is great variance between persons, certain generalizations can be made as to changes in the quality of image experience. As a person becomes less wakeful, reality-oriented, and committed to reason and problem-solving thought, images begin to occur more frequently, to attain greater vividness, and to escape directions of the will and limitations of censorship. The contents of images tend to be derived more and more from inner sources, less and less from external stimuli. In their organization they follow progressively more primitive or simple styles, and tend to be controlled more by wish or fear than the requirements of reality. In addition, there is a tendency toward fantasy elaboration of elementary sensations such as entoptic phenomena which may end in hallucination. As these changes occur, there is a gradual loss of the sense of self-direction of the course of image formation.

REFERENCES

1. Allers R, Teller J: On the utilization of unnoticed impressions in associations. Psychol Issues (7)2:121, 1960 (1924)
2. Amadeo M, Gomez E: Eye movements, attention and dreaming in subjects with lifelong blindness. Canad Psychiat Ass J 11:500, 1966
3. Aserinski E, Kleitman N: Regularly occurring periods of eye motility and concomitant phenomena during sleep. Science 118:273, 1953
4. Bakan D: On Method. San Francisco, Jossey-Bass, 1967
5. Barber TX: A Scientific Approach to Hypnosis. Princeton, Van Nostrand, 1969
6. ———: Imagery and "hallucinations": effects of LSD contrasted with effects of "hypnotic" suggestions. In Imagery: Current Cognitive Approaches. New York, Academic Press, 1971, pp. 102–130
7. ———, Calberley DS: Hypnotizeability, suggestibility, and personality. II. An assessment of previous imaginative-fantasy experiences by the As, Barber-Glass, and Shore questionnaires. J Clin Psych 21:57, 1965
8. Barr HL, Langs RJ, Holt RR, et al: LSD: Personality and Experience. New York, Wiley, 1972
9. Beres D: Symbol and object. Bull Menninger Clin 29:3, 1965
10. Berger RJ, Olley P, Oswald I: The EEG, eye-movements and dreams of the blind. Quart J Exp Psychol 14:183, 1962
11. Betts GH: The Distribution and Functions of Mental Imagery. New York, Columbia Univ Teacher's College, 1909
12. Bexton WH, Heron W, Scott TH: Effects of decreased variation in sensory environment. Canad J Psychol 8:70, 1954
13. Bleuler E: Dementia Praecox or the Group of Schizophrenias. New York, International Univ Press, 1950
14. Brady JP, Levitt EE: Hypnotically induced visual hallucinations. Psychosom Med 28:351, 1966
15. Brain R: Diseases of the Nervous System. London, Oxford Univ Press, 1955
16. Brauchi JT, West LJ: Sleep deprivation. JAMA 171:11, 1959
17. Bromberg W, Schilder P: Psychologic considerations in alcoholic hallucinosis. Int J Psychoanal 14:206, 1933
18. Brower D: The relative predominance of various imagery modalities. J Gen Psychol 37:199, 1947
19. Clark B, Graybiel A: The breakoff phenomenon. J Aviat Med 28:121, 1957
20. Cohen LH: Imagery and its relations to schizophrenic symptoms. J Ment Sci 84:284, 1938
21. Cordeau JP: Abstracted in Electroenceph Clin Neurophysiol 17:442, 1964
22. Coren HZ, Saldinger JG: Visual hallucinations in children. Psychoanal Study Child 22:331, 1967
23. Dement WC: Dream recall and eye movements during sleep in schizophrenic subjects and normals. J Nerv Ment Dis 122:263, 1955

24. ——, Kleitman N: The relation of eye movements during sleep to dream activity: an objective method for the study of dreaming. J Exp Psychol 53:339, 1957

25. ——, Wolpert E: The relation of eye movements, body motility, and external stimuli to dream content. J Exp Psychol 55:543, 1958

26. ——: Perception during sleep. In Hoch PM, Zubin J (eds): Psychopathology of Perception. New York, Grune & Stratton, 1965

27. Domhoff B, Kamiya J: Problems in dream content study with objective indicators. Arch Gen Psychiat 11:519, 1964

28. Doob LW: Eidetic imagery. A cross-cultural Will-o'-the-Wisp? J Psychol 63:13, 1966

29. Eagle M: Personality correlates of sensitivity to subliminal stimulation. J Nerv Ment Dis 134:1, 1962

30. ——, Wolitsky DL, Klein GS: Imagery: effects of a concealed figure in a stimulus. Science 151(2):837, 1966

31. Egdell HG, Kalvin I: Childhood hallucinations. J Child Psychol Psychiat 13:279, 1972

32. Eisenberg L: Hallucinations in children. In West LJ (ed): Hallucinations. New York, Grune & Stratton, 1962

33. Ellinwood EH: Amphetamine psychosis. I. Description of the individuals and process. J Nerv Ment Dis 144:273, 1967

34. Evarts EV: A neurophysiologic theory of hallucinations. In West LJ (ed): Hallucinations. New York, Grune & Stratton, 1962

35. Fisher C: Subliminal and supra-liminal influences on dreams. Amer J Psychiat 116:1009, 1960

36. ——: Dreams and perception: the role of preconscious and primary modes of perception in dream formation. J Amer Psychoanal Assoc 2:389, 1954

37. ——, Dement W: Studies on the psychopathology of sleep and dreams. Amer J Psychiat 119:1160, 1963

38. ——, Kahn E, Edwards A, et al: A psychophysiological study of nightmares and night terrors. I. Physiological aspects of the stage 4 night terror. J Nerv Ment Dis 157:75, 1973

39. ——, Kahn E, Edwards W, et al: A psychophysiological study of nightmares and night terrors. II. The suppression of stage 4 night terrors with diazepam. Arch Gen Psychiat 28:252, 1973

40. ——, Kahn E, Edwards A, et al: A psychophysiological study of nightmares and night terrors. III. Mental content of stage 4 night terrors. J Nerv Ment Dis 158:174, 1974

41. ——, Paul IH: The effect of subliminal visual stimulation on images and dreams: a validation study. J Amer Psychoanal Assoc 7:35, 1959

42. Fiss H, Ellman SJ, Klein GS: Effects of interruption of rapid eye movement sleep on fantasy in the waking state. Psychophysiology 4:364, 1968

43. ——, Goldberg FH, Klein GS: Effects of subliminal stimulation on imagery and discrimination. Percept Mot Skills 17:31, 1963

44. Forgus RH, Dewolfe AS: Perceptual selectivity in hallucinatory schizophrenics. J Abnorm Psychol 74:288, 1969
45. Freedman DX: On the use and abuse of LSD. Arch Gen Psychiat 18:330, 1968
46. Freedman SJ, Greenblatt M: Studies in human isolation. II. Hallucinations and other cognitive findings. US Armed Forces Med J 2:1479, 1960
47. Freud S: The interpretation of dreams. Stand Ed 4, 1953
48. Goldberger L: Homogeneous visual stimulation (Ganzfeld) and imagery. Percept Mot Skills 12:91, 1961
49. ———, Holt R: A comparison of isolation effects and their personality correlates in two divergent samples. New York University ASD Tech Rep 61:417, 1961
50. Goodwin DW, Alderson P, Rosenthal R: Clinical significance of hallucination in psychiatric disorders. Arch Gen Psychiat 24:76, 1971
51. Greenberg R: Cerebral cortex lesions: the dream process and sleep spindles. Cortex 2:357, 1966
52. ———, et al: The effects of dream deprivation. Presented to American Psychoanalytic Association, 1968 Annual Meeting, Boston, Mass
53. Gross J, et al: Eye movements during emergent stage I EEG in subjects with lifelong blindness. J Nerv Ment Dis 141:365, 1965
54. Haber RN: Eidetic images. Sci Amer 220:36, 1969
55. ———: Contemporary Theory and Research in Visual Perception. New York, Holt, 1968
56. ———, Haber RB: Eidetic imagery, imagery frequency. Percept Mot Skills 19:131, 1967
57. Hall CS, Vander Castle RL: A comparison of home and monitored dreams. Paper presented at the Association for the Psychophysiological Study of Sleep, Palo Alto, Calif, March, 1964
58. Havens LL: Placement and movement of hallucinations in space: phenomenology and theory. Int J Psychiat 43:426, 1962
59. Heaton RK, Victor RG: Personality characteristics associated with psychedelic flashbacks in natural and experimental settings. J Abnorm Psychol 85(1):83, 1976
60. Hoffer A, Osmond H: The Hallucinogens. New York, Academic Press, 1967
61. Holt RR: Imagery: the return of the ostracized. Amer Psychol 19:254, 1964
62. ———: The emergence of cognitive psychology. J Amer Psychoanal Assoc 12:650, 1964
63. ———: On the nature and generality of mental imagery. In Sheehan P (ed): The Function and Nature of Imagery. New York, Academic Press, 1972
64. Honorton C, Harper S: Pre-mediated imagery and ideation in an experimental procedure for regulating perceptual input. J Amer Soc Psych Res 68:156, 1974
65. Horowitz MJ: Visual imagery and cognitive organization. Amer J Psychiat 123:938, 1967

66. Jackson JH: In Taylor J (ed): Selected writings, vol 2. New York, Basic, 1958
67. Jansson B: The prognostic significance of various types of hallucinations in young people. Acta Psychiat Scand 44:401, 1968
68. Keith PR: Night terrors. A review of the psychology, neurophysiology, and therapy. J Amer Acad Child Psychiat 14:477, 1975
69. Kollar EJ, et al: Psychosis in dream deprivation. "Psychological, psychophysiological, and biochemical correlates of prolonged sleep deprivation." Amer J Psychiat 126:488, 1969
70. Kramer M: Manifest dream content in normal and psychopathologic states. Arch Gen Psychiat 22:149, 1970
71. Kubzansky PE: Discussion of papers presented at American Psychological Association Convention Symposium, "Sensory deprivation research: Where do we go from here?" 1964
72. Lindauer M: Imagery and sensory modality. Percept Mot Skills 29:203, 1969
73. Linton H, Langs R: Subjective reactions to lysergic acid diethylamide (LSD-25). Arch Gen Psychiat 6:352, 1962
74. Luby ED, et al: Model psychoses and schizophrenia. Amer J Psychiat 119:61, 1962
75. Mack JE: Nightmares and Human Conflict. Boston, Little, Brown, 1970
76. Maclay WS, Guttman E: Mescaline hallucinations in artists. Arch Neurol Psychiat 45:130, 1941
77. Maher BA: Principles of Psychopathology. New York, McGraw-Hill, 1966
78. Malitz S, Wilkins B, Escover H: A comparison of drug induced hallucinations with those seen in spontaneously occurring psychoses. In West LJ (ed): Hallucinations. New York, Grune & Stratton, 1962
79. Marrazzi AS: Pharmacodynamics of hallucination. In West LJ (ed): Hallucinations. New York, Grune & Stratton, 1962
80. McKellar P: Imagination and Thinking. New York, Basic, 1957
81. Mendelson JH, et al: Effects of visual deprivation on imagery experienced by deaf subjects. In Wortis J (ed): Recent Advances in Biological Psychiatry, vol 6. New York, Plenum, 1964
82. Miller SC: Ego autonomy in sensory deprivation, isolation and stress. Int J Psychoanal 43:1, 1962
83. Mintz S, Alpert M: Image, vividness, reality testing, and schizophrenic hallucination. J Abnorm Psychol 79:310, 1972
84. Offenkrantz W, Rechtschaffen A: Clinical studies of sequential dreams. I. A patient in psychotherapy. Arch Gen Psychiat 8:497, 1963
85. ———, Wolpert E: The detection of dreaming in a congenitally blind subject. J Nerv Ment Dis 136:88, 1963
86. Orne MT: On the social psychology of the psychological experiment: with particular reference to demand characteristics and their implications. Amer Psychol 17:776, 1962
87. ———: The nature of hypnosis: artifact or essence? J Abnorm Soc Psychol 58:277, 1959

88. Paul IH: The effects of a drug-induced alteration in state of consciousness on retention of drive-related verbal material. J Nerv Ment Dis 138:367, 1964

89. ——, Fisher C: Subliminal visual stimulation: a study of its influence on subsequent images and dreams. J Nerv Ment Dis 129:315, 1959

90. Pivik T, Foulkes D: "Dream deprivation": effects on dream content. Science 153:1282, 1966

91. Pötzl O: The relationship between experimentally induced dream images and indirect vision. Psychol Issues 7(2):41, 1960

92. Rapaport D: Cognitive structures. In Gill M (ed): The Collected Papers of David Rapaport. New York, Basic, 1967

93. ——: The Organization and Pathology of Thought. New York, Columbia Univ Press, 1951

94. Rechtschaffen A, Vogel G, Shaikun G: Interrelatedness of mental activity during sleep. Arch Gen Psychiat 9:536, 1963

95. Richardson A: Mental Imagery. New York, Springer, 1969

96. Roffwarg HP, et al: Dream imagery: relationship to rapid eye movements of sleep. Arch Gen Psychiat 7:235, 1962

97. Rossi AM, Sturrock JB, Solomon P: Suggestion effects on reported imagery in sensory deprivation. Percept Mot Skills 16:39, 1963

98. Sampson H: Psychological effects of dreaming sleep. J Nerv Ment Dis 143:305, 1966

99. Sarbin TR: The concept of hallucination. J Pers 35:359, 1967

100. ——, Juhasz JB: Toward a theory of imagination. J Pers 38:52, 1970

101. Schacter DL: The hypnagogic state: a critical review of the literature. Psychol Bull 83:452, 1976

102. Schultes RE: Hallucinogens of plant origin. Science 163:245, 1969

103. Schur H: The unconscious today; essays in honor of Max Schur. New York, International Univ Press, 1971

104. Shapiro D: Neurotic Styles. New York, Basic, 1965

105. Sheehan P: A shortened form of Betts' questionnaire upon mental imagery. J Clin Psychol 23:386, 1967

106. ——: Reliability of a short test of imagery. Percept Mot Skills 25:744, 1967

107. Shevrin H, Luborsky L: The rebus technique: a method for studying primary-process transformations of briefly exposed pictures. J Nerv Ment Dis 133:479, 1961

108. ——, Luborsky L: The measurement of preconscious perception in dreams and images, and investigation of the Pötzl phenomenon. J Abnorm Soc Psychol 56:285, 1958

109. ——, Stross L: The fate of fleeting impressions in dreams, waking images and hypnosis: a study of thought organization in different states of consciousness. Unpublished progress report, 1964

110. Siegel RK, West LJ (eds): Hallucinations: Behavior, Experience, and Theory. New York, Wiley, 1975

111. Silberer H: Report of a method of eliciting and observing certain symbolic hallucination phenomena. In Rapaport D (ed): The Organization and Pathology of Thought. New York, Columbia Univ Press, 1951

112. Singer J: The Inner World of Day-Dreaming. New York, Harper & Row, 1975

113. Slater PE, Morimoto K, Hyde RW: The effect of group administration upon symptom formation under LSD. J Nerv Ment Dis 125:312, 1957

114. Small IF, et al: Clinical characteristics of hallucinations of schizophrenia. Dis Nerv Syst 27:349, 1966

115. Solomon P, et al (eds): Sensory Deprivation. Cambridge, Mass, Harvard Univ Press, 1961

116. Spanos N, Barber T: Hypnotic experiences as inferred from subjective reports: auditory and visual hallucinations. J Exp Res Pers 3:136, 1968

117. Starker S: Effects of hypnotic induction upon visual imagery. J Nerv Ment Dis 159:433, 1974

118. Stoyva J: Biofeedback techniques and the conditions for hallucinatory activity. In Mcguigan F, Schoonover R (eds): The Psychophysiology of Thinking. New York, Academic Press, 1973

119. Suedfield P, Vernon J: Visual hallucinations during sensory deprivation: a problem of criteria. Science 145:112, 1964

120. Underwood HW: The validity of hypnotically induced visual hallucinations. J Abnorm Soc Psychol 61:39, 1960

121. Varendonck J: The psychology of daydreams. In Rapaport D (ed): Organization and Pathology of Thought. New York, Columbia Univ Press, 1951

122. Verdone P: Temporal reference of manifest dream content. Percept Mot Skills 20:1253, 1965

123. Vernon JA, Hoffman J, Shiffman H: Visual hallucinations during perceptual isolation. Canad J Psychol 12:31, 1958

124. West LJ, et al: The psychosis of sleep deprivation. Ann NY Acad Sci 96:66, 1961

125. Ziskind E: An explanation of mental symptoms found in acute sensory deprivation: researches 1958–1963. Amer J Psychiat 121:939, 1965

126. ———, Augsburg T: Hallucinations in sensory deprivation—method or madness? Science 137:992, 1962

127. Zubek JP (ed): Sensory Deprivation: Fifteen Years of Research. New York, Appleton, 1969

128. Zuckerman M, Cohen N: Is suggestion the source of reported visual sensations in perceptual isolation? J Abnorm Soc Psychol 68:655, 1964

129. ———, Cohen N: Sources of reports of visual and auditory sensations in perceptual-isolation experiments. Psychol Bull 62:1, 1964

130. ———, et al: Stress and hallucinatory effects of perceptual isolation and confinement. Psychol Monogr 76(30):1, 1962

Part II

Psychodynamics of Image Formation

4

EARLY CONCEPTS OF THE
ROLE OF IMAGES IN THOUGHT

It was once believed that thought was composed of images arranged by linear associational connections, and that persons could be typed according to the specific kind of image they habitually used. It was also believed that thought was conscious, directed by free will, and could be understood by introspection. This chapter relates these early theories and the observations that shattered them.

PHILOSOPHIC BEGINNINGS

Aristotle[4] considered images to be the basic elements of thought, connected by associational relevance. The mind determines the objects it will pursue or avoid by contemplation of these images, which exist in the mind in the absence of external objects. In this formulation, Aristotle advanced an enduringly important concept about images: they have the power to motivate a person to emotion and effort.

Later philosophers such as Locke and Hume formulated theories of cognition in which images were again basic elements. Locke[17] believed that thought developed as perception was recorded in residual images. These images were then recalled, as part of thought, and simple images could be recombined to form complex ideas. Hume[14] attempted to separate images from perceptions (he used the terms idea and impression) on the basis that perceptions had greater vividness, force, and liveliness. The image, however, was regarded as an exact copy of a perception. During sleep, fever, madness, or violent emotions the difference between images and perceptions was lost, and images seemed to be real.

Hume observed that memory must not only preserve perception as recorded images but must also retain some schema of their order in time and position in space. However, the images need not be recalled invariably in the order perceived; by reprocessing images into different combinations it was possible to imagine, as well as to recall accurately, the past.

Hartley[12] speculated that there was thought in imageless form through the use of word signification without sensory quality. He believed that word meaning was acquired through the process of labeling objects. Some word objects had "no proper ideas"; by this he meant that words such as pronouns and participles were not affixed to specific objects but were learned simply as words through speech or reading. Hartley thus presumed two overlapping systems for the representation of thought: words in nonsensory quality, and images of the various sensory types.

Mill,[23] like Hume, was interested in the difference between perceptions and images (he called them sensations and ideas). Sometimes he noted images were as vivid as perceptions, as in hallucinations or dreams. He regarded these as episodes in which thought escaped the laws of association and the government of the will. Ordinarily, thought was regulated by associational relevance. To define associational direction of thought further, Mill classified images as interesting (pleasurable or painful) and uninteresting (not particularly pleasurable or painful). Uninteresting ideas did not attract much attention, and trains of images were organized, in their flow, toward even more interesting images. In a sense, Mill regarded consciousness as a sensory organ that was attracted to interesting images just as it was attracted to interesting perceptions.

EARLY PSYCHOLOGY: IMAGES
AS THE ELEMENTS OF THOUGHT

In the late nineteenth century, many psychologists attacked the problem of thought with a stratagem based on Aristotelian science. They would describe the basic elements or "atoms" of thought and then find how these basic elements combined. They designated images as the primary elements of thought and trained introspectors to report as accurately as possible their streams of consciousness. For a while the theory became a self-fulfilling prophecy because thought is easily biased by the instructions of an authoritative person and the expectations of the subject. Since subjects were asked to describe the sensory quality of various kinds of images, they tended to report all of their thoughts as images. Thought in words was categorized by the image quality of the word: as a visual image if the word had the quality of being "seen," as an auditory image if the word had the quality of being "heard," and as a kinesthetic image if the word had the quality of being articulated.

In the above model of thought, images were assembled according to various laws of association. These laws suggested that once an image was in mind it would tend to call forth, as the next unit of thought, an image that was categorically similar, concretely similar, that occurred frequently, that occurred recently, or that had some perceptual continuity with the previous image. This second image would call forth a third, and so forth. Naturally, one image might evoke multiple associations, and multiple images might be "primed" by the conscious awareness of the preceding image. But, in general, thought proceeded by selecting the image highest in a hierarchy of activation.

DISCOVERY OF IMAGELESS THOUGHT

Marbe[21] and Külpe[16] at the University of Würzberg were among the first investigators to realize that their data contradicted the theory that images were the elements of thought. They used introspective reports to examine the processes occurring between a stimulus word presentation and a subject's reaction to it. Their subjects reported that they were sometimes aware of experiences hard to label as images. This conscious experience was not an image, not a word, and not even a clear awareness of will or choice—it was a kind of formless sense of predisposition. At other times, of course, they blurted out associations without awareness of any intervening conscious thought process.

Messer[22] tried to study the "dispositions of consciousness" that had not representational form. He groped toward the idea that much of thinking went on below the conscious level, and developed a model of conscious thinking as a sampling of these out-of-awareness processes with various degrees of clarity. His model, like Freud's,[9] considers consciousness as a kind of superordinate sense organ: consciousness samples thought.

The ideas of the Würzberg School about imageless and unconscious thinking outraged authorities in other academic centers of psychology. Wündt, the father of experimental psychology, responded with critical argument. He disputed the possibility of "imageless thought" and impugned the scientific methods of the Würzberg school. He, of course, was well aware of how easily introspective reports might be biased.[20]

Titchener,[31] another influential theoretician, seconded Wündt; he gave the verdict that there were no such things as imageless thoughts. The contents of thought called imageless by the Würzberg psychologists were actually "highly complex integrations of sensory components which faulty introspective techniques had failed to recognize." When introspection failed to yield any clear images, Titchener felt that images were nonetheless present but might be images of kinesthetic or spatial quality that were hard to recognize or describe.

Ach[1] tried to unite the opposing schools of thought by this type of formulation:

> When a content is only an imageless knowledge (immediately preceding or simultaneous with the meaning awareness) there exists in consciousness a visual, acoustic, or kinesthetic sensation (tension-sensation), or a memory image of the content. These sensations are image-representations in consciousness of the imageless knowledge. They are indicators of the meaning-content. The sensations may come without such meaning-content as pure sensory qualities.

Ach also tried to indicate the tremendous speed and multiplicity of thought:

> Furthermore, it happens at times that complex contents, the verbal expression of which would take several sentences, appear momentarily, like a flash of lightning.

The intensive experimentation by both sides of this image-imageless thought controversy resulted in two relatively new ideas which were highly important: (1) that there were determinants of conscious thought that operated outside of conscious awareness, and (2) that there were schemata, plans, expectations, attitudes, goals, and values that existed on a different level of abstraction than "elementary particles" of thought.

Bühler[7] formulated statements about cognitive schemata when he classified imageless knowledge as (1) consciousness of a rule, of knowing that one can solve a problem and how it is done, without actually having the steps in mind; (2) consciousness of knowing the meaning of something, intending it without having the meaning content clearly in mind; and (3) consciousness of relation.

Watt[32] was able to trace a mental set as it "left awareness." Upon beginning an experiment a subject might be completely conscious of the task set for him, but this awareness gradually tended to drop out of consciousness. At the same time, the mental set lost none of its effectiveness in determining the course of the subject's reactions. Thus, a vital controlling factor was found to exist that was not directly available to reflective self-awareness (consciousness).

Watt presented his subjects with a series of stimulus words and grouped their responses into three categories: (1) simple reproductions of the stimulus or the response (associated with rapid reaction time); (2) visual images after which came a spoken word (associated with longer reaction time); and (3) psychic word representations appearing between the presentation of the written word (optical) and the spoken reaction (reaction time between types 1 and 2). The vividness and frequency of visual images seemed to be dependent on the nature of the task in question. A subject who showed an absolute absence of visual images while performing one kind of task might show lively and detailed visual images with another.

Selz[27] summed up the accumulated experience and asserted both the possibility of understanding thought and the need to extend investigation of thought beyond the introspective reports of conscious awareness:

Together with the theory of diffuse reproduction, a conception of intellectual processes as a mere running off of images must also be abandoned. It is not images, not even the awareness of thoughts that have sometimes been designated as imageless "elements," that make up the constituent units of our system of specific responses; rather, these units are acts, intellectual operations that are just as needful of and amenable to analysis as the simple reflexes from which complex body movements are built up.

GESTALT PSYCHOLOGY: ANOTHER CHALLENGE TO THE ASSOCIATIONIST THEORY

The Gestalt school of psychology maintained and demonstrated that perceptions consist of entire patterns and forms rather than of particulate information that is pieced together into a whole.[15] Instead of sequential and associational assembly of bits from simple to complex, the Gestalt school suggests that thought, as well as perception, might be assembled holistically, from less clear to more distinct versions of the same form. This important focus on large-scale organization in perception and thinking was, perhaps, a final telling blow to the early theory that "atoms" of images were assembled by associational connection.*

Academic psychology was staggered by the idea of thought outside of conscious awareness, the conceptualization of endless levels of mental sets and determining tendencies, the multiple motives causing progression of thought along associational networks, and the unreliability of the intro-spective method that was required for collection of data. If such a bewildering array of variables had to be considered, how could thought processes ever be unraveled by scientific methods? Many psychologists despaired of the task and turned instead to the study of sensation (eg, visual psychophysics), human intellectual performance (eg, memory of visual images), and animal learning as measured by behavior (eg, condi-tioning to visual stimuli). Bakan[5] suggests that this flight was due, in part, to anxiety about investigating unconscious motives. The study of imagery itself was ostracized from academic psychology[13] only to return with a renewed interest in information processing.

THE CONCEPT OF IMAGE TYPES

One corollary of the theory that thought took place by forming se-quences of images was that persons differed in their habitual choice of sense modes for representation of thought. Common sense observation led to this formulation. Some persons obviously formed concepts pictori-ally while others generated thought as a series of words that seemed to be "heard" and scarcely ever had a picture in their "mind's eye."

Sir Francis Galton[10] was interested in how persons varied in their capacity to form mental images in different sense modes and conducted an interesting investigation by sending a questionnaire to prominent scientists and thinkers. Among other things, he asked his subjects to describe the vividness of their mental imagery as they attempted to recall, as clearly as possible, their morning's breakfast table with all its contents. He found a wide range of styles. Most people had not thought much about the sensory quality of their thoughts and were very surprised to find that everyone did not use exactly the same types of images as they did.

Galton, by careful questioning, was also able to demonstrate the presence of number forms, calendar forms, and synesthetic systems.

---

* An excellent reference to all the material covered so far in this chapter is Mandler and Mandler.[20]

Galton's diligent work on imagery led to the theory that each person used characteristic modes, so that persons could be typologized as visualizers, kinesthetes, audiles, and so on. The theory that persons have different styles of thought relates to the problem of differentiating personality; for if persons think in a different mode they will react to situations differently, remember differently, and behave differently.

When people describe their thought, they usually mention contents or ideas, but not the mode of representation. When asked what form his thought takes, a person is often puzzled by the question at first, but is usually able to go on to say whether a thought is a visual image, a word, whether there is a taste, movement, or tactile quality to the representation, and so forth. Persons unsophisticated in this type of discourse are surprised when told that all persons do not have similar experiences when thinking. A person who is used to a parade of visual images that are then translated into words may react with disbelief or even pity when told that some people think mainly in words. Persons who think mainly in words may wonder how it is possible to form visual images and, once formed, how any kind of rational thinking is likely to take place.

Anne Roe[24] used interviews to find out the representation of thought in various scientists. As an example of this type of approach, her results indicated that about one-third were visualizers, one-third were verbalizers, and about one-quarter were "imageless" in that they just knew something was going on without being able to qualify the nature of their representations. (The rest were mixed.) She found more visualizers among physical scientists, more verbalizers among social scientists.

Most persons, however, do not seem to have a discrete style; they use images of various sense modes, and they use words in a mixed fashion as appropriate to circumstances. In unusual cases, however, the reliance on a single style is easy to observe.

One of the best works on an extreme degree of single-style thinking is Luria's *The Mind of a Mnemonist*,[18] which describes in detail an extraordinary man whose thought was dominated by visual images. He could perform prodigious feats of memory using both eidetic visual perceptions and supplemental imagery. After seeing a table of numbers, he could retain the visual impression for years and read off numbers from the recalled image in any direction requested. When presented words, he remembered the visual images evoked by the sounds and then retranslated these images to reproduce the words he was asked to memorize and retain. Even mathematical or logical problems were solved through association of numbers with concrete objects. Simpler versions of the same mnemonic tricks are common. But what is of the greatest interest to us here is that this person was dominated by his cognitive style; he was *compelled* to form visual images and, at times, this actually interfered with volitional and goal-directed thinking. Only with great effort, and at times not even then, could he keep from elaborating visual images in response to any sensory stimulus. When reminded of that stimulus thereafter, he inevitably recapitulated the responsive images whether he wished to or not. These visual images were so vivid and so stable that sometimes he could not follow the meaning of what he was reading because images dominated his attention. Also, during his childhood, he periodically could not distinguish his images from perceptions. This kind of phenomenon might be found in a rare patient, who in psychotherapy might learn to "live with" his special disposition.

DISSENSION ABOUT THE RELIABILITY OF IMAGE TYPOLOGIES

In the research on images in thought conducted at the turn of the century, it was important to categorize subjects as to whether they were visualizers, audiles, kinesthetes, and so on. Experimenters devised many ingenious methods, but finally there was such a plethora of procedures for measuring images and image types that the psychologic literature became confused with little replication of promising experiments. In the midst of this confusion the American Psychological Association asked a special committee to standardize some of the procedures used in experimental work. J. Angell, chairman of this committee, took upon himself the long task of reviewing all the methods then in use for the determination of mental imagery.[2]

As described, many of the methods assumed that individuals could be typologized according to the type of images they used in thought. For example, one assumption was that measurement of whatever sense mode of stimulus presentation was easiest to memorize would indicate that person's habitual mode of representation. Thus, a person who did comparatively well memorizing a visually presented list was considered to be a visualizer, while a person who did relatively well on a list presented auditorily was assumed to be prone to use auditory images in thought. The same held true for the ability to maintain memorization during distractions in different modalities. A person who relied mainly on auditory imagery, for example, was thought to be more distracted by sound during a visual memorization task than he would be by visual stimuli during an auditory memorization task.

Creativity was thought to provide another means of typing subjects. Literary works could be studied for the sense mode of images most prevalently used as metaphors. Similarly, the ability of a person to create imaginary products in different contexts could lead to imagery typing. For example, a comparison could be made between relative ability to imagine things growing out of an inkblot, out of amorphous sounds, or out of movement sensations.

Angell's criticism of each of the above "objective methods"* is pertinent. He pointed out that many subjects could translate from one mode of imagery to another and, as a result of this effort, might remember a list they had translated better than one which was presented and recalled in the same type of imagery, without translation efforts. He also pointed out that intensification of the learning process might occur with efforts to concentrate during a distraction, actually improving learning rather than detracting from it. Angell concluded that, at the time, there were no objective methods of imagery analysis that were reliable.

Angell then went on to list more subjective methods, which usually required some degree of introspective report. He noted that subjects varied in their performances according to the ideas they had of what was expected of them by the investigators. Also, the images employed for describing one set of experiences sometimes differed from those used for another set. Subjects seemed able to shift their styles of cognition from one modality of imagery to another.

Concluding his summary of the methods then available, Angell made certain recommendations that are still worth following. Investigators should seek to ascertain all the forms of images that any individual could command at will, to determine the forms that person uses in daily life, and to determine the function of the subject's images in his thought processes. It was felt that no one of these aims could be realized by any simple, single, or quickly executed test. Even an extended group of tests would not yield such data if the subject were deficient in introspective powers. Angell suspected that the clear imagery types listed by Galton[10] were probably not to be found in experimental subjects. He indicated that the different image modes could be expected to shift and substitute for each other under slight changes of conditions: "This is not to deny the reality of types, but simply to urge that they do not follow with any great regularity the lines heretofore laid down. They represent problems we still have to solve, rather than solid foundations on which we can build."

---

*The methods were called objective because they resulted in scores of task performance rather than analysis of introspective reports.

At about the same time, Betts[6] was studying the ability to form vivid images in various sensory modes. He found a few people who formed thought in only one mode, but most of his subjects who reported vivid visual images also tended to form vivid images in other senses. Those with dim visual images tended to have dim images in general. Sheehan[28] confirmed these findings: persons with vivid images in one mode usually formed vivid images in general. Persons differed more in terms of general vividness of reported imagery than in specificity of mode of imagery.

Another approach to style concerns not so much the type of imagery but the contents, intensity, and emotional coloration. Singer[29] originated a means for exploring these aspects of style in his Imaginal Processes Inventory. By using this instrument to obtain reports from a large number of people, he was able to determine that there were consistencies of style, and identified three prominent ones.

The first was the "guilty-dysphoric style" in which waking fantasy life was dominated by images of guilt, fear, hostility, ambition, and conflict. The second style was labeled as "positive-vivid" since the factored items were usually associated with pleasant feelings and did not contain prominent themes of conflict. The third style was "anxious-distractible," in which contents intruded into awareness in a frightening or even bizarre manner, disrupting concentration on some other business. Singer's findings were replicated by Starker[30] on new subjects, and extended to include recurrent styles in dreaming.

These stylistic variations may be important in psychotherapy. The last chapter of this book includes a discussion of techniques in which the psychotherapist suggests that the patient form visual images of various kinds. For patients who have a positive affective style, such suggestions may tend to lead toward modification of currently negative moods to more optimistic and positive ones. If the patient has a habitual guilty-dysphoric or anxious-distractible style of imagery, the shift to image formation may be associated with a focus on regulation of trains of thought; on learning actively to control ideational and emotional themes which before had been experienced only passively. Also, with these patients, efforts to translate conflicted ideas into words may be especially important, as will be discussed in Chapter 5.

THE RELATIONSHIP BETWEEN
HALLUCINATIONS AND IMAGE STYLE

Despite the conclusions of such investigators as Angell and Betts, the concept of image types remained popular and led to some interesting research. Several researchers focused on the relationship of the mode of hallucinatory experiences to the person's ordinary style of thought images. Anthony[3] suggests, for example, that children with a visual tendency are more likely to develop syndromes such as hallucinatory night terrors while those with a motor tendency are more likely to become sleepwalkers.

Psychotic hallucinations were studied by Cohen[8] using the Griffitts word-image association test for prevailing mode of concrete images. In the Griffitts[11] test a subject is given a phrase and asked to report the content and sensory mode of his intrapsychic response. For example, the stimulus could be "whistle of a train" and the subject would report whether she had an auditory image response, such as hearing the whistle, or a visual image, say of a train. The results are scored in terms of the percentage of response in each sensory mode of thought image. Cohen contrasted schizophrenic patients who had reported hallucinations in different sense modes with normal subjects who did not report hallucinations. He found that the subgroup of visual hallucinators had less than the group average for visual thought images and that auditory hallucinators had fewer than average auditory thought images. In contrast to these negative correlations, kinesthetic hallucinations correlated positively with increased kinesthetic imagery, and "somatic hallucinations" correlated with increased "body imagery." Cohen concluded that "the relationships of imagery and hallucinations are different for the visual and auditory modalities than for the kinesthetic, tactual-temperature, and olfactory-gustatory modalities."

In 1945, Roman and Landis[25] reported another study correlating style of mental images with the modality of reported hallucinations. They used a standardized psychiatric interview that focused on the subjective intensity of various modes of images. They studied only auditory and visual hallucinations since these are most prevalent. Roman and Landis concluded, as did Cohen, that the results tended to contradict the hypothesis that hallucinations are exaggerations or projections of the person's usual thought images.

Based on these previous studies, Seitz and Molholm[26] conducted an extensive study of (1) persons with schizophrenia, (2) persons with alcoholic hallucinations, and (3) normal controls. They used the same test of concrete images developed by Griffitts and used by Cohen. In patients with auditory hallucinations, the mean percentage of auditory image responses to stimuli was less than the percentage in patients with no hallucinations. Similar results occurred in patients with visual hallucinations, who gave less visual responses than patients without visual hallucinations. Of interest, the numbers in the percentage data were quite similar to those reported earlier by Cohen. Seitz and Molholm concluded:

These findings indicate quite definitely that one of the factors on which auditory hallucinations may depend is a relatively low percentage of auditory imagery. According to this concept, most of those persons who attempt to resolve their personal mental conflicts by projecting them as auditory hallucinations would be found, if they were tested by means of an impersonal projective technique, to have had the hallucinations in a modality of imagery in which they were relatively deficient. . . . Not only do these findings disprove the old theory that auditory hallucinations are exaggerations of predominating auditory imagery, but they suggest the new concept that one of the factors responsible for auditory hallucinations is relatively deficient auditory imagery.

The data of these several studies were consistent, but the investigators may have misinterpreted these results since they did not consider defense and control. People who have symptoms such as hallucinations are likely to attempt to prevent lapses in control by suppression of image formation in the modality of the feared hallucination.* Also, the authors neglect to consider the attitudes of such patients. Many hallucinators will fear to disclose thought images in a modality that they have come to associate with a pathologic symptom. Certainly they will have already been questioned about their hallucinations. Thus, some patients who have had hallucinations will tend to report fewer responses in the image mode of the hallucinations. This is a good example of how difficult it is to interpret even replicated empirical data in the field of image formation in particular and thinking in general.

CONCLUSION

We can now summarize some of the hard-won findings of these early researchers:

1. Thought does not consist only of discrete image particles. Expression of ideas and feelings may take various forms of representation, some of which are imageless.
2. Thought is not limited, in construction, to sequential associations between basic elements; thoughts do not occur only one at a time, but rather, multiple thoughts may be experienced simultaneously.

---

* It is possible, however, that the investigators are correct in their interpretation of the results. While I consider this less likely, persons may have relatively more control over habitual image formation than over less habitual image formation. A "breakthrough" might occur in the less controlled modality. This topic, of control and defense, is discussed in more detail in Chapter 7.

3. Thought enters awareness (or consciousness samples thought) to various degrees. Many aspects of thinking take place out of awareness and are not available to introspective efforts.
4. Introspection alters the very thinking it seeks to study, and instruction on how to introspect alters thought even further.
5. There are hierarchical levels of thought organization ranging from definite images or words, to organizational schemata that assemble these presentations, to the regulatory influences that govern both.
6. Persons cannot be reliably separated into discrete image types according to a given sense mode. Few persons may habitually or even exclusively think in one mode. It does seem possible, however, to distribute people along a continuum from high to low capacity for forming voluntary images in general: some people form vivid images in several modes, others seldom have a clear image in any sensory mode.

We do not yet know why some persons use image formation more than others. We may speculate that some persons have constitutional factors that predispose them to heightened vividness or retention of images, or that reduce their capacity for regulation of image formation. Environment also must play a major role although we cannot yet chart the route of its influence. Probably important factors would include the kind of perceptual stimulation provided, the extent to which the infant used internal images as a substitute for perceptions (eg, of an absent mother), and the child's later capacity to acquire symbolism and language to substitute for images.

Infantile experiences at the separation-individuation phase of psychologic development may thus be very important influences on subsequent cognitive style.[19] Experience that involves perceptual shock or trauma would also influence subsequent emphasis on one or another form of imagery.

Finally, cultural factors will play a heavy influence and, at this time, our society has undergone a transformation from word orientation to image orientation, under the influence of television.

REFERENCES

1. Ach N: Awareness. In Mandler J, Mandler G (eds): Thinking: From Association to Gestalt. New York, Wiley, 1964, pp 201–207
2. Angell JC: Methods for the determination of mental imagery. Psychol Monogr 13:61, 1910

3. Anthony J: An experimental approach to the psychopathology of childhood: sleep disturbances. Brit J Med Psychol 32:19, 1959

4. Aristotle: Thinking; Recollection. In Mandler J, Mandler G (eds): Thinking: From Association to Gestalt. New York, Wiley, 1964, pp 9–15

5. Bakan D: On Method. San Francisco, Jossey-Bass, 1967

6. Betts GH: The Distribution and Functions of Mental Imagery. New York, Columbia Univ Teacher's College, 1909

7. Bühler K: Tatsachen und probleme zu einer psychologie der denkvorgänge. I. uber gedanken. In Mandler J, Mandler G (eds): Thinking: From Association to Gestalt. New York, Wiley, 1964, pp 162–164

8. Cohen LH: Imagery and its relations to schizophrenic symptoms. J Ment Sci 84:284, 1938

9. Freud S: The interpretation of dreams. Stand Ed 4, 1953

10. Galton F: Inquiries into Human Faculty. New York, Dutton, 1919

11. Griffitts CH: Fundamentals of Vocational Psychology. New York, MacMillan, 1924

12. Hartley D: Excerpts from "Observations on man." In Mandler J, Mandler G (eds): Thinking: From Association to Gestalt. New York, Wiley, 1964, pp 72–92

13. Holt RR: Imagery: the return of the ostracized. Amer Psychol 19:254, 1964

14. Hume D: Excerpt from "A treatise of human nature." In Mandler J, Mandler G (eds): Thinking: From Association to Gestalt. New York, Wiley, 1964, pp 51–69

15. Köhler W: The Task of Gestalt Psychology. Princeton, NJ, Princeton Univ Press, 1969

16. Külpe O: The modern psychology of thinking. In Mandler J, Mandler G (eds): Thinking: From Association to Gestalt. New York, Wiley, 1964, pp 208–217

17. Locke J: Excerpts from "An essay concerning human understanding." In Mandler J, Mandler G (eds): Thinking: From Association to Gestalt. New York, Wiley, 1964, pp 26–49

18. Luria AR: The Mind of a Mnemonist. New York, Basic, 1968

19. Mahler MS: Symposium on psychotic object relationships. III. Perceptual de-differentiation and psychotic "object relationships." Int J Psychoanal 41:548, 1960

20. Mandler JM, Mandler G (eds): Thinking: From Association to Gestalt. New York, Wiley, 1964

21. Marbe K: The psychology of judgments. In Mandler J, Mandler G (eds): Thinking: From Association to Gestalt. New York, Wiley, 1964, pp 143–148

22. Messer A: Experimental psychological investigations on thinking. In Mandler J, Mandler G (eds): Thinking: From Association to Gestalt. New York, Wiley, 1964, pp 148–152

23. Mill J: Excerpts from "Analysis of the phenomena of the human mind." In Mandler J, Mandler G (eds): Thinking: From Association to Gestalt. New York, Wiley, 1964, pp 94–124

24. Roe A: A study of imagery in research scientists. J Pers 19:459, 1951
25. Roman R, Landis C : Hallucinations and mental imagery. J Nerv Ment Dis 102:327, 1945
26. Seitz PF, Molholm HB: Relation of mental imagery to hallucinations. Arch Neurol Psychiat 57:469, 1947
27. Selz O: The revision of the fundamental conceptions of intellectual processes. In Mandler J, Mandler G (eds): Thinking: From Association to Gestalt. New York, Wiley, 1964, pp 225-234
28. Sheehan P: A shortened form of Betts' questionnaire upon mental imagery. J Clin Psychol 23:386, 1967
29. Singer JL: The Inner World of Daydreaming. New York, Harper & Row, 1975
30. Starker S: Fantastic Thought. Englewood Cliffs, NJ, Prentice-Hall, 1982
31. Titchener EB: Imagery and sensationalism. In Mandler J, Mandler G (eds): Thinking: From Association to Gestalt. New York, Wiley, 1964, pp 167-184
32. Watt HJ: Experimental contribution to a theory of thinking. In Mandler J, Mandler G (eds): Thinking: From Association to Gestalt. New York, Wiley, 1964, pp 189-201

5

MODES OF REPRESENTATION
OF THOUGHT

Visual images are only one form for representation of percepts, memories, ideas, and feelings. A given train of thought might include images of various sensory qualities, words without sensory quality, and implicit ideas, feelings, or predispositions. Examination of visual images alone would be misleading and would not result in an understanding of the motives for the train of thought or the utility of visual images in the thought process. Since an ongoing stream of consciousness may contain many modes of representation, it is desirable to formulate a model that shows the relationship of visual images to other forms of representation.

BACKGROUND

Freud[19] postulated that the earliest thinking in infancy was in hallucinatory images for purposes of temporary, if imaginary, gratification. In a parallel line of reasoning, Piaget[46] suggested that whenever the preverbal child experienced desire he might form in his mind an image, a kind of pseudohallucination that transformed or gratified the desire. Werner[62] and Lukianowicz[35] found resemblances among the thought patterns of children, primitive men, and psychotic persons in that all three groups use magical constructions and are prone to fuse inner images with perceptions of external reality. Werner also noted that when the child is around three or four years old, he begins to decrease physical manipulation of material, as a way of acting out thought, and instead begins to play make-believe games that probably involve thinking through images. Schilder,[54] like the other authors, also postulated that, in the development of thinking, images are gradually replaced by symbols and concepts with less sensory quality.

Most experimentalists and theorists in the last few decades have assumed a childhood progression from images to words, have paid little attention to the phases of image thinking, and have assumed that adult thinking depends largely on lexical signification. The image-imageless thought controversy described in the last chapter was dropped in favor of the assumption of the primacy of words.*

In one of the first works marking a resurgence of interest in thought processes, Humphrey[27] pondered over the assumption that thought proceeds in lexical form and reconsidered the place of image formation in cognition. He concluded that while thinking is permeated with language, it is not identical with word usage. He did not believe that images preceded words in adult thinking, but that images might either impede thinking by being "distractions" or might enhance thinking by connotative enrichment. Humphrey reasoned that perception involved images but, in the course of problem solving, the images were intellectualized. As this occurred, the images dropped away, became symbols or schemata, and eventually were transformed into imageless knowledge.

Not all contemporary investigators agree, however, about the primacy of words. For example, Vernon[61] studied the problem of the relationship of verbal language to thought processes by reinterpretation of 33 independent research studies involving 8,000 subjects. Among these subjects, some were deaf from birth, some acquired deafness after they had learned words, and some could hear normally. Thinking ability was, in these studies, measured by conceptual tasks such as nonverbal intelligence tests. Vernon takes a relatively extreme position when he concludes that "there is no functional relationship between verbal languages and cognition or thought process; verbal language is not the mediating symbol system of thought; and there is no relationship between concept formation and level of verbal language development."

Research has demonstrated the importance of images in learning and in retrieval of what has been learned. A series of research paradigms examined images and verbal processes as alternative coding systems for storing and recollecting information.[40,42] A variety of elegant experiments demonstrated that the matter was complex, but that images played an

---

*Lacan,[34] for example, suggests that the unconscious has a structure based on word representations.

important role in both learning information from stimuli[50,51] and in later recollection of that information.[11,16,29,56]

Tversky[60] has demonstrated that the same stimuli may be recorded in short-term memory, as either pictorial images or as words, depending on the anticipation the subject has, when he receives the stimuli, of what he is going to do with the information. Beritashvili[4] notes that when learning is accomplished by use and retention of mental images, then only a single trial is necessary for relatively permanent retention of what has been learned. He contrasts this with conditioned-reflex learning which requires multiple trials and is impermanent. Following methods developed by Paivio,[41] various investigators have found that nouns that are concrete and tend to evoke high levels of images in response tend to be recalled better than those with less image propensity.[21] A few investigators have not replicated these effects.[5,24]

A long-standing mnemonic device has been to link the information to be memorized to a concrete string of images. Some have suggested that unusual images help this process. In spite of such testimonials, bizarre images seem no better as a device for this purpose than common images.[25,55] Paivio[42,43] has suggested that images aid retention of information by providing a "conceptual peg" for classification both in storage and retrieval processes. Memory storage and retrieval can be aided by the concrete quality of image coding systems. Certain information is coded more optimally in the simultaneous organizations that characterize images, as contrasted to the sequential plans used to construct verbal information.

The course of development of such information processing during infancy and childhood has been the topic of considerable research.[44,52] Piaget[47] has shown that infants apparently have the cognitive capacity to retain mental images of once-seen objects that are temporarily removed from their environment. Mahler, Pine, and Bergman[38] have shown the importance of such stages in development of a coherent sense of self as related to others. Singer[57] has described how image construction is an important part of a child's assimilation and accommodation to the world, for it leads to an inner cognitive map.

Bruner,[9] in considering the course of cognitive growth during childhood, posits three systems for processing information and constructing inner models of the external world. He defines a thought representation as the end-product of information processing; the three forms of representation are labeled *enactive representation, iconic representation,* and *symbolic representation.* In using such terms, Bruner focuses on the level of concreteness of a representation. These extend from an enaction, the most concrete form, through an iconic representation, an intermediate form, to a symbolic representation, the most abstract signifier of meaning.

The model presented in this chapter is an elaboration of Bruner's tripartite system. Bruner focuses on the dimension from concreteness to abstraction of signification. Since I wish to focus on the subjective quality of thought representation, I have shifted the labels of the three systems to *enactive, image,* and *lexical* modes of representation, and consider the organization of these modes of thought (Fig. 5-1).

This model is similar to the SI (structure of the intellect) model put forward by Guilford.[20] Guilford's model is composed of three types of categories: content, operation, and product categories. What he calls the content category is closest to our present topic, the mode of representation. Guilford lists under content four headings: figural, symbolic, semantic, and behavioral. Behavioral content is similar to what will be here labeled, after Bruner, enactive; semantic to what is here labeled lexical; and figural

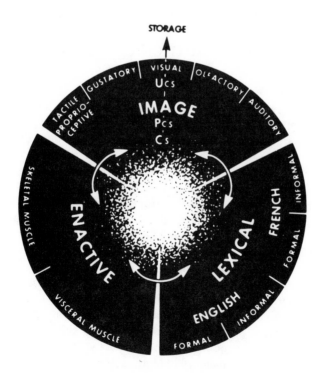

Fig. 5-1.   Systems for representation of thought.

is similar to what is here labeled image. Guilford's use of "symbolic" refers to numbers and letters which, in the present conceptualization, would fall into lexical representation. Once again the present model differs in purpose from Guilford's model: the intent is description of *modes* of representation of thought rather than the *contents* that are represented.

The use of the term "representation" in the following model will not conform to the suggestion of Beres and Joseph[3] that we define a mental representation as "*a postulated unconscious psychic organization* capable of evocation in consciousness as symbol, image, fantasy, thought, affect, or action." Here, the term representation will not be limited, as they suggest, to *unconscious* aspects of the organization of information. Use of the word "representation," instead, will follow Freud's general use of the word *vorstellung*, the use of "representation" by Piaget[47] ("the symbolic evocation of absent realities"), and, similarly, by Sandler and Rosenblatt.[53] *That is, "representation" will refer to an organization of information in a form that can be a part of conscious experience.*

REPRESENTATIONAL SYSTEMS

Enactive Thought

Infants act reflexively. Innate response mechanisms such as sucking, crying, clinging, following, and smiling are released by maturational sequence plus internal or external perceptions. Almost immediately, however, such responses lose their reflective quality and are modified by interaction with the environment. We may regard modification of motor response systems by experience as the rudiments or precursors of thinking, since the modification requires perception, response, and intervening change. Take, for example, a relatively reflexive motor response to a stimulus, such as withdrawal from pain. Through self-perception a memory of this response to this stimulus is retained. The recorded motor knowledge may be reactivated in subsequent situations that seem similar. Perhaps several possible motor responses are activated. Trial action may take place through relatively minor movements until the appropriate response is selected. These trial actions, through anticipatory tensing of various muscle groups, may be regarded as thinking through enactions. The memory pool for use as enactive representation would grow from two sources; memory of motor action by the self, and retention of mimicry responses to the motor activity of someone else.[54]

Several examples may clarify enactive representation as a mode of thinking that can be used by adults as well as small children.

A child wanted some candy that he had been emphatically told not to touch. As he tentatively reached for it with one hand, he made a stern reproving face and stopped his reaching with the other hand. The gestures and facial expression represent a train of thought: I want it, mother would say no, better not. The mimicry of mother's facial expression adds emotive power to the restraining ideas.

A person while conversing sought to use the expression "he likes to pin people down." The phrase, however, was apparently repressed for the moment. While attempting to recall the term, he made a hand gesture of pinning something down which represented enactively the desired thought. Then the words he sought entered his awareness and he was able to speak them.

While thinking of a coming tennis match, a person noted that he anticipated making various strokes by very slight muscle tensions and micromovements.

A woman patient was beginning to become aware of and to describe her sense of herself as physically and spiritually degraded and ugly. She paused in silence as she groped for words to express these emerging ideas. During this pause she grimaced. The grimace consisted of a peculiar tension that gaped one corner of her mouth. Next she became aware of this facial contortion. Only then did she realize that this facial gesture resembled, in form, an injury that had disfigured the once beautiful face of her mother. The enactive representation, the grimace expression, was the first conscious experience of this ideational complex. The enactive representation led to conscious thought experiences in visual and lexical form. These experiences contained memories of her mother and conceptualizations of her own identification with her mother and her mother's degraded (for other reasons) status.

Image Representation

Images allow continued information processing after perceptual events. In this constructive process, sets of information derived from perception, memory, and fantasy are combined, compared, and recombined in what could be called "thought by trial perception." Skill at refiguration through image formation allows one to review information for new meanings, to contemplate objects in their absence, and to seek new similarities and differences. Skill at conceptual manipulation by formation of visual images is useful to architects, painters, and surgeons. Skill at auditory image formation is useful in poetry and music, kinesthetic imagery in dance, gustatory imagery in cooking.

Visual images are excellent for representation of information about the form and spatial relationships of objects. As Freud[19] demonstrated for the plastic properties of dream imagery, this makes for ease in symbolization, condensation, and displacement. One can "play around" with the meanings of images. Words (and enactions) can be "played around" with too, but, in the case of words, the play is often in the form of auditory or visual images of words (eg, rhyme, rebus).

It is well known that images are useful for expressing the immediate quality and degree of emotion. This is especially true of complicated affective states which are hard to articulate (such as the patient's sense of psychic disintegration).[26] An example follows which illustrates how images express an affective state, how vivid unbidden images are often repetitions of traumatic perceptions, and how ideas and feelings warded off from verbal representation may emerge as images.

A 50-year-old man experienced a paralysis of one leg, with odd paresthetic sensations, as a result of a sudden cerebrovascular accident. In the hospital he was frightened, intolerant of his helpless state, but presented a blustery front with overt denial of the severity of his illness. He began to complain of recurrent unbidden images of a combat scene he had witnessed 25 years earlier. These occurred as nightmares and waking images that would be classified as pseudohallucinations. He had watched a smaller naval vessel alongside his own ship as it was wrenched apart by internal explosions. The intrusive images he now reexperienced were of the men on the deck who suffered terrible injuries. It was as if he could see again how their thigh bones were thrust into their abdomens by the massive vertical impact.

These terrible images were a compulsive repetition of a past trauma, triggered by his current stress and the ideational and emotional similarity of his current state. The images symbolized the warded-off ideas and emotions activated by his current illness. They would say, if translated into words, "Now I am to be the terrified victim, this paralysis makes me a helpless person, I am afraid of dying."

While not always as intrusive as in the above example, images may enter awareness in a spontaneous flow that seems mysteriously unguided by intention. This process, sometimes called automatic imagery, occurs continuously during everyday waking thought in some persons. Others experience such "inner movies" only during drug-induced hallucinatory states, during hypnagogic reveries, or in dreams. At least in some persons, censorship operates less keenly over image formation than over lexical representation.

Analysts, including Breuer and Freud,[8] Jung,[30] and Kubie,[32] attempted to use this property of image formation to skirt defensive processes and gain access to repressed mental contents. They simply told patients to think in visual images rather than words, and to report what images of memory or fantasy formed spontaneously. Even without such specific instructions, the emergence of previously repressed memories or fantasies is often in the form of image representation.

A related observation is that emotional responses to images of objects may be greater than those to purely lexical representations of object names. Sometimes emotional responses are delayed by inhibition of image formation until danger is past, as in the following example.

A mountain climber successfully maneuvered himself to safety after a rope broke. When he was back in base camp, he formed an image of what could have happened: the image depicted himself falling and being crushed on the rocks. On developing this image he felt intense panic, an emotion not present during the actual danger period when rapid and "cool" action was required.

Because of its emotion-evoking ability, image formation can also be used purposefully (although not necessarily consciously) to transform emotions.

A woman patient kept herself from feeling sexually aroused in the presence of attractive men by visualizing her mother's disapproving face. Vivid visualization made her feel disgust, but merely thinking words such as "mother" or "mother says sex is bad" did not generate sufficient emotion to provide her with a defense against her sexual excitation.

The use of images as a mode of thought representation increases in dreams, reveries, and hallucinogenic experiences, as noted in Chapter 3. Increased admixtures of primary process types of thinking are also noted in such altered states of consciousness. This double movement toward both greater use of images and greater admixture of primary process has led to a conceptual tendency to ally the two concepts. Thus, in psychoanalytic theory, visual images are often tacitly considered to be the characteristic mode representing primary process type thoughts. It should be emphasized, however, that visual images also may serve secondary process thinking.[2]

For example, some persons use images to represent conceptual problems, especially those involving spatial relationships as in architecture or geometry. Many persons also habitually rely on visual images for memory recall. The reader may wish to try to remember how many windows he has in his house. A usual maneuver for solving this problem is to visualize each room and count the windows in the image.

To recapitulate the main points of this section: image formation may be selected as a preferred mode of representation for several reasons. In addition to neurophysiologically determined capacities, and in addition to acquired cognitive styles, image formation may be used because of its special attributes in representing and processing information. It is close to perception and close to affect, and it allows memories to be treated "as if" they were current perceptions of objects. Image formation also permits disguises and shifts of meanings which, if represented in words, might be more difficult to disguise.

Lexical Thought

The lexical mode of representation is so familiar and yet so highly complex that only a few commonplace statements will be made to orient the place of the lexical system in the model of various modes of representation.

In the course of development, the relationship between words and what they signify is established. The child moves beyond the use of interpretation of sounds, inflections, and tonalities to include words as a means of thinking in the absence of real objects, and also in the absence of intense images of objects. The acquisition of lexical representation allows progression to new levels of conceptualization, abstraction, and reasoning.

Cognitive theorists regard thought in words as the most rational, secure, and conceptually clear form of thinking. Indeed, we have already mentioned Freud's formulation[8,18] that attachment of a word-representation to a thing-representation was the mechanism of raising an idea to the level of consciousness. While the present model is not strictly in agreement with that formulation, it is accepted that the clearest, most logical, and most communicable trains of thought occur when ideas and affects gain representation in lexical form.

In the present model, the lexical system is regarded as an epigenetic development from the earlier modes of enactive and image representation (in a manner similar to Erikson's[14] epigenesis of modes in zonal development). As will be discussed further below, the enactive and image modes also continue an epigenetic development *fostered* by the acquisition of lexical capacity. "Pure" lexical representation is conceptualized as action-less (no subvocal speech) and imageless (no auditory, visual, or kines-thetic accompaniments). As will also be discussed further, such "purity" is seldom found; rather there are conscious experiences that are relatively more or less "purely lexical" in the representational quality.

This point of view contrasts with that of such current theorists as Edelheit,[12] who suggests that the ego is a vocal-auditory organization with a structure determined by language. Such a model omits the important ego functions (and ego-organizing functions) of image formation and enactions that are *not* related directly to reception, manipulation, or production of words. While the phenomenology of conscious experience alone supports this disagreement with such language-based models of the ego, there is also experimental evidence.

Sperry[58] has studied patients after severance of the interconnection between hemispheres. The nondominant hemisphere continues informa-tion processing in (at least) visual-spatial modes, even though it is "de-prived" of access to the language and speech-determining centers of the major hemisphere. Furthermore, Freedman[45] has found, in studies of congenitally deaf children, that the relative absence of early language cues does not interfere noticeably with the processes of imitation, introjection, identification, and the internalized regulation of behavior. This does not mean, however, that development of the lexical system is not enormously important or even crucial to the processes of abstract reasoning. Fraiberg,[15] contrasting the effects of congenital deafness and blindness, finds that more early ego defects occur with deafness because, presumably, of the late acquisition of abstract conceptualization through word meanings.

Organization of Information in the Various Modes

Each system of representation will have intrinsic organizational tend-encies. As information gains representation, the mode selected may be that system which has the most appropriate organizational properties. As more or less the same information is translated from one mode to another, the organizational patterning of the information may change. For ex-ample, lexical representations tend to be organized in sequence, visual images tend to have a simultaneous arrangement of information. These organizational tendencies are not fixed, so that in addition to simul-taneous formats there is also sequential organization of images, and so forth.

Each system of representation may, because of its different organizational tendencies, separately influence the operation of memory. On the basis of extensive studies, Paivio[42] for example has presented a dual processing theory leading to dual memories, based on the organizational properties of simultaneous representation and sequential representation as described above.

In psychotherapy, the organization of memory by different encodings may be a pertinent issue to consider. A traumatic memory, for example, that has not been fully integrated into the person's inner assumptive world, may have to be recalled in terms of both its lexical and imagery memory sets. The goal is cross-translation of the meanings contained within these different aspects of the memory. As will be discussed in the final chapter of this book, in such instances the therapist may wish to suggest a shift from lexical thinking to image formation in order to expand upon a traumatic memory. While usually patients are asked to describe their visual images in words, they also may express them pictorially, as by drawing or painting. Indeed, in the study of sequential paintings by artists, as well as those by patients in art therapy, one can observe the emergence of traumatic memories without conscious recognition by the artist or patient that the forms depicted are related to traumatic perceptions.

The development of organizational capacities is an important feature in cognitive growth. So far, the modes of representation have been discussed in a particular order: enactive, image, and then lexical. This order was selected because it probably refers, crudely, to the sequence of onset of representational capacities from infancy to childhood. *But the early forms of representation, enaction and image formation, do not disappear as the new lexical capacity is gained. They do not remain at primitive organizational levels. They probably continue epigenetic development because the acquisition of lexical capacities increases the availability of schemata for organization of information in any mode.*

Within any system of representation there is an epigenetic development of information-processing capacity. As more and more information is processed, more and more ways of comparing and contrasting contents are developed. These "ways" are retained as organizational schemata after the particular information contents are either recorded in memory or forgotten. The development of these schemata of organization allows processing of more and more environmental stimuli, and this builds schemata of self, object, world, and interobject activities. This growth of cognitive structure is modeled in Figure 5-2.

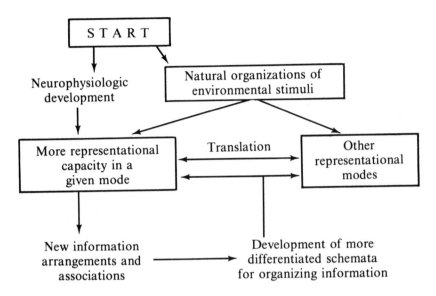

Fig. 5-2. Transactional relationship between mode of representation and organizational capacity.

While modes may share organizational formats, they will have certain intrinsic properties which are outlined in Table 5-1. For example, the usage of visual images for representation of information will foster development of spatial-simultaneous formats of organization (the capacity to order objects altogether). These formats will include ways of organizing information about the spatial-temporal contiguity of objects and their constancies, similarities, and differences. During *first* usage, such comparisons between objects will be time-consuming learning episodes; later such comparisons become automatic organizational tendencies with rapid processing characteristics.

Schemata of organization and programs for processing information that are developed in one system of representation will be useful in other systems of representation. Lexical representation, with its later onset than image representation, will first use formats already developed during earlier thought in nonlexical modes. For example, auditory image schemata—ways of categorizing which sounds are alike and which different—may be prototypic for organizing lexical representation (eg, organization by rhyme as in the clang associations of "primary process lexical thinking"

Table 5-1

An Outline of Modes of Representation

Mode	Subsystems	Sample Organizational Tendencies	Sample Statement	Sample of Complex Units of Represented Information
Enactive	Skeletal neuro-musculature Visceral neuro-musculature	By directionality and force, by operational end products	X does this	Gestures Facial expressions Postures
Image	Tactile-kinesthetic Olfactory-gustatory Visual Auditory	By simultaneous occurrence, spatial relationships, and concrete categorization of similarities and differences	X is like this, X is like Y, X is here and Y is there, X and Y happen together, X does this to Y	Introjects Fantasies Body images Relationship between objects
Lexical	Different languages	By sequentiality and linear structure; by abstract categorization	*If* X and Y *then* Z because X + Y → Z	Phrases or sentences Stories and histories

in some schizophrenic patients). The logic used in some choices of lexical representations for given objects may tend to follow visual image type schemata for comparisons of alikeness and difference. Later, the acquisition of communicative skills and connotative capacities will include the ability to order words by meaning rather than by image quality.

This development of lexical organizational capacity means building new sequential schemata out of elements derived from three sources: one includes the intrinsic and innate properties for lexical representation, what Chomsky[10] calls generative grammar. The second is derived from learning, and the third is epigenesis of enactive- and image-based schemata. The first and second sources, and the growing proportionate use of word representation, develop sequential organizational formats and lead to increased use of cause and effect reasoning. These organizational formats and reasoning "programs" can then be used for information processing in other modes, eg, in forming a sequence of visual images.

This formulation explains an apparent inconsistency in experimental data. Bruner's[9] theory suggested an epigenetic series of modes of representation. Based on this, some other investigators predicted that younger children would find image elaboration relatively more useful in problem solving then older children, and older children would find lexical elaboration more useful. Paivio[41] and Rohwer,[52] as reviewed by Reese,[49] performed a series of learning and memory experiments with children of various ages. They found results contrary to predictions: imagery elaboration was relatively less useful to the younger children than to the older children. These results were interpreted as contrary to Bruner's ideas on the course of cognitive growth. The present theory explains this: image formation is useful in such performance tasks only when it can make use not only of schemata fostered by that mode's own intrinsic properties, but also of schemata derived through the development of language.

Image representation aids in the formation of lexical organizational capacities, just as the acquisition of lexical organizational schemata enhances the ability to interpret, store, and retrieve information coded in image form. Children who are deprived of visual images due to congenital blindness may present behavioral patterns which illustrate impoverishment of lexical representation—in particular they have difficulty developing the first personal pronouns "I" and "me" in relation to the second personal pronoun, "you."[17]

Object Relations and Images

Visual images allow immediate depiction of objects in relationship due to the simultaneous organization of information in a single image. We usually characterize the objects of greatest emotional importance as self and other. Even a single image can instantly show self and other in some kind of transaction. Those transactions and images that are associated with important transactions will be repeated and, with repetition, will gain in structural clarity and development so that they come to act as organizers of new information.

Such schematic images can, for discussion, be considered as role-relationship models or two-person dyads. As an example, consider a sadomasochistic image which depicts an aggressor hurting a victim in some particular way. The sadomasochistic person who habitually uses this image schemata in fantasy or as a mode for interpreting current real experiences may identify himself at different times with different roles of the dyad. When he experiences some version of this repetitive image he sometimes links himself conceptually with the aggressor, sometimes with the victim. If one role is anxiety-provoking, the other role can be chosen for self-representation to reduce anxiety. This role reversal may still lead to some gratification because in childhood development persons learn both roles in transactional dyads. If either role is dangerous because of fear or guilt, then an undoing defense can be accomplished by shifting the designation of self from role to role and back again. The role-relationship model operates as an unconscious template for organizing information, whichever role is assigned to the self. Sometimes a story-like script is schematized, containing shifts from active to passive roles. This type of image schemata is what some refer to as an unconscious fantasy.[1,31]

One important aspect of image representation of object relationships is that the identity of the person need not necessarily be applied to *either* role. In other words, the person may experience the image without awareness as to who is hurt, who is hurting. Guilt or fear can be averted, inasmuch as the responsible person and the injured person are not the self or a particular other. Lexical representation, with its primarily sequential organization, identifies persons more clearly because word names are used.[36] Defensive operations also tend to be serial (if repression fails) and involve shifts in identification such as, "I hurt her; no, she hurts me." With such clarity of identity designation, the defensive operations are in danger of creating self-observable contradictions so that the aim—hurting —is kept relatively ambiguous. In image representation, the aim can be clear because the name is ambiguous. The fluidity and ambiguity of identification in image representation may be one reason that this system may represent impulsive aims that are inhibited from representation in the lexical system.

Regression

The present model allows clear specification of the varieties of regression that may take place in thought experience. The classification includes: (1) a return from later acquisitions of representational capacity to earlier systems of representation, for example, a retreat from words to images or enactions; (2) a return within one system to earlier contents, for example, a regression from a contemporary body image to a developmentally or organizationally primitive body image; and (3) a return within one system to earlier forms of control, such as low levels of inhibition. An example is a return to high-intensity representation (hallucinations) in the image mode. This regression in controls may include as variants: (a) a regression to dedifferentiation of reality and fantasy, (b) a regression to immediate discharge rather than imposition of delay, (c) a regression to memory and thought by drive organization rather than fidelity to reality, and (d) a regression from active organization and modification of perception to passive, unorganized, and unmodulated perceptual receptivity. The classification also includes (4) a return within one system to earlier modes of organization, such as a shift from complex systems of associational rules to simple rules of associational connection. For example, in some pathologic states, words may no longer be linked according to conceptual meaning and grammatical order but by phonic (rhyming) similarity.[37] This may include the variants of regression subsumed under (3).

Boundaries of the Systems

In normal conscious experience, in the average person, many modes of representation are used simultaneously without clear-cut division between systems. Enactions blur into image representations in the form of kinesthetic, somesthetic, and vestibular or visceral images. Image representation blends with lexical representation in the form of faint auditory, kinesthetic, or visual images of words. Words and enactive modes merge through subvocal speech. *What is represented in one system is freely and effortlessly translated into other modes of representation. But when there is a loss of functional capacity, or when defensive operations block one or another form of representation, then there is evidence in subjective experience of cleavage between systems.*

As an example of how organic pathology sometimes reveals the boundary between representational systems, some brain tumors or head injuries result in a relatively discrete loss of the ability to form visual images. This loss of visual representational capacity occurs without loss of word thinking or enactive capacities.[6,28] Persons with such injuries can still process information presented in verbal form and speak coherently. But they have great difficulty solving problems that require simultaneous and spatial organization.

As mentioned earlier, Sperry[58] has studied persons whose cerebral hemispheres were disconnected surgically (a radical treatment for severe epilepsy). He finds that after this procedure patients function as if they have two separate brains, in that there is loss of translation between image and lexical modes of representation. Stimuli can be presented selectively to either the dominant or nondominant hemisphere by masking certain areas of the visual field. Stimuli presented to the dominant hemisphere are processed better if they are in lexical form; stimuli presented to the nondominant hemisphere are processed better if they are in visual-spatial form (such as "how would you untie this knot shown here"). In a very dramatic demonstration, patients also "know" things with the hand ennervated by the dominant hemisphere (usually the left brain in right-handed persons) that they do not "know" with the hand ennervated by the other hemisphere. For example, suppose the patient is blindfolded and scissors are placed in his hand. The hand associated with the dominant hemisphere does not know how to make cutting movements but the person can say those are scissors. When the scissors are placed in the other hand, the person cannot verbally say what they are, but knows how to make cutting motions. Apparently in normal persons the hemispheres communicate with each other so that the "two separate brains" effect in these special patients does not occur.

An example of impaired translation between the systems for representation may also be found in organic pathology which leads to difficulties in the use of verbal information. These difficulties are called dysphasias. Clinicians identify three kinds of dysphasia: nominal, receptive, and productive. Nominal dysphasia is the inability to find the right word. If in a dysphasic person the intended idea is presented in consciousness as a visual image, the failure in nominal dysphasia can be conceptualized as a failure in translation from images to words. Receptive dysphasia is defective ability to comprehend the meaning of words expressed by others, although self-expression in words may be unimpaired. According to the model presented here, receptive dysphasia is an impairment involving the system for representing auditory images or an impairment in the processes of transition from auditory images to lexical meaning. In a similar manner, productive dysphasia, an inability to speak words already present in conscious thought, is a defect of translation between thought and the enactive representation of speech.

The assembly of a sentence depends on the lexical system. Deciphering what is heard or read, however, will require use of the image systems, either auditory or visual, because perceptual registrations must be held as images until appropriate labels are established. Also, enactive representations are necessary to movements for vocalization or writing. Ordinarily such enactive representations proceed automatically outside of awareness. When no automatic plan is available, however, some conscious enactive representation is required before execution of the motor behavior. In verbal communication then, there must be transitions among each system of representation. The different types of dysphasia that have been noted in organic brain impairments may reflect defective translation between systems of representation.

TRANSFORMATION FROM THE IMAGE MODE
TO OTHER MODES OF THOUGHT

Perceptions are retained for a short time, in the form of images, which allows continued emotional response and conceptual appraisal. In time, retained images undergo two kinds of transformation: reduction of sensory vividness and translation of the images into other forms of representation (such as words). Ordinarily the transformation of images is automatic. In extreme situations, however, transformation is not easily completed.

Clinically, we see that following a traumatic experience that is witnessed visually, certain distortions of ordinary cognitive experience may occur. Instead of becoming reduced in intensity, the images of the traumatic event may return to awareness with unusual visual vividness. Also, and this is significant, these vivid images apparently escape volitional control. At times they emerge in a peremptory manner in spite of efforts to avoid or dispel them. At other times there is an amnesia for the event; descriptive statements and recollection images cannot be formed at will. Sometimes amnesia and peremptory revisualization occur in the same person in separable phases after the traumatic episode. With recovery from the posttraumatic state the images become dim, the events can be discussed verbally, and the person regains the capacity to recall the events when he wishes to and, importantly, to repress the memory if he has to.

Failure of transformation could be discussed in terms of emotional stress alone were it not for the observation of very similar experiences in emotionally *neutral* settings. Peremptory and vivid formations of images occur not only after arousing perceptions but also after repeated perceptions. People who pick berries all day may experience involuntary but vivid images of berries when they are putting their minds at ease before falling asleep.[22] Students, after long hours at a microscope, may be troubled by returning images during moments of relaxation. Night drivers also report images of oncoming headlights while attempting to sleep later on. Skiers experience a similar effect in kinesthetic sensations: after a day on the slopes, while relaxing before sleep, they refeel muscle movements and changes in bodily position repeated so often during the day. Although the initial perceptions may be neutral or pleasurable, the later images are often unpleasant and hard to dispel.

These observations of vivid and peremptory visual images suggest that image transformation processes are overloaded either when the perceptions that form the images are extremely arousing or when certain (relatively novel) perceptual schemata are too frequently repeated. Observation of failures in transformation permits speculation about the processes involved.

In order to evaluate and to store perceptions by multiple markers for future memory use, perceptual images are transformed by labeling processes: they are assigned to various categories and translated into other representational modes, such as words, by association with relevant memories. When perceptions are simple and do not involve stress or conflict, the labeling processes are completed virtually instantaneously; otherwise the images might be put out of mind for the moment and stored in a special memory system for later review. Those images that overload transformation processes would then remain in an active image memory storage. Speculatively, this special storage would tend to press toward revisualization of those images until they are "worked through" and the storage system cleared for further records of experience. Some of the stored images might be reviewed and transformed in dream or preconscious thinking.[7,13]

In the case of traumatic or intensely arousing images, the association of strong emotions with the images would increase the difficulty of categorization and association operations. Whichever images were incompletely transformed in a given cognitive "effort" would remain in the active memory condition with its continued "push" for revisualization. Under repressive circumstances, release of images from the storage system would be inhibited. When inhibitions fail, the images would emerge in an involuntary manner, leading to unbidden or intrusive images.

CROSSING THE BOUNDARY TO CONSCIOUSNESS

Images are episodes of conscious experience, the results of image formation. The experiences are not necessarily exact replicas of the information as it is stored, retrieved, or assembled in nonconscious thought processes.[39] In his scholarly critique of the concept of mental imagery, Pylyshyn[48] suggests a cautious approach, one that avoids assuming either identical organization of information during nonconscious thought processes or the exclusion of images from a role in out-of-awareness cognition. He suggests, as a theoretical construct, a "descriptive symbol structure" that contains perceptual concepts and relations, but that has the abstract qualities of propositions rather than the particular qualities of images. These propositional representations do not correspond to the sensory pattern of perception but are already highly abstracted and interpreted. Knowledge would be stored in memory, and processed to a limited degree by such codifications. Memory retrieval would consist of activation of these codifications and transformation of the information into a mode representation.

Similar conceptualizations of unconscious and automatic transformations of information have been suggested by psychoanalytic theoreticians.[19,23,33] Unconscious and relatively automatic thought processes are much more rapid, but have a greater tendency to follow habitual routines than the slower process of conscious thought. Tomkins[59] has suggested a "recognizer function" which raises the level of conscious awareness when unconscious, automatic thought is stymied. The elevation of information to the realm of conscious experiences (such as images) can serve an adaptive function, as habitual patterns are altered by problem solving, new decisions, and the practice of new forms of attitude, self-image, role structure, and behavioral patterns.

The modes of representation, then, are the systems for conscious expressions of meaning. A cycle of thought, before it reaches a point of completion and termination, might episodically enter and leave the realm of conscious experience. When in a state of nonconsciousness, this set of information is probably stored in some codified form. We may never know if this code would "look like" an image if we could see it as well as we can see a holographic plate or the negative of a photograph. The holographic plate looks nothing like the image created by passing a laser light through it; the photographic negative does look like the pictorial product. But we can assume that whatever the form of codification, it has the property of reproducing the conscious images when it is properly activated.

This line of reasoning suggests that there may be codifications for nonconscious representations which relate closely but not exclusively to each mode of representation. Whether a given set of nonconscious but stored information can first enter awareness as image or lexical representations would probably depend on the code form, the state of activation of the biologic substrates of representational systems, and the cognitive structures and motivations influencing the cognitive processes of that moment.

SUMMARY

Thought is neither represented exclusively in images, as was once postulated, nor is it represented only in words. This chapter presents a model with enactive, image, and lexical modes of representation. Each has certain organizational tendencies and cognitive uses. The image systems, and their underlying organization, place them relatively close to emotion.

In ordinary thought, the modes interrelate flexibly. In extreme situations, illustrated by organic pathology and psychic trauma, the different modes are subjectively experienced in a less integrated form, and failures in transformation from one mode to another may occur. The goal of psychotherapy, when the condition is not one of severe organic impairment, is to reestablish continuity between ideas and attitudes in various modes of representation.

REFERENCES

1. Arlow JA: Unconscious fantasy and disturbances of conscious experience. Psychoanal Q 38:1, 1969
2. Beres D: Perception, imagination, and reality. Int J Psychoanal 41:327, 1960
3. ———, Joseph ED: The concept of mental representation in psychoanalysis. Int J Psychoanal 51:1, 1970
4. Beritashvili IS: Concerning psychoneural activity of animals. In Cole M, Maltzman E (eds): A Handbook of Contemporary Soviet Psychology. New York, Basic, 1969
5. Bowen C, Standing L: Imagery meaningfulness ratings of sentences: reliability and relationship to learning. Percept Mot Skills 42:479, 1976
6. Brain R: Loss of visualization. Proc Roy Soc Med 47:228, 1954
7. Breger L: Function of dreams. J Abnorm Psychol Monogr 72:5:641, 1967
8. Breuer J, Freud S: Studies on hysteria. Stand Ed 2, 1955
9. Bruner JS: The course of cognitive growth. Amer Psychol 19:1, 1964
10. Chomsky N: Aspects of the Theory of Syntax. Cambridge, Mass, MIT Press, 1965
11. Deno SL: Effects of words and pictures as stimuli in learning language equivalents. J Educ Psychol 59:202, 1968
12. Edelheit H: Speech and psychic structure. J Amer Psychoanal Assoc 17:381, 1969
13. Eissler KR: A note on trauma, dream, anxiety, and schizophrenia. Psychoanal Stud Child 21:17, 1966
14. Erikson EH: Childhood and Society. New York, Norton, 1950
15. Fraiberg S: Libidinal object constancy in mental representation. Psychoanal Stud Child 24:9, 1969
16. Frandsen A, Holder J: Spatial visualization in solving complex verbal problems. J Psychol 73:229, 1969
17. Freedman D: The influences of various modalities of sensory deprivation on the evolution of psychic and communicative structure. In Freedman N (ed): Communicative Structures and Psychic Structures. New York, Plenum, 1976

18. Freud S: The ego and the id. Stand Ed 19, 1961
19. ——: The interpretation of dreams. Stand Ed 3, 5, 1962
20. Guilford JP: Three faces of intellect. Amer Psychol 14:469, 1959
21. Gumenik WE: Imagery and association in incidental learning. Bull Psychonom Soc 3:241, 1976
22. Hanawalt NG: Recurrent images: new instances and a summary of the older ones. Amer J Psychol 67:170, 1954
23. Hartmann H: Ego Psychology and the Problem of Adaptation. New York, International Univ Press, 1939
24. Hasher L, Riebman B, Wren F: Imagery and retention of free recall learning. J Exp Psychol, Human Learning and Memory 2(2):172, 1976
25. Hauk P, Walsh C, Krolle N: Visual imagery mnemonics. Common vs. bizarre mental images. Bull Psychonom Soc 7:160, 1976
26. Horowitz MJ: Visual thought images in psychotherapy. Amer J Psychother 22:55, 1968
27. Humphrey G: Thinking: An Introduction to Experimental Psychology. New York, Wiley, 1951
28. Humphrey ME, Zangwill OL: Cessation of dreaming after brain injury. J Neurol Neurosurg Psychiat 14:332, 1951
29. Jenkins JR, et al: Differential memory for picture and word stimuli. J Educ Psychol 58:303, 1967
30. Jung CG: The Archetypes and the Collective Unconscious. New York, Pantheon, 1959
31. Knapp PH: Image, symbol and person. Arch Gen Psychiat 21:392, 1969
32. Kubie LS: The use of induced hypnagogic reveries in the recovery of repressed amnesic data. Bull Menninger Clin 7:172, 1943
33. ——: Neurotic Distortions of the Creative Process. Lawrence, Kansas, Univ of Kansas Press, 1958
34. Lacan J: The insistence of the letter in the unconscious. Yale French Stud Structural 36–37:112, 1966
35. Lukianowicz N: Visual thinking and similar phenomena. J Ment Sci 106:979, 1960
36. Luria AR: Higher Cortical Functions in Man. New York, Basic, 1966
37. ——, Vinogradova OS: An objective investigation of the dynamics of semantic systems. Brit J Psychol 50:89, 1959
38. Mahler MS, Pine F, Bergman A: The Psychological Birth of the Human Infant. New York, Basic, 1975
39. Natsoulas T: Concerning introspective "knowledge." Psychol Bull 73: 89, 1970
40. Paivio A: Mental imagery in associative learning and memory. Psychol Rev 76:241, 1969
41. ——: On the functional significance of imagery. Psychol Bull 73:385, 1970
42. ——: Imagery and Verbal Processes. Hillsdale, NJ, L. Erlbaum Associates, 1979

43. ———: Perceptual comparisons through the mind's eye. Memory and Cognition 3:635, 1975
44. Palermo D: Imagery in children's learning. Psychol Bull 73:415, 1970
45. Panel: The relationship of language development to problem-solving ability. J Amer Psychoanal Assoc 20:144, 1971
46. Piaget J: The Child's Conception of Physical Causality. New York, Harcourt, 1930
47. ———: Play, Dream, and Imitation in Childhood. New York, Norton, 1945
48. Pylyshyn ZW: What the mind's eye tells the mind's brain. Psychol Bull 80:1, 1973
49. Reese HW: Imagery and contextual meaning. Psychol Bull 73:404, 1970
50. Richardson A: Mental Imagery. New York, Springer, 1969
51. ———: Voluntary control of the memory image. In Sheehan PW (ed): The Function and Nature of Imagery. New York, Academic Press, 1972
52. Rohwer WD: Images and pictures in children's learning: research results and educational implications. Psychol Bull 73(6):393, 1970
53. Sandler J, Rosenblatt B: The concept of the representational world. Psychoanal Stud Child 17:128, 1962
54. Schilder P: Mind: Perception and Thought in Their Constructive Aspects. New York, Columbia Univ Press, 1942
55. Senter RJ, Hoffman RR: Bizarreness as a nonessential variable in mnemonic imagery: a confirmation. Bull Psychosom Soc 7:163, 1976
56. Sheehan PW (ed): The Function and Nature of Imagery. New York, Academic Press, 1972
57. Singer JL: The Child's World of Make-Believe: Experimental Studies of Imaginative Play. New York, Academic Press, 1973
58. Sperry RW: Brain bisection and mechanisms of consciousness. In Eccles JC (ed): Brain and Conscious Experience. New York, Springer-Verlag, 1966
59. Tomkins S: Affect, Imagery, Consciousness. New York, Springer, 1962
60. Tversky B: Pictorial and verbal encoding is a short term memory task. Percept Psychophys 6:225, 1969
61. Vernon M: Relationship of language to the thinking process. Arch Gen Psychiat 16:325, 1967
62. Werner H: Comparative Psychology of Mental Development. New York, International Univ Press, 1957

6

PSYCHODYNAMICS
OF IMAGE FORMATION

Some image experiences are not oriented toward reality, are not readily understandable by the self or others, and are emotional and idiosyncratic. These images are derived from a style of thinking that reflects internal motives more than external demands. Such image formation has been the province of psychiatric investigation and occurs prominently in the construction of dreams, hallucinations, delusions, myths, magic, and fantasy. When images are used in these fantastic forms of thinking they tend to be arranged by primary process types of association, with evidence of condensation, displacement, and symbolization. Image formation, in these circumstances, may gratify wishes; it may also express conflicted and fearsome ideas.

THE RANGE OF THOUGHT

The organization and regulation of thought has a spectrum from analytic, reality-oriented, logical thought to fantastic, wish-oriented, magical thinking. The forms of thought regulation that influence the latter end of the spectrum are called "the primary process," and the thought products are occasionally (and loosely) called "primary process thought." The forms of thought regulation that influence the reality-oriented end of the spectrum are called "the secondary process," and the products are sometimes called "secondary process thought." Freud devised these labels in a manuscript that remained unpublished until after his death, *The Project for a Scientific Psychology*[11] and used them in *The Interpretation of Dreams.*[8] For more recent reviews see Gill,[13] Holt,[14] and Noy.[23]

Primary and secondary processes are differentiated according to two key issues: the degree to which they impose delay of discharge on impulsive motives, and the organization they impose on the thought that intervenes between stimulus and response. In what follows, the stimulus will be regarded as an internal, impulsive motive; the response (also internal) will be in general a thought, in particular an image or series of images. What occurs between stimulus and response is the process of image formation.

PRIMARY PROCESS

The principal feature of primary process thought is its directness: the motives cannot be tolerated or restrained for long, they cannot be modulated, some kind of response is imperative, and the response need not be realistic. For example, the prototype of the first thought has been modeled, by Freud,[8] on the basis of hallucination. The infant is hungry and cries reflexively. In a short period of development, the infant associates the sight of the breast, or a bottle, or the mother's face with the relief of hunger pangs. In primary process thinking, the baby may temporarily relieve his motivational tension, in the absence of the gratifying object, by a hallucinatory recollection of the breast. Here is the principal influence of primary process: immediate gratification, by any means, with minimal delay, without detour or extended planning. These qualities of primary process thought lend it a magical quality and an orientation toward more pleasure, less pain, and neither too much nor too little tension. The adherence of ideas and feelings to word labels, images, and enactions is loose in primary process, more adherent in secondary process. For a review of this important topic in psychoanalytic theory see Holt.[15] This looseness of meaning permits the shifts in representation known as condensation, displacement, and symbolization (to be discussed below).

SECONDARY PROCESS

Secondary process forms of thought regulation are imposed gradually upon the primary process as the child develops. The child learns that immediate magical gratification is less optimal than delayed but real fulfillment. The child learns how to think realistically, and it also learns how to modulate motivation so that action can be delayed until the right time and the right place. These central characteristics (reality testing, ability to delay, and organizational ability) differentiate the secondary process from the primary process.[33] That is, instead of immediate wish-fulfillment, the child learns to use memory, reason, logic, assessment of meaning, appraisal of environment, comparison, hierarchy formation, rehearsal, planning, and other mechanisms aimed at optimum interaction with the physical environment. The child also develops thresholds of greater tolerance for drives and learns to modulate drives.

Like the primary process, the secondary process form of regulation serves the goals of maximum pleasure, minimum pain, and the right level of tension. But it subordinates these goals to the reality principle.[27] That is, the secondary process orients thought toward real possibilities and serves the goal of the greatest good over time.

COMPARISON OF PRIMARY AND SECONDARY PROCESS

Primary process is not necessarily disadvantageous. Suppose an explorer is lost and starving to death. In his extreme hunger he hallucinates a turkey dinner with all the trimmings. If he hallucinates when he should be lighting a signal fire, then this form of gratification is maladaptive in the long run. If, however, his signal fire is already lit and the hallucination helps him keep his will to live, then it is advantageous in the long run.

Primary process is also enormously advantageous to the creative process. Thought formation under the primary process is rapid and there is a relative absence of logical restraints. These two conditions make for many juxtapositions between one thought element and another in a given period of time. The rapidity of thought and the low requirements for conventional or reasonable association mean that a really novel combination of seemingly divergent ideas might be achieved while thought is under primary process mediation. Of course, secondary process mediation and revision might be necessary to complete the creative thought.[21]

As mentioned, primary process precedes secondary process developmentally. Primary process influence over thought probably rests on simpler structures and is never entirely lost. During situations of intense impulsive motivation, primary process influence may again become apparent in the final thought products. Also, when there is reduction in capacity for the high-level organization required for secondary process thought, primary process thinking may emerge. One example of the emergence of primary process influence occurs during dreaming sleep. Freud made one of his major contributions to science in his investigation of dream-thinking. He found that primary process thought is not disorganized, rather the primary process influence imposes its own style of organization.

In *The Interpretation of Dreams*,[8] Freud noted the central use of visual images in primary process thinking and certain characteristic mechanisms of primary process thinking in the formation of dream pictures. He described how dreams were wish-fulfillments, how latent thoughts were formed into the manifest dream by the dream work, and how the dream work used condensation, symbolization, and displacement to achieve disguised expression of usually censored ideas and feelings. These characteristic mechanisms of the primary process are easily achieved when thought is expressed as visual images and are also used to various extents in image thinking, in states other than dreaming.[6,12]

Though certain features often accompany thought influenced by the primary process, they should not be regarded as synonymous with primary process. For example, images are a frequent mode of representation in primary process thought but are not categorically limited to primary process thinking. Images are also used for representation that is influenced by secondary process. In an analogous relationship, condensation and displacement are mechanisms basic to the primary process, but they can also serve the purposes of the secondary process. This is even more true of symbolization which is used widely in both primary process and secondary process.[13,30]

CONDENSATION

Condensation is the compression of several latent meanings into a single manifest image. The simplest form of condensation is omission of some ideational elements, and allowing a part to stand for the whole. Usually, however, condensation includes an active process in which meanings fuse and form a composite. For example, the image of a face may be a composite, in which the eyes are derived from one person, the hair from another, and the overall facial expression from still a third person. Or, in another common type of condensation, ideas related to several persons can be relegated to a single person. A figure, in an image, may stand for the self now, the self as a child, and also for other persons.

DISPLACEMENT

Displacement is a mechanism that results in a change of relative emphasis. An unimportant idea or feeling may be accentuated, while an important idea or feeling may be diminished in intensity. This mechanism is so important to the image construction of dreams that, in interpretation, Freud warned against assuming that the most vivid or central element in a dream might be expressed, instead, in a fleeting, trivial, or peripheral detail. The purpose of displacement is to escape censorship by disguising ideas that are prohibited from clear expression.

SYMBOLIZATION

Symbolization is a process by which one object, feeling, or situation may be chosen to signify another. It differs from displacement in that the meaning is relatively fixed, and in that the meaning may be collective as well as idiosyncratic. For example, suppose a boy is angry at his mother because she disciplined him. If he slams the door or kicks the dog, the mechanism is displacement: instead of hostility toward his mother he is hostile to the door or the dog. If he fantasizes about a queen who comes to grief, he has formed a symbol for his mother. Like his parent, the queen rules her subjects, but queens are also common in stories so he can displace his hostility onto a convenient symbol and avoid recognition of the object of his hostility. Another kind of symbol would be to make a voodoo doll and stick pins in it.

Symbols may be selected for reasons of relevance, disguise, or simply because they are easy to visualize. For example, a king may represent the idea of fatherly authority and grandeur, small animals may represent children, a gun may symbolize a penis. Symbols that can stand for several meanings are often used in images because they also serve the mechanisms of condensation and displacement. Personal meanings may be different from cultural meanings. Thus, a gun in a dream may mean a penis, a source of harm or pain, a source of power, a threat, a memory about guns, or even a person named "Gunther." Only the context and the personal associations in each case reveals the significance of a symbol.

The following example shows data from a dream deprivation experiment where the subject did a series of six drawings, after first staring at a central dot (to reduce outward attention and encourage spontaneous images).

The subject was a nurse, who at the end of the experimental period was talking openly about her wish to meet a nice young man, get married, and have children. While she did not relate these thoughts during the early days of the experiment, they probably were not far from her awareness. Of course latent fantasies about sexual relationships are common to men and women in studies where subjects sleep in the laboratory.

On the evening of the third night in the laboratory and the first night of dream awakenings, the subject did a series of six drawings, one of which depicted a woman riding a porpoise through waves (Fig. 6-1). The theme returned the next morning in more abstract form (Fig. 6-2). Interestingly enough, she had forgotten the contents of Figure 6-1, done the previous evening. One day later, on the morning after the second night of a dream deprivation procedure involving multiple awakenings, she produced a drawing of fish swimming up a waterfall (Fig. 6-3). Two days later, after the sixth laboratory night and the fourth night of dream deprivation, she drew a balloon with a figure in the basket, in the fourth of six drawings (Fig. 6-4). The fifth picture of that set is Figure 6-5, a direct reference to pregnancy, and the sixth is Figure 6-6, a vase covered with vines.

These drawings are all symbolic of some phase of sexual relations, fertilization, and pregnancy. Without the associations the reader cannot be absolutely sure, but perhaps will accept the *possibility*, that in her fantasy thinking the fish swimming upstream could symbolize sperm, that the woman on a porpoise and the figure in a balloon might depict the ex-hilaration of intercourse, and that the vase could symbolize the female sexual anatomy (the fruitful uterus).

So far we have considered the range from primary to secondary process and certain thought mechanisms that occur frequently in the

Fig. 6-1.   Girl on a porpoise.

Fig. 6-2. Abstract version of porpoise.

primary process end of the spectrum: condensation, displacement, and symbolization. The next example, the dream of a patient in psychotherapy, shows these mechanisms and how they apply to both primary and secondary process thought. The dream was brief and reported as follows:

> I was sitting in a red Volkswagen bus with a friend (a man), and I have considerable difficulty adjusting our seats to the same level.

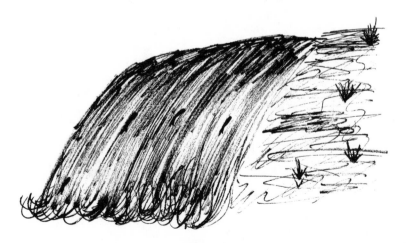

Fig. 6-3. Fish swimming upstream.

Fig. 6-4.   Ascending balloon.

Through associations to the dream images, it became clear that the red Volkswagen bus is a symbol that condenses several themes. She associated red to her friend's expensive red sportscar, a phallic contrast with the box-like quality of the bus. The Volkswagen bus was associated to "an intelligent way to carry a large family" but also a "low-status form of transportation." The bus symbolizes her self-concept: intelligent but low status.

The difficulty in adjusting seats to the same level is an action that also symbolizes current feelings. She fears that her friend might not be interested

Fig. 6-5.   Direct depiction of pregnancy wish.

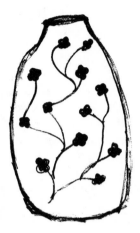

Fig. 6-6.   A vase.

in her because she is beneath his social level. She, on the other hand, wonders if she is not above him because of her greater intellectual quickness and sensitivity. The manipulation of the seat, the seat handle, and moving up and down referred to sexual intercourse. This portion of the dream could be a wish-fulfillment of erotic feelings as well as a statement about their sexual compatibility.

The dream shows secondary process as well as primary process organization of thought. It was the first conscious expression of a train of thought that emerged more clearly in subsequent therapy sessions. She and her boyfriend have fun sexually, but she wonders if they should consider marriage and family since they have trouble reaching the same level intellectually and socially. She regards him as superior because he is rich and upper class. She knows she is superior intellectually and is aware of her temptation to "cut him down." This train of thought is presented with marvelous simplicity and concreteness in the image of "difficulty adjusting our seats to the same level."

There was also displacement in the dream. Associations revealed that some of the sexual impulses were directed toward the therapist. "Not on the same level" referred to the difference between couch and chair, and "VW" referred to the therapist's car. There was displacement of emphasis from the patient-therapist relationship to the relevant relationship with the boyfriend.*

---

*The dream also had deeper meanings. The red color and being inside a car referred to particularly important childhood memories, and there were additional impulsive motives not cited here.

UNRAVELING THE MEANING OF IMAGES

Very often, the motives behind image formation are well disguised. The tracks are hidden and only the ingenious end-product, the image, enters awareness. To undo the work of symbolism, condensation, and displacement, the information inherent in every part of the image must be released. One key to this process is the free associative method.

Freud found a way of setting aside resistance and unraveling the concealments in the construction of dream images, which applies to all images. The essence of this technique is as follows. A person is asked to place his mind in a relaxed and uncritical state. He is instructed to report every thought regardless of its implications, apparent relevance, logic, or propriety. The therapist may break down the image report into phrases or components and give them back to the subject who reports his associations. When the associational chain seems to run dry, the next component might be presented.

With this method, information relevant to the image experience increases markedly. The information concerns both possible meanings behind image details and the attitude of the subject toward understanding various aspects of his experience. The observer and the subject listen to these associations with "the third ear," seeking meaningful patterns.

The additional information may provide clues that unmask the disguise achieved by condensation and symbolization. The observer and the observing part of the subject's psychic system notice which feelings and ideas emerge repeatedly as associations to various aspects of the image experience.* The following example illustrates how increased information from associations allows the interpretation of an image.

A psychotherapy patient was on the way to her session when she passed a sign on a window that read "Evangelist's Services." She had a visual image of a woman kneeling while a man prayed over her head. She burst into tears without knowing why. Even when she talked of her experience in the therapy hour, she could not understand her tears or her image. The therapist asked her to free associate even though the image experience was relatively simple. First, she was presented with the idea of a woman kneeling. When she seemed to run out of spontaneous associations to that part of the image, the therapist suggested the idea of a man praying. After the next pause she was asked what "over her head" brought to mind. Then she was asked to

---

* The technique of image interpretation is described further by Freud in *The Interpretation of Dreams*,[8] by Erikson,[3] Sharpe,[28] and by Saul, Snyder, and Sheppard.[26] Chapter 8 of this book provides illustrations of how the meaning behind formation of recurrent images may be unraveled.

associate to the words "evangelist" and "services." Here are several of her associations to each component.

A woman kneeling. Kneeling is a subservient position. I remember kneeling in church. A scrub woman kneels. The woman isn't looking up, maybe she is afraid to.

A man is praying. That seems silly, I don't believe in God anymore. I think of choir music and feeling inspired. Hands touch each other in prayer. The man is not touching her. It gives me a hypocritical feeling—about him, that is.

Over her head. Over someone means to be better than someone. She wants him to do something for her. But she can't see if he is. I can't see you either, because you're always looking at me and I have to look down (the patient faces the therapist but usually bows her head to avoid looking at him).

Evangelist. That's someone really inspirational, a little bit of a quack. I saw Burt Lancaster in a movie, he seduced Katherine Hepburn. People get all excited in evangelistic meetings. It's really dumb.

Services. Praying. Religious services. Stud services. I don't like that idea. A woman would go to an evangelist because she really was in need. I mean to deceive herself. The idea of a woman doing that is degrading. Like if she were really sexed up and had to fool herself by calling it religion.

From these associations one can make a tentative formulation of at least one meaning of the image. The patient alludes several times to the feeling of humiliation: kneeling is "subservient," someone better than another, "really dumb," "degrading." There is also the hint of sexual excitement: inspiration, touching, stud services, and the patient's insightful remark about a woman being "sexed up."

The combination of the affects associated with the image contents suggests this interpretation. She is beginning to feel attracted to the therapist (as part of a reliving in the transference of a prior set of experiences). She feels inferior intellectually because she is emotionally "sick." She also feels, guiltily, that she is coming for love rather than for treatment, and feels hypocritical because she has always believed that psychotherapy was a hoax and a waste of time. At the moment she is afraid that she will reveal her sexual excitement, to herself and to the therapist. She fears that she will express her yearning for love and receive either a humiliating rejection or become a sucker swallowing the hoax of psychotherapy in return for artificial affection. When she saw the sign "Evangelist's Services," the perceptual stimuli acted as a trigger for these latent thoughts, which influenced the formation of an image that condensed, displaced, and symbolized her feelings. While the thought content was sufficiently disguised, the image nonetheless released enough accompanying emotions so that she wept in response.

GRATIFICATION THROUGH
IMAGE FORMATION

As stated earlier, both primary process and secondary process regulate image formation. When primary process influence is preponderant, the impulsive motives act as imperative stimuli, moving toward resolution not so much as soon as is feasible, but "right now," whether feasible or not. Sometimes a person cannot achieve gratification from the external environment, and he turns to internal sources. One internal, immediately workable source is image formation. These images are derived from memories of situations or fantasies that gratified similar desires or needs in the past.

Freud[11] illustrated this process, in a hypothetical, primitive form, by conceiving of the infant's "first" thought process as a hallucination of the maternal breast. In this model, as mentioned earlier, the baby associates seeing the breast with the ensuing relief from his pangs of hunger. When this association and the relevant perceptual images are adequately recorded in memory, when hunger pangs are strong, and when the breast does not immediately appear, the baby "hallucinates" the absent breast by reviving the memory trace. This image, with its association of relief from tension, momentarily reduces hunger-anxiety and helps the baby tolerate the delay until the next feeding. Rapaport[24,25] considers such hallucinatory image formation of a previous perception associated with gratification as the prototype for all later thought. Holt[14] points out that such hallucinations, if they occur, would be really gratifying because the infant would suck, and thereby comfort himself, on his own lips and tongue.

Less primitive kinds of gratification occur in daydreams about sex and success in everyday life. Here is a typical example:

A scientist had devised an ingenious but laborious experiment. It would be a major contribution to his science if the conclusion he anticipated were reached. It was necessary, however, for him to spend a great deal of time in the laboratory. He frequently became bored, fatigued, and irritated and found himself thinking of reasons to leave the laboratory, such as for coffee. He resisted these impulses by returning to a visual daydream of himself, modestly accepting the honorarium that was offered for the solution to the problem he hoped to solve. The man who offered the award, as demonstrated by the patient's associations and description of the visual images during psychotherapy, resembled his father.

The images involved in the fantasy took but a few seconds, but left him feeling refreshed. He repeatedly used the fantasy to stimulate himself. The visual and implicit sensation of being given something of value by the older man changed his mood and increased his motivation by reminding him of an eventual reward for the arduous work and by gratifying in fantasy his frustrated wish for closeness and identification during lonely moments. The daydream also granted him his father's permission to do well. As suggested by Joseph,[16] the fantasy was a trial action modified to provide gratification.

Visual fantasies can provide a safe outlet for impulses that might be dangerous if they were discharged in real action. The employee who is submissive in reality, but imagines telling off his boss, is one example. Similarly, images can be used to gratify prohibited desires or to attain in fantasy what is unobtainable in reality.

Image formation for gratification may occur with or without accompanying actions. Many wishful visual fantasies occur during masturbation, which provides real physical gratification. In fact, the frequent association of fantasy with the physical act of masturbation leads some persons to suppress fantasy activity because they unconsciously endow the act of fantasy with guilt. Other persons indulge frequently in fantasy, even to the disruption of daily tasks, and such activity has earned the nickname "mental masturbation."

This type of gratification through image formation also occurs in the context of sexual intercourse. For example, some persons are unable to achieve orgasm unless they have certain visual fantasies during love making, including images of a person other than their actual partner. This type of fantasy allows indulgences of impulses that the person would not put into real action because they conflict with other motives such as those of ideals and conscience.

A young married woman was sometimes sexually frigid. At other times she was able to achieve an orgasm during intercourse with her husband. Her only route to sufficient erotic excitation for orgasm was to have a specific visual fantasy during love making. In this fantasy she pictured herself as a prostitute permitting humiliating acts to be performed upon her for money. She felt guilty and tried to avoid recall of these fantasies or acknowledgment of their implications. She also feared revealing the images to the therapist because she was ashamed of them and feared that they might be regarded as abnormal. Also, translation of the images into words would destroy the compartmentalization of her mental life: she would have to recognize the images and their implications, and that meant that she might have to give up her only current route to sexual pleasure.

Image formation, even in daydreams, is not exclusively dominated by sexual or aggressive urges. The gratification may be compliance with the rules of conscience or concepts of the ideal self. Also, the gratification may be that of mastery, such as completion of a difficult problem or task.[20] The internal activity itself, separate from contents, may be a pleasurable compensation for reduced external stimulation.[29]

Psychoanalytic theory has focused largely on the issue of gratification through image formation because of Freud's insistence that, whatever evidence of problem solving might be present in the *manifest* dream, the *latent* dream thoughts and the dream work involved a striving for wish-fulfillment. In a broader view we might regard image formation as motivated thinking which may alter mental states in varied ways. Pleasant images may increase rather than decrease longing; unpleasant images may motivate avoidance.[1,31]

EXPRESSION OF EMERGENT CONCEPTS AS IMAGES

A new thought may gain representation in any mode: enactive, image, or lexical. Clinicians observe, however, that thoughts involved in an impulse-defense conflict often enter awareness first in the form of visual images.

Freud used this observation during an interval when he wished to give up hypnosis but had not yet developed the free associative method. Breuer and Freud[2] believed that repressed memories of traumatic experiences provided the basis of hysterical symptoms. To relieve the symptom, they wanted patients to recall the memory and undergo a working-through of the emotions involved. Freud gave up trance-induction and simply used suggestion. He pressed his hand on the patient's forehead and told him a picture would come to mind when he released the pressure:[2]

> Once a picture has emerged from the patient's memory, we may hear him
> say that it becomes fragmentary and obscure in proportion as he proceeds
> with his description of it. The patient is, as it were, getting rid of it by

turning it into words. . . . (If) a picture of this kind will remain obstinately before the patient . . . this is an indication to me that he still has something important to tell me about the topic of the picture. As soon as this has been done, the pictures vanish like a ghost that has been laid. (pp 280–281)

Freud later developed the method of free association and abandoned suggestion. He continued to pay attention to visual images and, in *The Ego and the Id,*[5] stated:

We must not be led away . . . into forgetting the importance of optical memory residues . . . or to deny that it is possible for thought processes to become conscious through a reversion to visual residues and that in many people this seems to be the favored method.

Freud[7,10] observed that when a memory is repressed, there often emerges into consciousness an unusually vivid (überdeutlich) visual image of a relevant object. In an instance from his own experience, he was blocked in the recall of the name of the artist Signorelli but saw instead an ultraclear thought image of the artist's self-portrait. This kind of vivid image partially expresses, but also screens from awareness, conflicted memories or ideas. That is why they are sometimes called "screen memories."[5,9]

Later psychoanalysts also noted that images sometimes are the first vehicle for expression of repressed mental contents.[17] They also emerge in resistance to expression of ideas in words.[2,22] Kanzer[18] suggests that there may be an oscillation between image formation and lexical representation and that image formation tends to occur during transitions in the state of consciousness. One common experience in the conduct of insight therapy is that patients may report a vivid visual image during the seconds after they heard an interpretation.

Warren[32] and Kepecs[19] have noted how visual images present new material, yet also seem to be a form of resistance to having this material emerge. Both analysts asked patients to describe what they noted in their minds during moments when they lapsed from verbal reports. Patients often responded with reports of visual images. One of Kepecs' patients reported that her mind had gone blank, so he asked her to describe the blankness. It appeared that it had a particular substance, like looking at a closed door. The patient then recalled that she had followed her father into the bathroom, hoping to see what a penis looked like. The door was shut in her face. A similar motive, the wish to look, was currently active and directed toward the analyst. The image of the blank, closed door was a partial expression of this motive, in the form of a memory that also reminded her that looking was prohibited.

Here is an illustration of how images may serve as the first expression of conflicted thoughts.

A young woman in her twenties had been in therapy for a character disturbance for over a hundred hours. One day when entering the office, she imagined herself as being without her head and, after a silence, said she had nothing to talk about and that no thought would come to her. She then had an image of herself with a button on the side of her head. The button was pressed and little white letters sorted into bundles came out of her mouth. She felt like an automaton.

Her next associations concerned people being laid off work because of "motivation." She laughed and said motivation was a slip of the tongue for "automation." Next she reported an image of a word game like Scrabble. Then she said, "That was like trying to sort words meaninglessly."

The therapist asked if the slip, "motivation" for "automation," could have to do with her feelings about therapy. She replied that she felt treatment might be discontinued because of her apparent lack of motivation. She said her feelings of being like an automaton doing the therapist's bidding must have been behind the image of entering without her head emitting meaningless words. She felt forced to talk but wanted to say nothing. Why should she tell the therapist how bad off she was when he cared so little for her? Then she spoke more freely about a recent accident in which she was nearly killed. She had resisted mentioning this episode during several previous therapy hours.

This same patient could also alter her perception to achieve certain gratifying sensory effects. During a different period of therapy, she found her attention focused on a brass bookend on a shelf behind the therapist's head. Next she had a thought image of the bookend striking the therapist's head.

She realized, as a consequence of verbalizing this image, that she was angry at the therapist for his failure to congratulate or reward her for recent therapeutic progress. The therapist's "brass-headedness" seemed to be a connecting associative link. She then revealed her capacity to purposively change the direction of gaze of a single eye. This allowed her to move, in her internal double image, the bookend toward and away from the therapist's head. She was thus capable of partially gratifying her hostile urges by forming images of bashing in the therapist's head.

There are many other instances in free association when a patient reports a visual image that represents a repressed urge or idea. Of course, this effect is not limited to images. Recall the slip of the tongue in the above example. The patient may describe the image and report associations to it before he realizes the full impact of the idea and associated feelings. Sometimes, however, the image is understandable at once:

A young surgeon was launching himself into private practice and was forcing himself to work extremely long hours. Although the success and financial gain were highly gratifying, and although he was propelled by an intense ambition, he periodically thought about his long hours without knowing why he was bothered. While falling asleep after a hard day of work, he experienced a hypnagogic hallucination. The image was a yellowish, lifeless hand like those he saw during autopsies. He instantly awoke and felt that the image was a message to the ambitious and driving part of himself from some other aspect of his personality. The message was clear to him: he would kill himself if he maintained his current hectic pace.

Why should some conflicted ideas gain representation first as visual images and not as lexical thoughts?* To summarize, image formation is a more primitive system, and it tends to be under the influence of a primitive system of regulation, the primary process. Images may be harder to inhibit, and they may also be easily disguised through the mechanisms of condensation, displacement, and symbolization. Lexical representation develops later, when prohibitions have been internalized and inhibitory systems and the secondary process have developed. Also, words tend to be clear, once they enter awareness: images may be fleeting and poorly recorded in memory. Finally, images are more likely than lexical representation to provide partial gratification because they are more analogous to perception. Perhaps these remarks can be accepted as preliminary approaches to the question of how thoughts emerge into conscious experiences. The topic will be reconsidered in what follows.

CONCLUSION

This chapter focused on the expression of impulsive motives as images. As inner motives develop into images, the thought process may follow primary process or secondary process types of organization. Some aspects of the impulsive motives may be disguised by condensation, symbolization, and displacement. This disguise can often be unraveled using the free associative method. The images may serve as partial gratification of wishes, and they may also be the first expression in awareness of emergent and previously hidden ideas or feelings.

---

* The expression of emergent ideas is not exclusive to image formation, of course, and certainly it is not exclusive to visual images. Any of the concepts expressed in this chapter may be equally applicable to other forms of imagery such as auditory images, olfactory images, and so forth.

REFERENCES

1. Arieti S: The Intrapsychic Self. New York, Basic, 1967
2. Breuer J, Freud S: Studies on hysteria. Stand Ed 2, 1955
3. Deutsch F: Instinctual drives and intersensory perceptions during the analytic procedure. In Lowenstein RM (ed): Drives, Affects, Behavior, vol. 1. New York, International Univ Press, 1953
4. Erikson EH: The dream specimen of psychoanalysis. In Knight RP, Friedman CR (eds): Psychoanalysis, Psychiatry, and Psychology, vol. 1. New York, International Univ Press, 1954
5. Freud S: The ego and the id. Stand Ed 19, 1961
6. ———: A mythological parallel to a visual obsession. Stand Ed 14, 1957
7. ———: Hysterical phantasies and their relation to bi-sexuality. Stand Ed 9, 1959
8. ———: The psychopathology of everyday life. Stand Ed 6, 1960
9. ———: The interpretation of dreams. Stand Ed 4, 5, 1952
10. ———: Screen memories. Stand Ed 3, 1962
11. ———: The psychical mechanism of forgetfulness. Stand Ed 3, 1962
12. ———: Project for a scientific psychology. In Bonaparte M, Freud A, Kris E (eds): The Origins of Psychoanalysis. New York, Basic, 1954
13. Gill MM: The primary process. Psychol Issues Monogr 18/19, 5:60, 1967
14. Holt RR: The development of the primary process: a structural view. Psychol Issues Monogr 18/19, 5(2-3):344, 1967
15. ———: A critical examination of Freud's concept of bound versus free cathexis. J Amer Psychoanal Assoc 10:475, 1962
16. Joseph ED: An unusual fantasy in a twin with an inquiry into the nature of fantasy. Psychoanal Q 28:189, 1959
17. Kafka E, Reiser M: Defensive and adaptive ego processes: their relationship to GSR activity in free imagery experiments. Arch Gen Psychiat 16:34, 1967
18. Kanzer M: Image formation during free association. Psychoanal Q 27:465, 1958
19. Kepecs JG: Observations on screens and barriers in the mind. Psychoanal Q 23:62, 1954
20. Kris E: On preconscious mental processes. In Rapaport D (ed): Organization and Pathology of Thought. New York, Columbia Univ Press, 1951, pp 474-493
21. Kubie LS: Neurotic Distortion of the Creative Process. Lawrence, Univ Kansas Press, 1958
22. Lewin BD: Dream psychology and the analytic situation. Psychoanal Q 24: 169, 1955
23. Noy P: A revision of the psychoanalytic theory of the primary process. Int J Psychoanal 50:155, 1969
24. Rapaport D: The conceptual model of psychoanalysis. In Knight RP, Friedman CR (eds): Psychoanalytic Psychiatry and Psychology. New York, International Univ Press, 1954

25. ———: Consciousness: a psychopathological and psychodynamic view. In Abramson HA (ed): Problems of Consciousness. New York, Josiah Macy Jr. Foundation, 1951, pp 18–57
26. Saul L, Snyder T, Shepard E: On reading manifest dreams and other unconscious material. J Amer Psychoanal Assoc 4:122, 1956
27. Schur M: The Id and the Regulatory Principles of Mental Functioning. New York, International Univ Press, 1966
28. Sharpe EF: Dream Analysis. London, Hogarth, 1949
29. Singer J: Daydreaming. New York, Random House, 1966
30. Stekel W: The polyphony of thought. In Rapaport D (ed): Organization and Pathology of Thought. New York, Columbia Univ Press, 1951
31. Tomkins S: Affect, Imagery, Consciousness. New York, Springer, 1962
32. Warren M: The significance of visual images during the analytic session. J Amer Psychoanal Assoc 9:504, 1961
33. Zern D: Freud's considerations of the mental process. J Amer Psychoanal Assoc 16:749, 1968

7

REGULATION OF IMAGE FORMATION

Ordinarily people are not aware of the ways in which they regulate the vividness and contents of their images, but they do become aware of images that are unusually vivid, or images that depict contents they wish to avoid. When such images occur, a person may feel as if he or she has lost control of his or her thinking. Such episodes occur in everyday life, as when a person cannot dispel a recurrent melody, or when a person cannot recall an image of a familiar object.

In states of psychopathology, recurrent unbidden images, even hallucinations, may torment a person, or there may be total amnesia for important memories. By studying lapses in control, we may deepen our understanding of the processes that regulate image formation. In particular, in psychotherapy, the clinician aims at understanding the differences between failures of control efforts, defensive maneuvers that prevent emotional distress by inhibiting or distorting thought processes, or coping efforts aimed at deliberately keeping emotions or actions within adaptive limits. Therapists intervene to move control from failure to defense, and from defense to coping. Many of their interventions affect control processes, either to get at warded-off trains of thought and feeling, or to facilitate the patient's adaptive self-regulation.

A CONCEPTUAL MODEL OF
IMAGE FORMATION

Most theoreticians have suggested multiple input models of the image system.[1,2,44,56,59,60] The common denominator is dual input, ie, the image

116

forming systems meld perceptual and memory inputs. But it is helpful to break down the sources of information even further, in order to examine different aspects of regulatory processes.

Information enters the visual system from at least four and probably five sources, as shown in Figure 7-1. One source is perception. Perception includes the reception of external visual signals, as well as stimuli that arise within the body such as floaters in the anatomic eye itself or excitations of the optic pathways (entoptic images). A second source is summarized by the term "memory." This includes the schemata necessary in the construction of perceptual images[44] and the storehouse of long-term memory. This storehouse includes recollection of events, recall of fantasy, and reconstructions using various fragments of memory. The third input is from codings retained from prior episodes, episodes retained in a kind of short-term or active memory with a property of recurrent representation. Recent shocking visual perceptions, such as of traumatic incidents, are retained in this type of memory. The fourth input is translation from thought cycles occurring in other modes. The hypothetical fifth source is from parallel image forming systems. Entry of information from a primary process type of image formation into an image system that has been regulated by secondary process is the instance

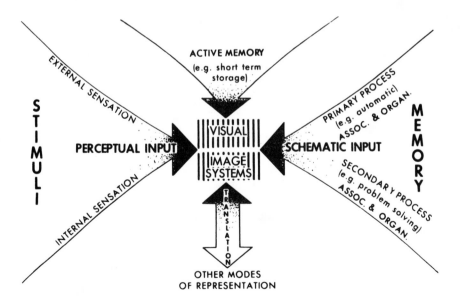

Fig. 7-1 Model of inputs into the image systems.

of concern here. Defensive aims can be accomplished through the regulation of each of these forms of input.

As a metaphor for the image system itself, consider a series of matrices upon which images may be formed. Unless these matrices are activated, no image appears in conscious experience. The degree of image vividness depends on the degree of activation, reduplication of images, or rhythmic repetition. The matrices may be activated from the various input sources. Perhaps there might be a gradient. Certain matrices might be turned toward perception, but accessible, in states of high intensity, to memory images; others might be turned toward internal image formation, but accessible to perception images under situations of very high stimulus input (or a low barrier against stimulus input).

The information resources and inputs, the various perception and image formation processes, and the apparatus for image formation would be interrelated by feedback processes. This feedback would include provisions for matching perception images with memory images and searching for a "best-fit" composite image. This feedback would also involve sensorimotor control systems, especially those involving schemata for eye movements, head position, proprioception, and other modes of sensation.

To prevent excessive entry or flooding with stimuli from external or internal sources, regulatory influences would affect transmission of information at all levels of this model. Such regulatory influences would also amplify or "seek out" stimuli when required by states of need. Regulation would exert its main effects on control at the sites of information input, and could take place by either active inhibition or active facilitation to modify content, organization, or vividness of image formation.

These basic regulatory mechanisms, inhibition and facilitation, would each have a range of settings. The setting, ranging from very high to very low, would depend on current neurobiologic capacity and psychologic motives. For example, fatigue might reduce the ability to facilitate in spite of strong psychologic motives for amplification of the process. Inhibition and facilitation can be exerted in concert or in conflict.

Perception could be "tuned up" by facilitation while memory activation or fantasy was "tuned down" by inhibition. Or, a given portion of a process could be in a state of excess facilitation with deficient inhibition producing a situation analogous to an uncontrolled car, going too fast without brakes or steering. A combination of excess facilitation with excess inhibition would be like pressing on the gas pedal and the brakes at the same time.

Hernandez-Peon[26] suggests that from a neurophysiologic viewpoint a major occurrence in mental development is the progressive differentiation of inhibitory and facilitory mechanisms. Gardner[18] and Holt[28] arrive at the same conclusion from a psychoanalytic point of view, and suggest that such a model of reciprocal control may clarify theoretical problems involving the energy-structure duality. Gardner sees mental processes activated in hierarchically organized "columns of structures." In alert wakefulness, activation is greater in upper process levels of a column. At these upper levels processes are regulated by fine controls of inhibition and facilitation yielding secondary process thought, as described in the previous chapter. Lower levels are regulated by the more primitive controls that characterize primary process.

In summary, this model of a central image-depicting apparatus is somewhat differentiated: part shows preferential receptivity to perception, part to internal image formation. Two basic sources, external and internal, may provide contents to this apparatus. The entire system can be regulated through inhibitory and facilitory influences at various locations. These active regulatory operations may operate at high or low levels, synchronously or in conflict, with refined or gross control processes. Their operation depends on both neurobiologic influences and psychologic motives.

OVERCONTROL: LOSS OF VOLITIONAL ABILITY TO FORM IMAGES

Suppose, in what follows, that the neurobiologic structures that subserve the various parts of the model are intact and capable of the normal range of function and that variations in function are due to psychologic influences.* A person may fail in his conscious desire to obtain images from either perception or memory. Such a failure could be due to excessive inhibition, or deficient facilitation.

---

* Influences on image formation from alterations of biologic substrates will be considered in Chapters 9, 10, and 11. This model presumes that subjective experience alters regulatory levels such as thresholds of excitation. Since these regulatory mechanisms have an electrophysiologic or biochemical basis, the model presumes that conscious experience can causally affect brain processes. While many neural scientists have tended to reject such hypotheses and have preferred to regard consciousness as an "epiphenomenon," investigators such as Sperry[57] have emphasized the need for models that show an interaction between consciousness and neurobiologic processes and that consider the directive role of consciousness in determining the flow pattern of cerebral excitation.

Inability to Generate a Memory Image

A young marine stationed on a Pacific Island became panicky because of strong sexual impulses toward the native girls he worked with. He tried to conjure up an image of his fiancée in the United States but was unable to do so. He could, however, form images of his home, his mother, his father, and other close acquaintances. He became panicky and felt that the girl was completely gone from his memory. He could remember their dates and could visualize places they had gone, but he could not remember what her appearance was like.

In this example, the marine consciously attempts to facilitate internal image formation (remember his fiancée), but volitional facilitation is weak in comparison with unconscious inhibition (forgetting his fiancée). Put more simply, one set of his motives (unconscious) wants him to forget his fiancée and have a good time with the local girls. Another set of motives (conscious), the part he identifies as "himself," says that he will be happier in the long run if he remembers his fiancée and forgets the island girls.

Inability to Generate Perceptual Images

A woman consulted an ophthalmologist because of tunnel vision: she could see objects directly in front of her but not at the periphery of her gaze. As the objects were further from the center of her glance, they became grayer and less distinct. No neurologic deficits were found, and no known neurologic disease could account for her impairment of perception. Psychotherapy uncovered the fact that she was afraid of seeing particular sexual scenes and that this specific fear had generalized to vision, leading to inhibition of images of peripheral perception. The symptom was relieved when her specific fear was brought to light.

The two previous examples indicate how a lapse of control characterized by inability to facilitate, or excessive inhibition, may involve processes that form images from either memory or perception.

UNDERCONTROL: LOSS OF VOLITIONAL ABILITY TO PREVENT IMAGE FORMATION

The next two examples indicate either a failure to inhibit or instances of excessive facilitation.

Inability to Prevent an Internal Image from Forming

When a young, adolescent girl tried to pray at night, she was troubled by a vivid, intrusive image of God's penis, hanging down from heaven as an inverted erection, pointing at her like an accusatory finger. The intrusion occurred only during prayer, especially when she tried to recite the prayer beginning, "Our Father who art in Heaven. . ." She was frightened both by the contents of the image and by her inability to dispel it.

A similar inability to prevent images may occur from the side of perception.

Inability to Stop Perception

A 10-year-old boy watched, terror stricken but unable to remove his gaze, while his father slaughtered piglets whose mother had died. As his father disemboweled each piglet, he threw the guts into a bucket. During that night, the boy screamed and complained that he was seeing it over again in his dreams. During the next day, he told his mother that he could not forget seeing his father cut up the pigs. Both parents recalled that the child stood and stared wide-eyed at the event even though they urged him to leave. He seemed unable to take his eyes off what was happening and, afterwards, he seemed to be in a state of shock.

PSYCHOPATHOLOGY

A loss of control over image formation is one of the important symptoms of psychopathology. It is useful, conceptually, to consider loss of control from two points of view even though any given clinical syndrome will contain elements related to both points of view (and others as well). One point of view considers formal properties, especially the vividness of images and the problem of differentiating internal image formation from visual perception. Failures in this differentiation are commonly called a loss of reality testing. The second point of view focuses on contents: the key issue is the intrusive entry into awareness of unbidden images.

REALITY TESTING

When we vividly experience a perceptual image, localize it as external, and recognize it as plausible, then we have no trouble saying "it is real." When we vaguely form an image and know it is intrapsychic and fictive, then we have no trouble saying "I imagine it." But let one part of the triad—vividness, localization, and plausibility—be incongruent with the other factors, and the question of reality occurs. For example, suppose an image is depicted with a vividness that resembles the intensity of perceptual images. In the model presented earlier, this vividness might include activation of the perception-oriented portion of the image depiction structures. Suppose that in spite of this vividness there is not sufficient information about whether the image contents have entered the depiction structure from the side of perception or the side of memory. And, in addition, suppose the image contents are appraised as unlikely to be real: an angry pink elephant charging down Main Street. The person who experiences the image is faced with a problem: is the elephant real or imagined? He must find a way to test the difference, to find the true origin of his image in order to plan or execute appropriate behavior. Reality testing has great conceptual importance in psychiatry because hallucinations and delusions are regarded as "failures in reality testing." This phrase, coined by Freud in 1911,[13] has been so overworked that one gets the impression that there is some discrete, single reality-testing apparatus that is working well, weakly, or not at all. Instead, there are at least three clinically discrete operations to test the reality of images. I discuss these next under the headings (1) automatic reality testing, (2) checking, and (3) logical appraisal and learned counterweights.

Automatic Reality Testing

I use this phrase to refer to the effortless and immediate differentiation usually made between perceptual images and memory or fantasy images. This automatic differentiation is suggested in the model by placement and vividness. Perceptual images are placed at different locations in the area of image depiction and have a greater vividness than thought images. Additional information may be provided by the direction of input: perceptual images are derived from binocular gaze and are altered by eye movements and blinking. Subjectively, perceptions seem to be a passive experience (although we know that physiologically and cognitively the process is active, ie, requires regulation). Internal images are more often willful, or at least there is incipient or implicit planfulness; they follow internal motives rather than external or physical events, and they come from within.

Thus, in ordinary circumstances, several different sets of information differentiate external and internal sources of input. When the different sets agree that the episode of experience is from one source and not the other, then there is automatic, seemingly effortless labeling of what is real and what is unreal. When the different sets of information disagree, then a person activates the additional process of checking.

Checking

Suppose an image is depicted with unusual vividness, yet it is not clearly a perception. Automatic differentiation of the two possibilities is not successful. A variety of processes can check out the image, including altering the level of facilitation or inhibition of the two basic sources of image material.* For example, the person may inhibit the perceptual input by closing his eyes or shifting his glance. If this reduces vividness, then the image probably came through this external channel. Of course, checking is not always successful or correct, as shown in one of the following examples:

Successful Check by External Perception Inhibition

A man walking late at night visualized moving lights. Was he seeing flying saucers, he wondered? He closed his eyes—the lights remained vivid in his awareness, so he knew they were not really coming from the night sky.

Unsuccessful Check by External Perceptual Inhibition

A woman awoke with a start. There beside her in bed was a giant crab. She shut her eyes, the crab disappeared. But when she opened her eyes it was still there. She repeated this three times: the crab was there whenever she opened her eyes. Convinced that it was real, she screamed, awakening her husband. While she told him of her experience, the image faded. (Why cessation of hypnagogic hallucinations sometimes occurs with eye closure is unknown.)

Facilitating perception is another method of testing reality, as when a person may "look closer" at the image to see if this makes it increase in vividness, or when he may try to dispel what he thinks are internal images. As with inhibition, none of these methods is invariably successful.

Internal Inhibition to Check Reality

A patient stared at his girlfriend and felt her face was turning into a dog's head. He tried mentally to plastically restore her face to its usual shape. The

---

* Martin[41] considers this process as alteration of thresholds, thus keeping Freud's metaphor of the stimulus barrier. Unlike Freud,[11] Martin suggests a stimulus barrier not only to perception, but also to internal images.

dog-like features disappeared. When he relaxed, he had a repetition of the same impressions. Again he could make it go away with an effort of will. He decided his mind was playing tricks on him.

Internal Facilitation to Check Reality

A student taking LSD saw his girlfriend's hair change into snakes. Somewhat whimsically, although he was a little frightened, he mentally commanded the snakes to smile with pleasure and give their heads a little shake. When they did so, he relaxed and felt this was part of his "trip," and not a menacing reality.

Sometimes internal image formation can achieve great vividness and even apparent external localization. Automatic and checking types of reality testing fail to distinguish the source of image input. A sense of reality and unreality can still be preserved, albeit with less stability, by use of logical appraisal.

Logical Appraisal and Learned Counterweights

When an internal image is both very vivid and subjectively seems to occur "outside," a person can still test reality by appraisal of image contents. The appraisal of content as "not real" may counterbalance the effects of unusual vividness of internal images and may be based on logical calculation ("I never saw a purple cow before"), on previous experience ("I sometimes hallucinate crabs when I am just awakening"), or on consensual validation ("No one else here seems to see a Martian"). Many schizophrenic patients come to know the contents of their hallucinations and, though they continue to hallucinate, develop counterweights that help them to distinguish a perception from a hallucination. They thus reduce the deleterious effect of hallucinations on their behavior patterns by repeating a formula such as "whenever I think I see my brother it is probably a hallucination."

Progressive Loss of Reality Testing

Inquiry into the development of hallucinations sometimes indicates two rather different routes. In one type, gradual deterioration in the differentiation of image sources begins with intensification of internal image experiences. Images become progressively more vivid and automatic processes become insufficient. For a while checking may maintain a sense of what is real and what is unreal, but if loss of control continues the person appraises vivid images as unreal only through logical inference. As logical inference becomes less reliable, a single image may fluctuate so that the experience seems now real and now unreal. Finally, hallucinations always seem like real perceptions.

Deterioration of Reality Testing Beginning as Intensification of Inner Images

A woman entered the hospital with an involutional melancholia, a type of depressive psychosis in which hallucinations and delusions sometimes occur. Her husband had died some years ago, leading her into immense grief and loneliness. For a while after his death, she was saddened but able to care for herself in spite of her former dependency on him. She still regularly set two places for dinner and laid out his clothes. At times she indulged herself in the pleasant daydream of talking to him at dinner. At other times she tried, sometimes in vain, to rid herself of such visions.

Next she began to see her husband out of the corner of her eye, or hear him speak. She would turn with a start, look quite carefully, and determine that no one was there. Next she hallucinated him visually for hours on end it seemed, but still retained a sense of reality by reminding herself of his death. Finally, however, her sense of reality was entirely lost, and she had both pleasant and unpleasant hallucinations of him.

Another form of progressive deterioration in reality testing begins with distortion of perception. Blurring may occur as well as changes in size, shape, vividness, and color. Persons in this condition often complain of depersonalization and derealization. Illusions may occur which can deteriorate into hallucinations as an end result. Regaining the reality testing capacity may at times retrace the course of the original deterioration.

Deterioration of Reality Testing Beginning as Perceptual Distortion

A man was upset when his wife left him, and he became suspicious of men at work. He spent several days in morbid ruminations. One morning, when he went out for the paper, the sunlight seemed brighter and buildings had a fiery edge. When he looked at people they appeared dark and blurred, while the edges of their contours were bright as if surrounded by an aura or halo. He began to feel people were especially interested in him: he had fleeting illusions of faces watching him from windows, began to hear accusing voices, and felt as if he were Jesus. Finally, he formed delusions of persecution and grandiosity and hallucinated leering faces and religious figures.

The regulation of vividness of internal images, as indicated in the above examples, is one of the major problems to confront the discrimination processes. I will mention briefly two current hypotheses which account for loss of control of vividness: the release theory of neurobiology, and the purposive theory of psychodynamics. They are not contradictory.

Undercontrol of Vividness: The Release Theory

Many studies of the evolution and development of the nervous system indicate that primitive patterns of function remain but are held in quiescence by inhibition and patterns of function acquired at a higher developmental level. Jackson[30] suggested that vivid internal images, such as hallucinations, also derived from primitive functions of the nervous system. When higher cortical functions, such as those subserving lexical thought or thought in images that were parsimonious in vividness, were disrupted as in fatigue, toxicity, or disease, then the lower cortical functions, including those subserving image formation of hallucinatory vividness were activated as the result of failure of inhibition.

West[59,60] summarized contemporary views of this hypothesis in his general theory of hallucinations and dreams. He postulates that vivid internal images tend to occur when (1) the nervous system is in a state of relative arousal or excitability, and (2) when there is insufficient input from perception to occupy the image-forming apparatus or to inhibit entry of internal images. For example, in sensory deprivation when the subject may be awake but have little perceptual input, internal images tend to gain in vividness. Similarly, in dreams, there may be greater cortical arousal without perceptual input resulting in unusual vividness of internal images.

A variety of other authors have supported this theory of a continuum from normal alert waking thought to states of hallucination. This continuum is characterized by increasing general excitation of the central nervous system, as well as relative shift in activity. For example, Hartmann[24] has suggested an ascending norepinephrine-controlled system in the brain that ordinarily inhibits the emergence of vivid image activity and also affects the capacity for reality testing of image experiences that do occur. Fischer[8] has contrasted such adrenergic hyperarousal states, in which he agrees that vivid images such as hallucinations tend to occur, with serotonogenic states characterized by tranquility and hypoarousal. Winter[61] concurs with the theory that hallucinations tend to occur when there is hyperexcitement of the central nervous system, and suggests that this condition creates an overload of visual stimulation relative to the information-processing capacity.

The release theory is not incompatible with the model suggested at the beginning of this chapter. Vividness of internal images could occur under various circumstances. Internal input could be facilitated with unusual intensity in states of organic irritation or high motivation. Internal input could undergo relatively low inhibition due to organic diminution of inhibitory capacity or because of a low psychologic defense level. The matrices for image formation could have a shift in gradient so that internal images were favored. Scheibel and Scheibel[53] suggest that a shift in dendritic biasing could accomplish this effect. Finally, external perceptual inputs could be modified in a way conducive to increased vividness of internal images: there could be global reduction of input, a high signal-to-noise ratio of input (see Chapter 9), and input that triggers and intensifies psychologic motives.

Undercontrol of Vividness: Purposive Theory

Purposive theories of increases in vividness of internal images have been advanced from neurobiologic as well as psychoanalytic points of view. Neurobiologically, increased vividness of internal images in states of perceptual reduction may be useful for maintaining arousal by supplying a source of stimulation that acts as external perception. This is in contrast to the release theory which states that the vivid images are the *result* rather than the *cause* of high arousal.

Psychoanalytic theories of vivid events such as pseudohallucinations or hallucinations tend to focus on the meaning and purpose of the *contents*. The increase in vividness per se has been designated as part of a two-fold process called "topographic regression."[14,19] One aspect of topographic regression is conversion of thoughts in words to thoughts in images. The second step occurs in hallucinations. The "sense organ of perception" is stimulated from within, and thoughts, thereby, become as vivid as perceptions. Perceptual regression, in terms of enhanced vividness or apparent perceptualness of thoughts, may make fantasies appear more real and also make reality more like fantasy (since the two are no longer distinguished).[3,9,52] For instance, the woman in the example on page 125 may have greater gratification by hallucinating her husband because, during the hallucination, her sad loss is magically undone. The increase in vividness of the image of her husband, and her ensuing appraisal of the image as a real perception, avoid feelings of grief.

UNBIDDEN IMAGES

Another type of loss of control of thought, regardless of increased vividness, is intrusive, *unbidden visual images*. This term avoids the connotations of Gordon's earlier term, "autonomous imagery,"[21,22] which indicates that the images entered awareness under their own autonomy, in contrast to images formed consciously and volitionally. Unfortunately, the word autonomous conveys the almost opposite meaning in psychoanalytic theory, where autonomous ego functioning, for example, refers to mental processes that are carried out independently of id, reality, or superego influences. In psychoanalytic theory, a loss in ego autonomy over image formation means what Gordon called autonomous images.[25,42,48,49]

In terms of content, people form either voluntary, spontaneous, or intrusive images. Voluntary images are deliberate, for example when a person tries to recollect a familiar person or scene. Less deliberate are spontaneous images, which emerge without conscious effort: they seem to pop into the mind, are perhaps related to the stream of thought, and do not seem particularly intrusive or distressing. They often occur when the mind is drifting.

In contrast, unbidden images seem to "intrude" into awareness. Their presence is often distressing and their meaning may be obscure. They range from hallucinatory vividness to a dim quasi-sensory quality. A person may exert various defensive maneuvers against continuation or repetition of the image, but efforts to dispel it may or may not be successful. These images seem unwanted or alien to the very person who forms them.[51]

Emotional responses to unbidden images range from extreme pleasure to great pain and may include feelings of ecstasy, surprise, awe, anxiety, fright, or panic. The experience of the images may lead to anxiety over the lapse in control in addition to the emotions expressed in, and responsive to, the contents of the images. While the majority of reported unbidden images are deemed unpleasant, some unbidden images herald remarkable creative achievements. Such creative responses often arise after a period of struggle with an apparently unsoluble problem. Lewin[39] points this out in retelling Kekule's experience of a creative unbidden image while in a drowsy state:

> Kekule had been puzzling over the linkage of carbon atoms in forming the benzene ring, as the story goes. Then he dozed and saw snakes form a mouth-to-tail chain. The front snake took the hind snake's tail in its mouth. He realized the carbon atoms must be linked together in such a chain to

account for the various properties of benzene and awoke with a start knowing he had solved the problem.

Lewin also retells the story of William Lamberton, who had worked for two weeks unsuccessfully on an algebraic problem. He gave up and decided not to think of it again. For a week he succeeded in his resolve. Then on awakening one morning from sleep, he had an unbidden image that solved the problem in an unusual way: the solution was geometric rather than algebraic and was seen as a picture projected onto a painted-over blackboard some distance from him. As Kubie[38] has observed, such creative solutions are not uncommon during dream thinking and often take a visual form. Kris[35] would regard such creative products as "regression in the service of the ego"; Weissman[58] would regard creative products as regression in the service of the ego-ideal rather than the ego. The following section describes less desirable regressions.

Pathologic Forms

Freud devoted his earliest studies[15] to the effects of unconscious wishes on symptom formation. In several places he describes repeated and peremptory images; for example, in "A Mythological Parallel to a Visual Obsession,"[12] he describes a young man in whom the products of unconscious mental activity have become conscious as obsessive images.

Hollender and Böszörmenyi-Nagy[27] studied acute and chronic schizophrenics with hallucinations and noted that in the acute state of hallucinatory schizophrenia the

> ego's own reaction . . . is not always at one with the hallucinated experience. The initial response is that of fear bordering on panic. To some extent this state may persist for a considerable period of time and is responsible for much of the anxiety (and perhaps depression) noted in acute schizophrenic episodes. To an extent, the ego maintains its observing function and reacts to its own experience (the hallucination) as something foreign, strange, or "crazy."
>
> [Later the hallucinations] are fitted into the ego's previous orientation by use of a variety of theories. . . . When this type of reconciliation has occurred, the hallucinations are no longer regarded as "crazy" (by the subject).

In the next chapter I shall describe the unbidden image syndrome in detail. It will help to consider in advance three points of view which explain unbidden images as (1) sequels to psychic trauma, (2) eruptive expressions of usually repressed ideas and feelings, and (3) a means for transformation of feeling states.

Unbidden Images as Sequels to Psychic Trauma

Breuer and Freud[5] first considered repetition of trauma in their theoretical model for hysteria. They followed Binet's therapeutic technique of directing a patient's attention back to the moment when the symptom (of hysteria) first appeared. They insisted that abreaction (reliving the experience) was the significant aspect of this therapy. If there were no impediments to abreaction, the mental disturbance caused by the trauma was dissipated through absorption of the memory into the usual complex of memory storage and associations and the well-known ways of "working-off emotions" (expressing anger, experiencing grief, and so forth). The dissipation of pathologic or "strangulated" emotion was prevented by two basic types of situations—defensive and hypnoid:

Defensive. Social situations prohibited expression of the emotion or else the trauma was associated with something so personally painful that the patient "repressed" it. The trauma itself was specified as fright, shame, or psychic pain.

Hypnoid. The trauma took place during a hypnoid state. Freud became more dubious about this second type of situation and later repudiated the idea as superfluous and misleading.[31] Actually, the hypnoid state idea had been put forward in 1890 by Moebius[5]:

> The necessary condition for the (pathologic) operation of ideas is . . . a special frame of mind. . . . It must resemble a state of hypnosis; it must correspond to some kind of vacancy of consciousness in which an emerging idea meets with no resistance from any other. . . . We know that a state of this kind can be brought about not only by hypnotism but by emotional shock (fright, anger, et cetera) and by exhausting factors (sleeplessness, hunger, and so on).

Recurrent intrusive dreams, a prominent symptom of the traumatic neurosis of World War I, called Freud's attention to what appeared to be a new kind of repressive failure. In traumatic dreams as in wish-fulfilling dreams, ideas or memories repressed by day gained expression during sleep. But the breakthrough was clearly unpleasant; the traumatic dream appeared to be an exception to the pleasure principle. Thus, Freud hypothesized the principle of the *repetition compulsion*.[11]

The compulsion to repeat trauma worked as follows. A harrowing or frightening experience exceeded a person's state of preparedness and/or capacity to master the resulting stimulations and affects. A temporary protective mechanism shunted the experience out of awareness where it resided as a kind of undigested foreign body; the memory traces were still extremely vivid and the affects were still of potentially overwhelming intensity. At some later date, the "repetition compulsion" asserted itself— the person relived the experience repeatedly until it was mastered—until associated feelings such as helplessness diminished. Until such mastery of affects, recall of the experience tended to evoke very vivid images. With mastery the memory traces were processed for storage in the usual way: they were stripped of sensory intensity and related to various schemata and concepts. Arlow[2] has suggested that, to some extent, the traumatic images always remain in unconscious fantasy and are "looked at" inter- nally whenever potentially similar situations arise. Bibring[4] and other psychoanalysts* suggest that the repetition of trauma is for the purpose of working off the trauma by mastery and acceptance.

Greenacre[23] notes that overwhelming visual experiences in childhood may daze and bewilder the child and undergo compulsive repetition in fantasy. If incompletely mastered, these visual traumas may lead to a symptom complex of visual disturbances, headaches, and halo effects. Niederland,[45] Krystal,[36] and Chodoff[6] studied concentration camp victims of the Nazis and, concurrent with other symptoms, found that intrusive visual images of concentration camp scenes persisted for decades. These intrusive images sometimes occurred after a relatively symptom-free interval.

Psychologic responses to great stress differ in various personality types but seem to have a course that can be abstracted.[7,16,29,46] The first response to perception of the stressful life event is often an emotional outcry. But a common next phase is one of ideational avoidance accompanied by emotional numbing. Only after this global denial period may intrusive and repetitive thoughts, such as unbidden images associated with the event, emerge with attendant pangs of emotion. With oscillation between periods of relative denial and relative intrusion, the person may enter a working-through period in which the images related to the stress event

---

* See Furst[17] or Horowitz[29] for a complete review.

gradually lose their peremptory and intensive quality. The phases, then, are characterized by periods of both overcontrol and undercontrol over the contents stored in active memory, a form of memory storage that has an intrinsic tendency toward repeated representation.

Continued clinical studies of psychoanalytic patients who reported traumatic experiences revealed that traumatic memories sometimes serve as partial screens for ideas and feelings that are currently dangerous or anxiety provoking.[20,40,50] By attending to the traumatic memory, the patient may externalize and project into the past what is current and internal; he thus escapes full recognition of the present conflict. Owing to such motives, even a dormant memory may be revived as a current image.[47,55] The intense vividness and traumatic contents of revived images lead to arousal of a feeling state resembling the emotions produced by the original experience. The feeling state generally includes a sense of impending danger which may be used to motivate preparation of defenses against emergent but threatening mental contents.[43,54]

Unbidden Images as an Eruptive Expression of Usually Repressed Ideas and Feelings

Concepts that are not presently conscious may be dormant and easily activated, or they may be repressed and held from consciousness. In the state of repression two forces, at least, are present. One force presses for expression of the idea or feeling, the other force presses against expression. In the model presented at the beginning of this chapter, the urges for expression would facilitate a particular internal image; the motives for avoidance of contemplation would inhibit it. The high level of facilitation and of inhibition results in a dynamic equilibrium with the image held out of awareness.

Disruption of the equilibrium could result in a sudden release of previously inhibited images. The intrusion of these images into the conscious stream of thought would be experienced as an unbidden image. The sudden release could arise from a rapid change in motivation or from a change in the capacity to inhibit. For example, perception of a current sexually arousing situation might increase the impetus to express sexual strivings; or ingestion of alcohol might reduce inhibitory capacity.

Psychoanalytic theoreticians such as Kubie,[37,38] Arlow,[2] and Knapp[34] suggest that there may be continuous unconscious daydreaming in visual images. The processing of these images might lead to some sudden activation, catapulting the unconscious image into consciousness. The conscious self might regard this intrusion as an attack of unpleasant stimuli. In this regard there is a similarity, in subjective experience, between the reception of external traumatic perceptions and the reception of internal "dangerous" ideas or feelings. Both are regarded as unwelcome intrusions.

Image Formation to Transform States of Mind

Image formation is well suited to the tasks of disguise or transformation of feeling states.[32] For example, while remaining unaware of his own purpose, a person might form an unbidden image in order to raise his level of anxiety. Freud describes such breakthroughs as the result of switch-off processes in his paper, "Some Neurotic Mechanisms in Jealousy, Paranoia, and Homosexuality"[10]:

> The pathogenic phantasies, derivatives of repressed instinctual impulses, are for a long time tolerated alongside the normal life of the mind, and have no pathogenic effect until by a revolution in the libidinal economy they receive a hypercathexis; not till then does the conflict which leads to the formation of symptoms break out. . . . I should also like to throw out the question whether this . . . does not suffice to cover the phenomenon which Bleuler and others have lately proposed to name "switching." One need only assume that an increase in resistance in the course taken by the psychical current in one direction results in a hypercathexis of another path and, thus, causes the flow to be switched into that path.

Klein,[33] in his paper on peremptory ideation, develops this switch-off model into an ideomotor cycle with various types of sequences and linkages. He calls the region of start of the cycle a "primary region of imbalance." The series of steps in the cycle are cognitive efforts aimed at terminating the imbalance through some kind of switch-off such as a thought (eg, an image), an action, or a perception. If the primary region of imbalance has extreme intensity, its effects have a peremptory quality. Such intensity is gained due to inadequate completion of the cycle, especially dense or converging facilitations at the primary region of imbalance, or repeated interruption of the cycle due to inhibitory negative affects (eg, anxiety, guilt, and so forth). The processes involved in the cycle may be either in or out of awareness, and Klein emphasizes the special properties of repressed trains of thought: they endure without fading and have a special kind of impetus. Klein postulates that repression tends to interrupt the cycle, the lack of switch-off terminations results in increased intensity of the primary region of imbalance, and peremptory ideation such as unbidden images result.

A vignette may help to illustrate these three explanatory viewpoints for loss of control over the contents of images.

Recurrent Unbidden Images in a Neurotic Patient: The Intrusive Mother

The patient, a young married woman, complained of a recurrent unbidden image of her mother's scowling face. This image occurred at the moment of vaginal penetration during sexual intercourse with her husband. The image of her mother's scowling face appeared before her, as if it were several feet over the bed. The images were quite vivid, but she knew they were generated in her own mind. The first time they occurred, she reacted by crying and feeling frightened. Later, even though she knew the images would occur, she found that she could not prevent or dispel them. The images dissipated "of their own accord" in a minute or less. This symptom persisted for a long time and, even when she "got used to the image," she still experienced disgust, shame, and anxiety when it appeared. As the image faded, she could suppress her disgust, reestablish genital arousal and reach a sexual climax "in spite of her mother!"

By piecing together material from psychotherapeutic work, it is possible to give some idea of the latent thought processes that led to development of the unbidden image. While these thoughts were not consciously experienced, they can now be given the following expressive form:

I am sexually excited by my husband. But whenever I think of my husband, I am reminded of my father toward whom I also have had sexual feelings. I feel and felt that sexual feelings toward my father are wicked and dangerous. I might be caught doing or thinking something bad, or he might hurt me with his big penis. Mother would disapprove strongly of my images and make me miserable if she found out about them. After all, sex is disgusting. What I want is wrong, and I had better not allow myself to get excited. Maybe if I think of how bad she would make me feel if she were to catch me thinking erotically, that would scare the sexual feelings out of me. Just imagine her seeing me; that makes me feel disgust, shame, and anxiety.

Now consider the case with regard to the trauma, repressive breakthrough, and transformational explanations.

Trauma.   As it happened, the patient once had a traumatic perceptual experience when her scowling mother caught her masturbating. Sexual arousal reminded her of the earlier event, reactivated the vivid shock memory, and released the associated images into awareness.

Expression of Repressed Mental Contents. Symbolically, her husband represented her father, and sexual excitation toward her husband was unconsciously and magically regarded as sexual excitation toward her father. Her sexual impulses led to guilt, and both feelings were repressed. The sexual excitation involved in intercourse activated the repressed feelings and also lowered her defensive capacity (due to the altered state of consciousness). Only the more defensive aspect of her feelings erupted: her guilt as expressed by imaging her mother's face.

Transformation and Disguise of Affective State. The image of her mother's scowling face did not directly express her sexual wishes toward her father. In fact, it did not directly express guilt feelings as her own but rather projected them onto her mother. Forming the images evoked feelings of fear, disgust, and shame, which reduced her sexual excitation. Thus, by forming the image, she avoided sexual feelings. At a more conscious level, she tried to suppress the fearsome images and regain arousal.

Summary. The intrusive mother became a symbol that condensed not only the train of thought summarized earlier, but also other trains of thought. For example, in the course of her psychotherapy it became clear that the image was used not only to transform sexual arousal to fear, but also to satisfy exhibitionistic wishes. She defiantly wished to show her mother that she was having sexual activities in spite of the mother's prohibitions. At the conscious level she wished none of these things but only to have a mutually gratifying experience with her husband. The emergence of less conscious and less adaptational motives was therefore experienced as a loss of control over the contents of her thought.

SUMMARY

Sometimes image formation appears to get out of hand. The internal images gain in vividness so that they are hard to distinguish from perceptions. Or they express ideas and feelings that the person wishes to avoid. In many instances unbidden images combine both features: unusual vividness and an alien quality. Thus, they are a central problem for any theory of image formation. Three explanations—traumatic repetition, breakthrough of repressed ideas or feelings, and defensive transformation of feelings—have been outlined. The next chapters present more detailed examples of unbidden images and attempt to examine the explanation in greater depth.

REFERENCES

1. Antrobus J, Singer J: Mind wandering and cognitive structure. Paper presented to NY Acad Sci, October 20, 1969
2. Arlow J: Unconscious fantasy and disturbances of conscious experience. Psychoanal Q 38:1, 1969
3. ———, Brenner C: Psychoanalytic Concepts and the Structural Theory. New York, International Univ Press, 1964
4. Bibring E: The conception of the repetition compulsion. Psychoanal Q 12:486, 1943
5. Breuer J, Freud S: Studies on hysteria. Stand Ed 2, 1955
6. Chodoff P: The German concentration camp as a psychological stress. Arch Gen Psychiat 22:78, 1970
7. Cobb S, Lindeman E: Neuropsychiatric observation after the Coconut Grove fire. Ann Surg 117:814, 1943
8. Fischer RA: Cartography of inner space. In Siegel R, West L (eds): Hallucinations. New York, Wiley, 1975
9. Freeman T, Cameron JL, McGhie A: Studies on Psychosis. New York, International Univ Press, 1966
10. Freud S: Some neurotic mechanisms in jealousy, paranoia, and homosexuality. Stand Ed 18, 1962
11. ———: Beyond the pleasure principle. Stand Ed 18, 1962
12. ———: A mythological parallel to a visual obsession. Stand Ed 14, 1957
13. ———: Formulations on the two principles of mental functioning. Stand Ed 12, 1958
14. ———: The interpretation of dreams. Stand Ed 4, 1953
15. ———: Project for a scientific psychology. In Bonaparte M, Freud A, Kris E (eds): The Origins of Psychoanalysis. New York, Basic, 1954
16. Friedman P, Linn L: Some psychiatric notes on the Andrea Doria disaster. Amer J Psychiat 114:426, 1957
17. Furst SS: Psychic Trauma. New York/London, Basic, 1967
18. Gardner RW: Organismic equilibration and the energy structure duality in psychoanalytic theory. J Amer Psychoanal Assoc 17:3, 1969
19. Gill M: Topography and systems in psychoanalytic theory. Psychol Issues Monogr 10, 3(2), 1963
20. Glover E: The screening function of traumatic memories. Int J Psychoanal 10:90, 1929
21. Gordon RA: An experiment correlating the nature of imagery with performance on a test of reversal perspective. Brit J Psychol 41:63, 1950

22. ———: An investigation into some of the factors that favor the formation of stereotyped images. Brit J Psychol 39:156, 1949
23. Greenacre P: A contribution to the study of screen memories. Psychoanal Stud Child 3-4:73, 1949
24. Hartmann E: Dreams and other hallucinations; an approach to the underlying mechanism. In Siegel R, West LJ (eds): Hallucinations. New York, Wiley, 1975
25. Hartmann H: Ego Psychology and the Problem of Adaptation. New York, International Univ Press, 1958
26. Hernandez-Peon R: Psychiatric implications of neurophysiological research. Bull Menninger Clin 28:165, 1964
27. Hollender MH, Böszörmenyi-Nagy I: Hallucination as an ego experience. Arch Neurol Psychiat 80:93, 1958
28. Holt RR: Comments made during the panel "Psychoanalytic Theory of the Instinctual Drives in Relation to Recent Developments." Reported by Dahl H: J Amer Psychoanal Assoc 16:613, 1968
29. Horowitz MJ: Stress Response Syndromes. New York, Aronson, 1976
30. Jackson JH: Selected writings of John Hughlings Jackson. Taylor J, Holmes G, Walshe FMR (eds): New York, Basic, 1958
31. Jones E: The Life and Work of Sigmund Freud, vols. I, II, III. New York, Basic, 1953, 1955, 1957
32. ———: Fear, guilt, and hate. Int J Psychoanal 10:383, 1929
33. Klein GS: Peremptory ideation: structure and force in motivated ideas. Psychol Issues 5:80, 1967
34. Knapp PH: Image, symbol and person. Arch Gen Psychiat 21:392, 1969
35. Kris E: On preconscious mental processes. In Rapaport D (ed): Organization and Pathology of Thought. New York, Columbia Univ Press, 1951, pp 475-493
36. Krystal HK (ed): Massive Psychic Trauma. New York, International Univ Press, 1968
37. Kubie LS: The relation of psychotic disorganization to the neurotic process. J Amer Psychoanal Assoc 15:626, 1967
38. ———: Neurotic Distortion of the Creative Process. Lawrence, Univ Kansas Press, 1958
39. Lewin BD: Remarks on creativity, imagery and the dream. J Nerv Ment Dis 149:115, 1969
40. Malev M: Use of the repetition compulsion by the ego. Psychoanal Q 38:52, 1969
41. Martin RM: The stimulus barrier and the autonomy of the ego. Psychol Rev 75:478, 1968
42. Miller S: Ego autonomy in sensory deprivation, isolation and stress. Int J Psychoanal 43:1, 1962
43. Murphy WF: A note on trauma and loss. J Amer Psychoanal Assoc 9:519, 1961
44. Neisser U: Cognitive Psychology. New York, Appleton, 1967

45. Niederland WG: Clinical observations on the "survivor syndrome." Int J Psychoanal 49:313, 1968
46. Popovic M, Petrovic D: After the earthquake. Lancet 2:1169, 1964
47. Rapaport D: Emotions and Memory. New York, International Univ Press, 1967
48. ———: The theory of ego autonomy: a generalization. Bull Menninger Clin 22:13, 1958
49. ———: The autonomy of the ego. Bull Menninger Clin 15:113, 1951
50. Reider N: Percept as a screen; economic and structural aspects. J Amer Psychoanal Assoc 8:82, 1960
51. Sachs LJ: A case of obsessive-compulsive neurosis showing forced visual imagery. J Hillside Hosp 5:384, 1956
52. Schafer R: Aspects of Internalization. New York, International Univ Press, 1968
53. Scheibel M, Scheibel A: Hallucinations and brain stem reticular core. In West LJ (ed): Hallucinations. New York, Grune & Stratton, 1962
54. Schur M: The ego in anxiety. In Lowenstein RM (ed): Drives, Affects, Behavior, vol. 1. New York, International Univ Press, 1953, pp 67–103
55. Sears RR: Functional abnormalities of memory with special reference to amnesia. Psychol Bull 33:229, 1936
56. Segal S: Imagery, Current Cognitive Approaches. New York, Academic Press, 1971
57. Sperry RW: A modified concept of consciousness. Psychol Bull 76:532, 1969
58. Weissman P: Creative fantasies and beyond the reality principle. Psychoanal Q 38:110, 1969
59. West LJ: A general theory of hallucinations and dreams. In West LJ (ed): Hallucinations. New York, Grune & Stratton, 1962
60. ———: A clinical and theoretical overview of hallucinatory phenomena. In Siegel RK, West LJ (eds): Hallucinations: Behavior, Experience, and Theory. New York, Wiley, 1975
61. Winter WD: The continuum of CNS excitatory states, and hallucinosis. In Siegel RK, West LJ (eds): Hallucinations: Behavior, Experience, and Theory. New York, Wiley, 1975

8

UNBIDDEN IMAGES

Why do I yield to that suggestion
Whose horrid image doth unfix my hair
And make my seated heart knock at my ribs
Against the use of nature? Present fears
Are less than horrible imaginings.
SHAKESPEARE: *Macbeth I.iii.*

Unbidden images have a certain irony. The person who forms them disowns them and regards them as unwelcome intrusions. An incomplete analysis would suggest that these experiences are simply eruptions of impulsive motives. Analysis of the underlying psychodynamics, however, reveals that a variety of unconscious regulatory maneuvers modulate image formation. By detailed study of cases, such as those reported in this chapter, it is possible to infer the cognitive operations involved, and to understand why images are experienced as intrusions.

I asked psychiatric inpatients whose complaints centered on pathology of image formation to participate in a study of their thought processes and symptom formation.* If they consented, certain research methods supplemented their regular treatment program. Research study interviews

* I thank Dr. Norman Mages and the staff and patients of the Mount Zion Medical Center Psychiatric Inpatient Service for their help. Judy Payne, R.N., and Carol Farwell, R.N., made special contributions.

were separate from psychotherapy interviews. The patients understood that their psychotherapist received information from the research interviews, and vice versa. This freed the investigator to inquire into thought processes that might, at that moment, not be directly relevant to the psychotherapeutic process.

The focus was on developing detailed descriptions of current subjective experiences, thought processes in general, image formation in particular, and the responses to external events and psychotherapeutic interventions. The interviewer used both free associative methods and direct questioning, as seemed appropriate. In addition, various ancillary procedures examined control over image formation.

A visual evocation task gathers information about voluntary, spontaneous image formation in a semi-structured situation which includes three sets of instructions. In the first set, the patient is asked to form first an image of a person, then a pleasant image, then an unpleasant image, and lastly an image from earliest childhood.

The second set of instructions in this task uses emotional words as stimuli for image formation. Generally, the patient is asked to repeat a phrase beginning with "I feel" and ending with a different label for emotion, such as "angry." Five types of emotion are presented, as indicated by the following words: pleased, fearful, angry, ashamed, and gloomy. Thus, the patient would first say, "I feel pleased," allow himself to form a spontaneous image, and then report what image occurred to him. This would be repeated for each word. To avoid repeating the same words with successive tasks, four matched sets are used, each containing different words. For example, the first set consists of satisfied, anxious, resentful, guilty, and depressed. The second set is pleased, fearful, angry, ashamed, and gloomy. There were two additional sets of adjectives.

The third part of the visual evocation task provides a looser structure: the subject is only told *when* to form images, not what *kind* of image to form. The patient is told that when an instruction is given to form an image, he should just let his mind rest and allow a spontaneous image to develop and grow in vividness. Half a minute is given for silent imagery formation, followed by one minute of description of the image. Then about one minute is spent drawing the image that is produced. This is repeated six times. Later, associations to certain images can be requested.

In each set, the patient is told to allow images to spring into his mind in response to whatever suggestion is given and that he should describe in detail his actual subjective experience. If necessary, he is asked additional questions as to how vivid the image was, whether it was in color, what was in the background, whether he himself was visualized, what the mood was like, how old he was at the time depicted, and whether the image was fleeting, durable, surprising, expected, from imagination, or from memory.

After a patient describes an image experience, additional data may derive from a drawing of the image. Information is often available in the graphic product which amplifies or corrects the verbal description. One way to obtain drawings is the dot-image sequence,[4] in which patients stare at a dot in the middle of a page, draw what comes to mind, and produce a series of six pictures. Another technique for obtaining a graphic series over time in withdrawn or nonverbal patients is interaction drawing.[5] The patient and therapist jointly draw on the same page and usually take turns. Ideally, they continue the process of joint drawings several times a week. Interaction drawing can obtain more imagery production than the patient ordinarily gives in interviews or in his own free drawings. The responses of the therapist stimulate counter-responses, decrease the distrust and distance experienced by the patient, and also can be used to counter or diminish his defensive maneuvers.

Projective tests consist of visual stimuli that are presented to the patient who is then asked to report his internal image responses. The most common form is the inkblot, such as the Rorschach or Holtzman inkblots. The blots are symmetric splotches of form, color, and shading. While they do not actually depict any particular object, they are suggestive and certain usual responses have been catalogued for each stimulus. The patient reports what forms are suggested to him, and from his responses some inferences can be made about his current impulses, defenses, conflicts, thought processes, and cognitive style.

These several methods are ways to add to clinical impressions of a patient's spontaneous communications. Manipulation of image formation through instructions and situations may add information about the degree of control the patient has over this aspect of thinking.

ISABEL: A CASE OF TRAUMATIC PERCEPTION

The case presented here is a good illustration of how images derived from a traumatic perception may serve defensive functions.

Isabel, a married woman in her twenties with three children, was hospitalized on a psychiatric ward because of confusion, panic, and recurrent frightening images. Her diagnosis was hysterical psychosis. She complained of "seeing an old man who had died in her home." The images, always of the old man, frightened her and occurred in two forms. In one, the old man looked angrily at her; in the other he was dead. These same images came as hallucinations or pseudohallucinations and also as illusions, hypnagogic visions, and recurrent nightmares.

The old man depicted so intensely and repeatedly was a boarder in her home and had died there a year previously. After his death, the patient was upset but did not receive psychiatric treatment. Within a few weeks she felt better. Then, almost a year later, the unbidden images of the old man returned and were associated with panic, confusion, and disordered thinking and behavior. The onset was a dream of the old man, and afterward he came to "haunt" her during the day.

She originally met the old man while walking her children in the park. He was friendly toward them, and after a brief conversation she found out that he was on social security with no place to live. As she had an empty room in her home, she invited him to purchase room and board. For a while all went well, and he even helped with babysitting. Then he became bedridden with a chronic debilitating illness. She had to care for him as his physical health and mental functioning deteriorated. He became incontinent of urine and feces. Also he was easily enraged. During his rages, he accused her of tormenting him, robbing him, and giving him poor care. At times she responded with equal rage and, for instance, tried to persuade her husband to punish the old man physically.

The night before the old man died, she had dreamed that her little girl was killed by a car. In her subculture this was known as a "deathdream" and meant that someone would die. She thought of this when, in the morning, she found the old man dead. Since her mother and sister had insisted at times that the patient's dreams were prophetic, she believed that she had caused the man's death. She felt the recurring visualizations were his ghost returning to haunt her.

Hospital Course

Initial Phase. During the initial phase of hospitalization, the intrusive image of the old man was the principal content of her communications. She usually was in a confused and panicky mental state, pacing about while wringing her hands and sobbing anxiously. She gave little history other than repeated fragmentary descriptions of her images. Any questions about other aspects of her life were twisted back to this topic or ignored. Her speech was blocked and punctuated by pleas for reassurance and protection against the images.

She found references to the old man in every aspect of her waking life. For example, during an interview she looked suspiciously at some papers. When asked what was there she said, "a chair," and on further inquiry drew an outline of a chair by connecting some random marks on the papers. In the angry image the old man is seated in such a chair, she added.

In an effort to see if the visual evocation task might obtain more information, she was asked to do the first set. The first instruction was "form an image in your mind's eye of a familiar person." She said several times that she could not do this. Then she said, "Oh, the head of the old man! Bald, a scary face!" She got to her feet, raised her hands to cover her face, and sobbed. While crying and pacing back and forth, she said that she had had angry thoughts about the old man because he swore at her. When he yelled at her she wished he would die; when he did die she knew she had killed him. His ghost haunted her. She needed help. After these remarks she told of her "deathdream."

She then frequently related this story to members of the ward staff in order to gain repeated reassurances from nurses that she was not to feel guilty about having the dream, that the death and dream were coincidental, and that there was no such thing as a ghost. This repetition deflected attention away from other considerations about why she was in the hospital.

Second Phase. During the second week of hospitalization the patient was considerably less panicky. She cried less, her pleading behavior diminished, but she still reported illusions: she thought other persons on the ward were the old man, especially if she saw them unclearly or in the corner of her eye. Also, she sometimes walked up and down the halls and peeked into rooms, claiming to see the old man within them. Recurrent unbidden images of him continued as intense thought images or pseudo-hallucinations. Recurrent dreams of him screaming at her troubled her sleep. A drawing she made of the recurrent images is shown in Figure 8-1.

As she became more coherent in interviews, she began to describe her brittle temper, her impulses to hit people, and her fear that part of her body was dying. The image evocation task was repeated during this phase. Her comments revolved around preoccupation with the old man theme. For example, when asked to form a visual image in response to the concept of "I feel angry" she replied:

I don't know—the old man is looking at me real mad. He said "damn you."
I hit him a couple of times. He got mad and then he threatened to get me.

At this point rapport with Isabel was good enough so that she could take a projective test, the Holtzman inkblots. This is a series of 42 cards; a

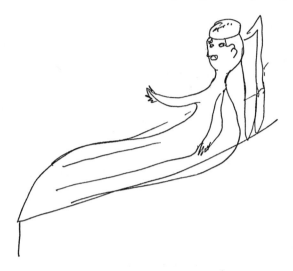

Fig. 8-1.   The old man screaming.

single response is obtained for each card. Her response to seeing ten of the inkblots was "I don't know"; she saw unpleasant faces in eleven of the cards. In seven of the cards she saw spiders, bugs, or reptiles. Her responses were instant without careful scrutiny of the contours and shapes. Almost every card seemed to frighten her. Because of this latter observation, she was asked to pick out the card that frightened her the most. When she selected an inkblot and was asked what she saw in it now, she said, "two children hanging." (Previously her response had been "two people dancing.") She then said, "No, I don't mean that, I see people dancing or sitting down." She got up and began to cry and pace about.

After a while she was asked what had come to mind to cause this reaction. She said that what she had seen made her think of how her sister had tried to hang herself. Her words came in seemingly unrelated fragments; she described how her mother used to beat her and how mean people could be toward children. When asked what she had meant about two children hanging, she denied saying that, and insisted that for her the card represented two people dancing.

The next day, she reported a dream of the old man saying angrily, "Let me take care of her." This time, however, there was a new element in her dream. A little boy crawled on the floor in the background. She identified him as her son. This was a startling bit of information because she had previously given a history of having two daughters without mention of a son. She reported a second dream of fighting with her sister. When asked what she thought these dreams might mean, she replied in an evasive manner:

> She (sister) hits when she gets mad. My sister was like that. I don't hit people when I get angry. No, oh, I guess I did throw a hanger at my husband. He slapped me because it nearly got into his eye, and I told him that I hated him. I cried for five hours. Then the old man said, "Who's that baby? He should have hit you more." The old man was real mean after that.

During subsequent psychotherapy sessions she described memories of various traumas at the hands of her sister, her mother, and her stepfather. Perhaps these were partly fantasy, partly real. She was regarded as the black sheep of the family and was accused of having an evil eye or being like a witch. She had rheumatic fever as a child and spent long periods alone in bed. As she recalls, she spent most of this time daydreaming in visual images. Being weaker than her sister when she emerged from bed, she was often beaten up. She sometimes hated all members of her family and attempted to suppress her rage.

During the research interviews in this phase, the interviewer asked her to draw pictures of the old man image. This she began with reluctance, but then continued with intensity. She said that drawing the images helped her to work through some of her feelings, and she hoped that she was now shielded from the images.

Third Phase.   Isabel continued to improve, her thinking seemed to be less confused, and she comported herself reasonably well on the ward. She was sent home for a trial period but returned after only a few hours, weeping and frightened. She spoke brokenly and would not report what had happened at home. The next day she remained unwilling to say what had happened or how she was feeling but did agree to repeat again the visual evocation task. Once again, the evocation task resulted in information. It was clear by this time that her thought was predominantly in visual images with poor capacity for abstract thought in lexical concepts. After repeating the stimulus phrase, "I feel lonely," she reported this image:

> My little boy, he's crawling. He fell off the bed, the crib. I didn't know what to do. He's crying. I'm trying to catch him, I wasn't there in time.

She indicated by her manner that this image represented something of considerable importance to her but refused to elaborate. The next day she reported a dream of the old man lying in his bed, saying that she had tried to kill him. As in the previous dream, she saw a little boy in the background and began to explain who he was. Her drawing of this dream is shown in Figure 8-2. Note the similar lines on the head of the old man and the boy; similar lines occur in the old man drawing of Figure 8-1.

The little boy was her son. Because of mental retardation and uncontrollable behavior, she and her husband had sent him to a state hospital. She recalled the scene at a commitment hearing. The judge said that the boy looked too normal to be hospitalized. She replied that she was going to leave the boy there and let the judge see for himself. Her husband was surprised that she would just leave the boy, but she simply walked out. The boy, held for observation, was committed because he was violent.

Fig. 8-2.   The old man with a boy in the background.

She cried and said that she had to commit him because he was so violent, he would have killed someone, but she felt very badly. Then she blurted out, "Instead of hitting him or doing something drastic, I had to put him away." She then refused to talk further.

That night she dreamed of both her little boy and herself feeling anxious and crying. She said that now she thought of him whenever she saw children on the street. Also, instead of seeing the old man, she now had ugly images of her son eating disgustingly and sloppily as he used to. She began to cry again and, in a fragmented manner, continued her story. When her son was only a few months old, she had left him in his crib with the railing down. While she sat across the room sewing, he squirmed to the edge of the crib and, as she watched horrified, fell to the floor hitting his head. After that he began to show signs of mental retardation.

Quite likely, the etiology of the mental retardation occurred at birth or before and the fall was incidental. Naturally, however, she experienced considerable remorse and sadness and felt at fault. She now told of a daydream she had had intermittently since the accident, in which she goes crazy, is sent to the same state hospital, is reunited with her son, and nurses him back to health.

During this phase, as she talked about her past history and her symptoms, there were juxtapositions of association and slips of the tongue suggesting the symbolic similarity of the old man and her son. It was shortly after the boy was committed that she asked the old man to move in, and the old man was given the boy's room. Both the boy and the old man had periodic rages and threatened violence. Both were sometimes incontinent of feces or urine, and she hated them both when she cleaned up their messes.

Next, in psychotherapy, she began to admit her fears that she might fall into a rage and hurt her two daughters. She had previously kept these ideas hidden, but her husband confirmed that she had spoken to him about them prior to that hospitalization, and that she did have periodic rages. She was afraid that she would become so intensely angry that she might assault her daughters and inflict upon them some injury equivalent to the ones she felt she had inflicted upon the old man and her son.

Isabel continued to improve, but, whenever the threat of discharge became too intense, her condition tended to deteriorate. She would become fearful and pleading, would sometimes say that she was now having the old man images again, and would act helpless and demanding. With each regression the fear she experienced about her aggressive impulses toward her two daughters was reinterpreted. Arrangements were made for a housekeeper and babysitter to be added to the household.

With this buffer she was able to maintain her improvement and accept discharge from the hospital. During the ensuing period she continued psychotherapy, did well, and it was eventually possible to give up the housekeeper and babysitter.

Case Discussion

In this section the clinical material is related to the explanatory points of view suggested in the previous chapter.

Unbidden Images as Sequels to Traumatic Perceptions. The content of Isabel's unbidden images derived from the traumatic perception of the old man dead or screaming. But the images were not simply repetitions of trauma. The images returned a year after the old man's death when current strong hostile impulses toward her daughters had achieved dangerous proportions and she had a realistic need to avoid emergence of these impulses into behavior. The images of the old man served as a screen that partially expressed and partially prevented awareness of her dangerous impulses.[3] The unconscious role structure or "latent thoughts" included an injuring party, herself, and an injured party, her children (earlier her son, now her daughters). In the images of the old man as dead, the injured party became the old man instead of her children. In the images of the old man screaming angrily at her, the roles were reversed: she became the injured party, he the one who would injure. By forming the image of his anger she frightened herself and scared away her own anger. This reversal of roles also correlated with childhood memories in which she identified herself as the injured party.

From this material, we can see that because of their special propensity for vivid revisualization, images of traumatic experiences may come to serve as symbols or screens for other concepts. The process may be retrospective or prospective: previous traumatic images may be revived to serve contemporary purposes (as in this case) or new traumas may tend to remain unmastered because they have become associated with previous memories and conflicts.

Expression of Repressed Ideas and Feelings. The image of the old man is at once a disguise and a breakthrough of repressed ideas and feelings. If, for conceptual clarity, we artificially label the repressed idea-feeling as "I'd like to hurt those girls (like my mother hurt me)," then in awareness the old man images express part of the repressed idea, "Somebody is angry, somebody is hurt." In an analogous compromise, the patient projects the impulsive feeling—anger—onto the old man. The defensive feelings—dread and guilt—she experiences as her own. In spite of partially successful defensive operations, the breakthrough of some of the repressed contents leads to her subjective sense of loss of control. Her dangerous ideas, denied expression in words, gain partial expression in images.[6] Additional defensive efforts inhibited translation of the images into words.

The other repressed thoughts may be partially expressed in the image. She feels inadequate to the demands of taking care of small children and would like to be taken care of. If she were to scream crazily, like the old man, perhaps she would have her burdens lifted and be taken care of (eg, by hospitalization). The recurrence of the images may be reinforced by this secondary gain.

Transformation and Disguise.   The above case illustrates the disguise of roles and the transformation of hate to fear. Persons do sometimes reduce anger by making themselves afraid or, in other situations, may reduce fear by making themselves angry. Fear, guilt, and hate stand in a particular relationship to each other; any of these affects may be generated to avoid experience of the other two.[7] A person may generate fear to reduce his own guilt or hate. He may make himself hate to reduce his guilt or fear or both.

Isabel projected her own rage onto the old man and formed images of him to produce a feeling of danger. Danger led to fright which, together with the resultant altered state of consciousness, reduced her feelings of hatred.

Summary

So far I have used traditional psychodynamic language to interpret or infer the latent meanings of the manifest images and the motives for the image formation. We have some idea why the images occurred and why they were subjectively experienced as unbidden. But we are not yet clear about the cognitive operations and sequences required in the image formation process. For example, some aspects of the repetition remain unexplained. The old man image expressed, yet disguised, dangerous ideas and feelings. It condensed past and impending traumas. But why was this one image so easily triggered?

This image recurs possibly because it is "tried and true." Put less colloquially, connecting links between elements in an ideational cycle that reduces displeasure or increases pleasure tend to remain in a state of latent facilitation. A predisposition to follow the same pathway in subsequent trains of thought remains. This predisposition can be considered to be a schema and will tend to structure subsequent ideational responses to similar stimuli. Thus, activation of the beginning of a train of thought may lead to the same end result, such as the same unbidden image. With repetition, the end result (the unbidden image) may come to stand as a symbol for the entire train of thought.

As described in Chapter 7, Klein[8] suggests an ideational cycle model of peremptory ideation. He suggests a "primary region of imbalance" that leads to a series of ideas aimed at reducing the imbalance by producing some kind of switch-off thought, action, or perception. Following Klein, a provisional outline of an ideational cycle can be constructed. The region of imbalance consists of feelings of hatred which might lead to a certain expectable course of thought. The first element in this conjectured train of thought might be the idea of hurting her child. Next in this sequence might be a plan of how to hurt the child. These fantasies might lead to certain perceptual expectancies. For example, there might be the idea, "The next time I catch her doing something bad, I'll beat her." The need for the excuse, "when she does something bad," is the result of a compromise between raw aggression and mitigating forces such as conscience. When actual perceptions match expectancy, the plan of hurting the child may be released and the assault carried out. As a consequence of aggressive actions, hatred is reduced, and the cycle of ideas is temporarily deactivated because of the reduction in the pressure of the emotional motive.

The cycle of ideas that would diminish hatred by hurting a child is not carried out in awareness. The concept of hurting her child is too dangerous to contemplate, especially since Isabel realizes that her control is insufficient to control her rage and since she still feels very guilty over the idea of damaging her son. To avoid completion of this ideational route, she transforms some of the ideas pressing for expression. The idea of hurting her daughter is transformed into the idea that she herself has been hurt, eg, by the images of the old man. This is reinforced by her childhood memories of being hurt when she was a daughter.

In an alternate ideational cycle, the dangerous assaultive ideas are transformed into the concept of her being assaulted by using the vivid traumatic memories of the old man raging at her. The guilt feelings are expressed in the image of finding the old man dead. Both images lead to fright at an intense level. The fear, the warning pangs of guilt, and the secondary gain of being cared for herself diminish rage feelings. This secondary cycle can be activated to avoid the primary ideas of child assault. Repeating the thought cycle leads to condensation of the elements into a single symbol, the old man image. In a sense, she forms the image instead of the whole train of thought. Thus the images serve as a defensive mechanism against, as well as an expression of, primitive impulses.

NED: A BEATING FANTASY

The following case illustrates how unbidden images occur as a symptom in a schizophrenic patient. In contrast to Isabel, who was not schizophrenic, the communication is less clear, and the thought processes are less cohesive and organized. In spite of the basic difference in psychopathology, however, some of the same explanatory principles remain relevant to the symptom of unbidden images.

Ned, a 17-year-old, entered the psychiatric ward because his behavior had become progressively more withdrawn, aggressive, and strange. He was considered to have a schizophrenic disorder.

During his hospitalization, Ned revealed recurrent unbidden images in which he depicted his father beating his mother. The contents consisted of his mother bleeding from the nose, his father with an outstretched hand; and sometimes he depicted himself, as a small helpless bystander. These images sometimes lasted for the unusually long period of half an hour.

The presence of these images was not known to the staff during the first weeks of hospitalization. He entered the clinical research study because of his many bizarre statements about his body, which suggested a disturbed body image. Later, we found that these remarks also referred to the images. For example, he frequently repeated his initial complaints: his nose or his rectum was bleeding on the inside, someone had beaten him up, his nose was connected to his penis, his stomach and his bladder and his penis were connected.

Ned's bodily concern was not surprising, for he was abnormally short in height. For many years this impairment was thought to be due to defective formative processes secondary to hormone imbalance. To correct the defect, he received weekly injections of hormones in the buttocks. After several years, his growth pattern and his x-rays revealed that hormones were not to blame. He was told that the suspected disorder was not present and so he did not have to return for further treatment.

Ned had grown to like and depended upon his physician and the nurses of the clinic. He missed them when the regular visits stopped. After a few weeks he returned, complaining of a pain in his ear. Examination showed an infection and an antibiotic was prescribed. As a side effect, Ned developed buzzing in his ear. This progressed to painful hearing and finally to auditory hallucinations. He would hear his uncle's voice saying, "You've got to be patient, Ned, you've got to be patient."

About this time he had outbursts of destructive behavior toward objects in the home. He stared into space, stayed in his room, and then stayed in bed. His speech was bizarre, and these symptoms led to the hospitalization.

The Beating Images

Ned was seen in interviews that sometimes incorporated drawings, interaction drawings, or visual evocation procedures. The first indication of the images occurred during an interview on the 32nd day of hospitalization. He started to talk about having "crooked thoughts" which consisted of "pictures coming into my head by surprise." When asked what the pictures were about, he changed the topic abruptly. Later in the interview he was asked to do the visual evocation task and agreed. When asked to visualize a familiar person he said he could see (ie, image) his father and his mother, and that both were red. His facial expression became distracted and he said, "No, maybe they were bright green."

When asked for a pleasant memory, he said he saw his mother kissing him a lot. For an unpleasant memory he reported, "Blood, just blood, it's red." In the second part of the visual evocation task, he was given various emotional words and asked to say whatever image came to mind about each. In response to the word "angry" he said only, "beat, pulling and kicking, she gets upset." At the end of the session he said plaintively, "My nose is bleeding from the inside, my bowels don't work. I'm bleeding on the inside. Can you help me with my crooked thoughts?"

There was little additional information about the images until the 53rd day of hospitalization. He saw two patients scuffling and became panicky. A nurse comforted him, and he told her it was like seeing his father beat his mother when he was a young boy. He added that he had continued to see his mother bleed ever since. In interaction drawings he drew a more striking picture than usual: a frog being cut open as in a dissection. On completing the drawing he looked up and said, very sincerely, that he realized his parents had a hard time so he wasn't going to let their arguments bother him anymore.

About a week later, I said that I noticed him lying in bed a lot and was interested in what went on in his mind. (His posture was unusual; he lay on his back but in a tense manner, with knees bent and hands very tightly clasped over his abdomen.) He said he stayed there to keep from thinking about his father hitting his mother. With encouragement, he then described how he once came home and found his mother covered with blood. It probably was because it came from her nose, he continued, because she didn't hold it up and because his father "did not keep patience."

He said he saw this again in his mind often, usually in color—the blood was very red. He also saw himself standing off to one side with a "question mark expression on my head." Talking of these images made him sad and anxious; those were his usual feelings while having them. He thought it might have happened when he was four or five. He then started talking about his hormone shots.

After talking of the injections he said that he had no thoughts while he was in bed, but sometimes he would just have the image for half an hour or so. I asked him to draw it sometime. He said he would if he could use stick figures; the image was not in stick figures but that was all he could draw. He drew the picture shown in Figure 8-3: his father with an arm into the face of his mother, the spiral of blood, himself off to one side. He said the drawing of the picture made him nervous, he had hit his father once, he had wanted to hit his father, but he was afraid his father would beat him into a nothing.

The next day he said he wished to stop drawing with me and just talk. He said the images troubled him whenever he was not doing much, like when he brushed his teeth. He knew he should just forget it, but when the images came his stomach hurt. He then drew pictures of how his internal organs were connected to his penis and to his nose. Then he reassured me: the images meant nothing; his father had told him his mother was having a bloody nose. Then he added wistfully, "But why was she crying?"

Fig. 8-3.   First drawing of the beating.

In later sessions he talked more of the images for a few days, then devoted his comments to other topics. A little over a month after telling me of the images he went on an extended home visit. He seemed relatively rational before leaving, but he returned in a regressive state before his pass was over. He reported having intrusive images of the blood and the beating.

The next day I found him in bed. He smiled, sat up, and said, "I was freezing out my thoughts." He was troubled by the image, so I said we could try and see if drawing it helped him control it. He seemed hesitant but agreed. He selected a yellow felt tip pen from several I carried with me. This gave the dimmest possible line. He drew his mother as a small figure (Fig. 8-4). When asked to repeat the image, he took a purple pen and drew it twice the size (Fig. 8-5). He was then asked to write words that described each person. The words for his father were "mean, ugly, filthy, dead, misunderstood, and dishonest." The words for his mother were "helpless, innocent, helpful, means well, bad temper, and kind." He liked to describe himself with these same words.

I asked him to draw the image again. He did so showing only the head of his mother. He said that really she was kneeling down, but he didn't

Fig. 8-4.   Second drawing of the beating.

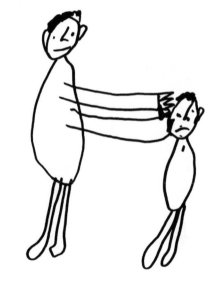

Fig. 8-5.   Third drawing of the beating.

Fig. 8-6. Interaction drawing of the beating.

Fig. 8-7. His father beating his mother.

know how to draw it. Would I help? He gave me his pen saying that "she faces toward him on her knees." I drew in a simple kneeling body (Fig. 8-6) and asked him to draw it himself. He did and added blood pouring from his mother's head plus arms which he had previously omitted (Fig. 8-7).

Ned went on to tell how the images sometimes came as the whole thing, sometimes only in pieces such as faces, or as just the red color. He drew some of the variations he experienced. In one there were two heads of different sizes and an elongated penis-like shape between them (Fig. 8-8). He also drew the one as "only blood" (Fig. 8-9).

In the days that followed our detailed redrawing of the images, Ned said they no longer bothered him. Perhaps he was able to suppress the image, perhaps this was a suggestion or positive transference, possibly he mastered the ideas and feelings, and possibly he simply wanted to avoid a repetition of our encounter together with the image. He improved gradually, as he had before the home visit, so there is no way to attribute this to the drawing intervention. He was discharged to outpatient treatment and, six months later, remained outside of the hospital and in school.

Case Discussion

Ned's recurrent image of the beating can be considered under each of the points of view developed earlier.

Fig. 8-8.   A variation of the beating
image.

Fig. 8-9.   Only blood.

The Image as a Repetition of a Traumatic Perception. As with Isabel, there was a possibility that Ned's images were memories of traumatic perceptions. We knew that violence in his family sometimes occurred. Ned seemed to recall an assault on his mother by his father. He also had a fear of losing control of his own rage, like his father.

Expression of Repressed Mental Contents. The recurrent image reflected the idea, "I am watching my mother being beaten by my father." Each person in the statement may stand for Ned himself, as pointed out by Freud.[2] Ned expresses hostile sadistic impulses, in a disguised way, by identifying himself with his father as he holds the images in mind. He may also identify with his mother in the image. This latter theme resonates with the situation that occurred before his hospitalization. He felt rejected by the doctor who prescribed injections. He wished to return to the state of being injected by the doctor. The image of "somebody" being beaten is a disguised version of his wish to submit, be injected (beaten), but attended to (nurtured, or loved) by the doctor. Deprived of the doctor, and withdrawn from father and mother, he must find a way to console himself.

One way of self-consolation is fantasy and/or masturbation. Unfortunately, these processes were also dreaded as dangerous, and as symbols of guilty activity. The timing of Ned's images provides a clue to their relevance to masturbatory wishes. The images came most often when he was alone in his room and unoccupied with a task. He usually would lie in bed, and at such times wanted to masturbate. As he described this in an interview, "I had to resist myself." He was afraid that he might have caused his deformity by excessive masturbation and was fearful of giving in to his urges. While he did not describe his masturbation fantasies in terms of content, he said that the excitement caused a turmoil of terrible thoughts. Beating is also a pun for masturbation: his age group uses such expressions as "to beat off" or "go beat your meat" to refer to this act. Paradoxically, while the beating images may signify masturbation, the anxiety they engender is used to nullify sexual arousal and to avoid masturbation.

Use of imagery may, nonetheless, have had a reparative aim. One aspect of Ned's thought disorder was a relative incapacity, at times, for thinking in orderly sequences of words. There were thoughts he wished to avoid, but he may also have had an incapacity to facilitate word organization. By facilitation of images he had a "fallback" position. He could think in images rather than face the danger of mental chaos: a turmoil of disorganized and dangerous lexical ideas and feelings. The images could be maintained with some clarity; they avoided verbal conceptualization of the dreaded ideas of his own hatred and avoided total disorganization.

MARY: THE EARTHQUAKES

The following case illustrates two interesting clinical phenomena: (1) how phases of repression may alternate with phases of recurrent intrusive images; and (2) how two sets of unbidden images, that superficially appear different, may have an underlying unity.

Identification of the Patient

Mary, a divorcée in her middle twenties, was admitted to the psychiatric ward shortly after childbirth. She had stayed at a home for unwed mothers until the child's birth. After delivery she was mute, apathetic, and remained in bed for days. She responded to encouragement by greater activity, but talked tangentially and bizarrely. When social workers asked her to decide the fate of her baby, she said she wanted to have the child adopted, but she refused to discuss necessary procedural details. Because of her recalcitrance, as an interim measure, the baby was sent to a foster home and Mary remained in the home for unwed mothers. Three weeks later, using an overdose of pills, she attempted suicide. After a day of intensive treatment on a medical ward, she was transferred to psychiatry.

The Syndrome of Unbidden Images

One of Mary's chief complaints on entry to the psychiatric ward was that she was "having earthquakes" and wanted them to go away. These "earthquakes" were a synesthetic experience consisting of intrusive visual and kinesthetic images plus associated emotions. In the visual images of "the earthquake," she was injured or hollow in her abdomen and the victim of various crushing injuries (such as the ceiling falling in). Another version was that some bad organ or object was in her abdomen, such as "a yellow hair-ball." She also felt as if her abdomen were churning and as if she were shaking and the room were moving. The associated feelings were dread, fear of sudden death, depersonalization (a sensation of personal unreality), and feelings of hopelessness and emptiness. In addition, Mary reported distorted visual perception: when she looked at other people they appeared to twist at the stomach "as if they were being shifted or churned by an earthquake"; when she looked at the walls they seemed to buckle or move. Although these various experiences were frightening and seemed real, within moments she could check the sensations by carefully looking around, and would then decide that an earthquake was not really in process. Although her hospitalization occurred in San Francisco at the time of an earthquake scare, her symptom had other determinants.

In addition to her earthquakes, Mary later reported another set of unbidden images. In the second set she was not the injured victim, but the dangerous aggressor: she had repeated images of people, buildings, or cars exploding, or of herself shooting or stabbing people in their stomachs. She experienced these images as involuntary and intrusive but felt that she enjoyed them, "in a smirky evil way." The aggressive images seemed less peremptory than "the earthquakes" which frightened her the most.

Both sets of images recurred in spite of her efforts to suppress them. She was reluctant to say much about them other than giving brief descriptions of the content. She acted as if she did not acknowledge them as meaningful, purposive, or self-generated. Rather, they were alien, to be removed, mysterious, and not to be understood.

Past History

Parental and environmental instability were important factors in Mary's early life according to the history given both by her parents and the patient herself. In her first year of life, several different persons cared for her. When she was one year old, she went to live with her grandparents. At age three she was returned to her parents for six months and then remitted back to the grandparents. Again at age five or six she returned to her parents' home. During this time a baby brother was born. Four additional younger siblings followed who occupied the center of attention. She was expected to care for all of them while she, herself, was very neglected.

Throughout childhood and adolescence she had a difficult time finding her own identity and role. She disliked her family and felt like Cinderella: always working on the chores and childcare, getting no love or attention. In adolescence she vacillated between "good" and "bad" self-concepts. The "good" identity included religious activity, plans to become a missionary, and development of her musical and sewing talents to an above average degree. The "bad" identity included parental defiance and passive compliance with promiscuous and drug-taking friends. After two broken love affairs, several vacillations from positive to negative self-concepts left her very depressed. She was married once, wanted children, but could not become pregnant. Her husband beat her, and she also was violent. After divorce she periodically felt very inadequate and, in despair, attempted suicide at least twice.

She became pregnant in a passive, happenstance manner, but decided to carry the baby to term. Shortly before delivery she said the baby was to be adopted, but refused to discuss matters beyond this point with a social worker. Following delivery the topic of adoption of the baby was broached many times, but she would not discuss it beyond abrupt agreement. Instead she might withdraw, begin to talk in a bizarre manner, or have a temper tantrum. During this period her "earthquakes" became intense; she said she had had them on and off since adolescence.

The Meaning of the Images and the Psychodynamics of the Image Formation

The way Mary labeled her unbidden images, "my earthquakes," suggests that she wished to communicate (at least to herself) or regard the experience as a disaster. The reasons for selecting the label "earthquakes" were revealed in the course of her hospitalization; the label reflects a traumatic experience which predates the symptom. The images, in turn, became "used" for screen purposes.

When Mary was 15 years old, a strong earthquake occurred. She was in a third-story school classroom at the time. For several seconds the blackboards moved on the walls, and the windows buckled, opened, and closed. The experience triggered a dangerous internal image. She realized it was an earthquake and had the sudden intrusive thought, "I hope the house falls on them [her family] and crushes them all to death"; the thought was accompanied by a vivid visual image of such an event. She was very frightened, vowed to forget her thoughts, and made penances. One penance was to imagine herself as the victim in her earthquakes; she has the inner churning, she is crushed, she has the hole in her body.

Thus, as with Ned and Isabel, content derived from a "traumatic" perception is depicted in the intrusive images. The images are not, however, simply repetitions of the trauma. They are revived again and again as a vehicle and screen for the expression and concealment of other ideas and feelings. Her rage toward her parents, her repeatedly frustrated wish to have them take care of her, and her wish for revenge (at being neglected) were present at various times throughout her childhood, adolescence, and adult history. During the earthquake she experienced these ideas intensely, and the traumatic moment, with its associated fright, was recapitulated whenever some aspect of this set of ideas or whenever similar feeling states were triggered by current situations. The concept of the earthquake also serves as a useful symbol for other important ideas and feelings to be described below.

Expression of Repressed Ideas and Feelings. In the previous cases, the sudden expression of images that partially expressed previously inhibited ideas or feelings led to the subjective feeling of unbiddenness or loss of control over thought. Mary is of special interest because during her hospitalization she had relatively clear phases in which unbidden images alternated with complete regression. These phases show the double-sided coin of loss of control: at times she could not think about certain concepts; at other times she could not prevent herself from thinking of them.

As indicated earlier, Mary had two sets of unbidden images. In one set her role was passive: she depicted herself as injured. These images expressed the latent idea that something inside her abdomen was missing or damaged. The latent emotions included anxious dread and depression related to feelings of being hopelessly deprived of nurturance or affection, and fear of losing herself and her baby. The image of her damaged belly symbolizes several themes: her overwhelmingly destructive hunger, her fear that she is beyond rescue, her wretchedness at having lost her baby, and possibly also her sensation of the baby kicking before she was "emptied" by childbirth.

Mary's second set of images makes her role active and destructive. She machine-guns people and blows the middle out of buildings and cars. These images express the latent idea of retaliation and the latent emotion of rage and blame toward others for not gratifying her needs.

Expression of such ideas and feelings had been a problem for Mary since childhood since her fear, helplessness, and rage were intense, persistent, and morally taboo. She was shuffled back and forth from parents to grandparents, feeling angry and depressed at each "rejection" and loss. When she returned to her parents, a new baby occupied their attention. She imagined she had been sent away because of the coming of this baby. For years after her return home, her mother continued to produce babies which, from Mary's point of view as a child, deprived her of love. In order to remove these rivals she developed fantasies of ripping the insides out of her mother. These thoughts were repressed since, as part of the talon principle (an eye for an eye), she feared that she would be destroyed in the same way because of her evil urges.

The above constellation of repressed ideas and feelings were, by and large, dormant until triggered by her pregnancy, isolation, and childbirth. These experiences exicted implicit thoughts or questions such as: Who will feed the baby? Who will feed me? As she identified herself as both mother and baby, these questions generated dread, expressed in the passive set of images, and rage (no one will) expressed in the active images. These images partially express the dangerous ideas and emotions and hence are experienced as alien, intrusive, and menacing. She must disown the images to disown her impulses and her pain.

Hospital Course

The phases noted in the course of Mary's hospitalization will be described next to illustrate successful and unsuccessful inhibition of the images. Such phases of symptom, symptom remission, and symptom recurrence are not uncommon in psychiatric hospitalizations. Acute symptoms subside in the safety of the ward leaving a plateau that includes denial of illness. This avoidance of thoughts or discussions relevant to illness distinguishes the plateau phase from stable reintegration of psychologic controls. Movement within psychotherapy or around discharge planning reactives conflict and may lead to symptom flare-up. After such turbulence, patients commonly achieve a more stable integration.

Phase I: Intrusive Images, Passive Injured Type. On entry to the ward she complained of unbidden images and feelings that she labeled "earthquakes." She was cooperative, but passive, and periodically seemed to have a clouded state of consciousness during which she was withdrawn, inattentive, and unwilling or unable to concentrate. Her emotional expressions in her face, posture, and tone of voice indicated mild depression, but she would not speak about how she felt. This phase lasted three days.

With one of the nurses, she started interaction drawing to further communication of her current thoughts through pictures. Figure 8-10 is the first drawing produced. Mary drew a cracked head; the nurse drew a similar head with a similar line or crack. Mary added an icebag to her head and a flower to the head drawn by the nurse. Mary's later comments indicated that the cracked head was an earthquake reference.

Phase 2: No Unbidden Images. From the fourth through the eleventh days of hospitalization Mary seemed rational and cooperative. She recalled having the earthquakes but said the symptom was gone. She talked a little of her past history but specifically avoided mention of her pregnancy, the baby, her previous marriage, or plans for leaving the hospital or adopting the baby. She did report feeling sad and empty. When the

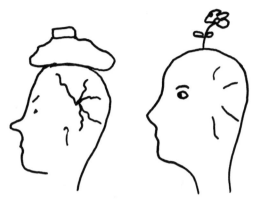

Fig. 8-10. The cracked head.

psychotherapist referred to "forbidden" topics, eg, the pregnancy, she cried and became silent. She remained rational, however, in all her communication and, on a questionnaire to assess confusion in thinking and intrusiveness of thought in general, she scored in a normal range. Tasks that measured perceptual attention, memory, and perceptual matching were also performed with high levels of concentration, attention, and exclusion of intrusive thoughts.

Figure 8-11 is one of the interaction drawings from this plateau period. Mary drew mountains and a rising sun, the nurse a road. Mary drew pine trees and a walking figure. The nurse added another figure; Mary drew a detour sign. The nurse added a side road. Mary added a "Dairy Queen." Such food references were common; many of her drawings showed themes like a child who had dropped his ice cream cone. The nurse, as with the road after the detour sign, would add a helpful path. Mary would block this "help" in a passive-aggressive manner during this phase.

Phase 3: Eruption of Hostile Images. During her psychotherapy hour, Mary was asked how she felt about her baby, and what was going to become of him. She wept, became angry, then confused, and stayed in a clouded state of consciousness for some hours. Thereafter, she reported intrusive, angry thoughts in the form of images. She saw herself machine-gunning people and blowing up buildings and cars. She visualized herself as having a hairy yellow mass in her abdomen; she saw others as plastic manikins without middle sections. She felt depersonalized, and others also seemed unreal. She threw a temper tantrum, threw her treasured

Fig. 8-11.   A drawing from a period without intrusive images.

musical instrument out the window, and messed up her room. During this period she did cooperate with cognitive testing: she reported herself confused with intrusive thoughts on the questionnaire, made perceptual errors, and had intrusive thoughts while attempting to attend to the perceptual stimuli of the task.

Figures 8-12, 8-13, and 8-14 are the second, fifth, and sixth drawings from an interaction drawing session conducted immediately after the psychiatric interview in which the baby topic was brought up. The patient depicted an exploding building and car. She dropped a boulder on the ambulance "dispatched" by the nurse and depicted a fire behind a wall drawn by the nurse. In Figure 8-13 Mary drew a picture that she called "bombing the baby." The nurse added a child figure pointing at the fight; the patient dropped a bomb at it. In Figure 8-14 the nurse repeated the bomb theme. The patient drew a baby carriage where the bomb would drop into

Fig. 8-12.   Explosion.

it. The nurse added a nurse and a warning figure which the patient labeled "deaf mute." She added a firecracker for good measure.

About two weeks after these drawings of "baby bombing," the patient asked to see her drawings. Her comments while looking them over were recorded. Here are her comments about this part of the series:

Fig. 8-13.   Bombing the baby.

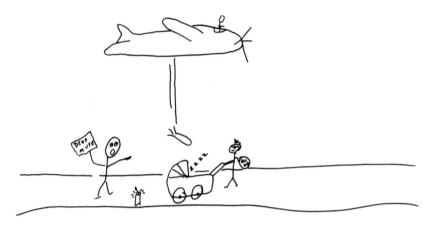

Fig. 8-14.   Repetition of the bomb theme.

The nurse had drawn some little people, like a child or children. So I bombed him. I dropped a bomb on him. (Shown next picture.) Yeah. She decided to keep on with the bomb. So I decided to bomb the baby carriage. And she drew a man trying to warn the nurse about the bomb that was falling. Only he was a deaf-mute and couldn't say anything. And I threw a firecracker for him and then she drew glasses on the nurse. So I colored them in and said she was blind. It's going to get bombed anyway, I don't care.

The angry impulses are clearly depicted in these drawings. There is also a despairing quality of hopelessly intense, insatiable need. The "bombing" pictures were made on the first day of a three-day period of intrusive thoughts revolving predominantly around destructive visions. The airplane theme emerged again toward the end of this period in an image that expresses poignantly the feeling of hopeless dependency. During the visual evocation procedure she was asked to report whatever visual images might form in response to the stimulus concept, "I am afraid":

I am an airplane. Looking for a place to land, but no place to land. I do see two places, one bigger than the other, but can't land on either, running out of fuel. I am the plane, silver, the air is transparent black.

Phase 4: Reinhibition of the Images Associated with Confusion.   The angry images subsided in three days. She reported no images and said she was hardly thinking at all. She sat staring at the floor and the wall and said there was a lid on her mind. During conversations and psychotherapy interviews she was dull, preoccupied, and confused. Apparently she inhibited the images but at the expense of a kind of confused "nonthinking." While she reported no intrusive images during this period, one of several interaction drawings made did show destructive themes. This is shown in Figure 8-15.* The nurse drew the figure outline. Mary drew in the face with crossed eyes, lines on the forehead, and the speech balloon, "my girdle is killing me." This remark was a joke about the slenderness of the figure but also a reference to her own abdomen (still distended from the

Fig. 8-15.   A girdle that cuts.

---

* The numbers in the illustration are annotations to indicate serial order. Circled numerals indicate Mary's drawing, uncircled numerals are the nurse's drawing.

postpartum period). The nurse drew a girdle, Mary added arms with knives that dripped blood.

This period lasted about a week, while the psychotherapist was supportive and deliberately avoided distressing themes. Then he again broached the "toxic" topics.

Phase 5: Reactivation of Unbidden Images.   When the baby issue was brought up by the psychotherapist, Mary avoided talking. Afterwards she was angry and reported many intrusions of her "earthquakes." These were probably not only recurrent unbidden images; they were also used by Mary to punish the therapist and to appear as if she were made ill by his intervention. The unbidden images were now, to an extent, "bidden unbidden images." Her drawings revolved largely around destructive and injured themes. While she would not discuss these ideas or feelings in words, she drew expressions of ideas of desertion, hunger and yearning, hopelessness and despair, and destruction involving the abdomen. Figure 8-16 provides one example. Mary drew a man holding a knife, and

Fig. 8-16.   Man with a knife.

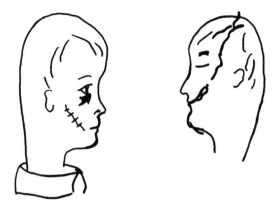

Fig. 8-17.   The rejecting male and the injured female.

in his mouth is an uptilted cigarette. This upturned cigarette is a repetitive theme: note for comparison Figure 8-17. One head seems to be a rejecting male, the other the injured female.

Phase 6: Inhibition of Images Again.   Mary once again reported that the images were gone. She was confused, abstracted, and forgetful. At times she was overheard by staff groaning aloud or saying "no" to herself. This was now the sixth week of hospitalization. She flirted, at other times she had temper tantrums. She still refused to discuss her baby, so the adoption procedures could not proceed.

Phase 7: Hostile Images Again.   Then she began to report the hostile images again. They still came of their own accord, but she said she kind of enjoyed them "in a smirky evil way." She began to speak of the images as her own ideas and thought of producing the fearsome hole of the "earthquakes" in other persons (see Figs. 8-18 and 8-19). In Figure 8-18 Mary drew a gun, and the nurse responded with a target. Mary made the target into a belt of a person and added a bleeding hole. The nurse added the head behind the gun. Then Mary changed to a new sheet of paper.

The nurse drew a circle (Fig. 8-19). Mary scribbled inside it and drew worm-like forms (worms in holes was another repeated theme). The next day, Mary and the nurse drew Figure 8-20. It indicates Mary's passive-aggressive behavior and the hostile and orally deprived themes. Mary drew the artist, the nurse a picnic basket. Mary drew the bear, the nurse a box. Mary added honey in the bear's paws. The nurse added another

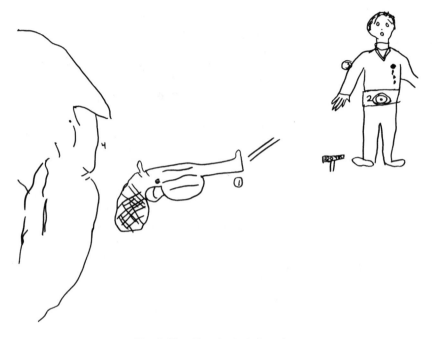

Fig. 8-18.   Put the hole in others.

"friendly" figure. Mary provided an alligator to threaten him, labeled the box "biskits," and staked down the figure so it could not escape. Finally, Mary drew a bird, the nurse added legs, and Mary drew a hunter with an arrow piercing the bird's belly.

Phase 8: Emergence of the Underlying Ideas, Turbulence, and Resolution.   The above period lasted five days. Then an anniversary: two months after the birth of her baby. Mary berated her therapist for not curing her faster, had a temper tantrum, entered a state of clouded consciousness, and behaved in an infantile manner. She dreamt of floating away with her baby to another planet because she could not keep it on earth: this was her first deliberate mention of the baby. She said, "Now the stopper is out, and the poison gas is loose." She felt very depressed and began talking of the baby. She also talked more of the earthquakes. In the drawings she showed an elephant stomping a man (Fig. 8-21), a crushed head (Fig. 8-22), and scenes of oral poignancy (Fig. 8-23).

At times, while she was thinking of her troubles, she also avoided them by entering an altered state of consciousness. She did this by staring at

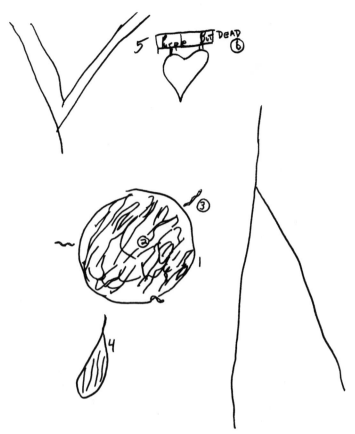

Fig. 8-19.   Worms in holes.

Fig. 8-20.   Food versus injury.

Fig. 8-21.   Elephant stomping a man.

some visual form such as a door jamb or a patch of sunlit floor. She said she felt "less awful while afloat" and that "when awake she feels disintegrated." She felt "phony" and "in parts," illustrating this with Figure 8-24 in the drawing sessions. The nurse added a feminine figure which Mary made toothless and breastless.

Mary began to talk things over in psychotherapy. She expressed the feelings previously depicted only in the images and her communication of their contents. She decided that her baby should have a permanent home

Fig. 8-22.   Crushed head.

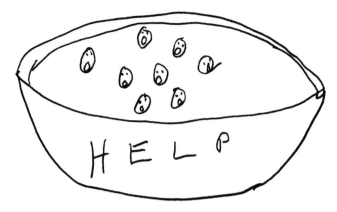

Fig. 8-23. Help.

that she herself had never had. She signed papers so that he could leave a temporary foster parent home and be adopted. In interaction drawings she deliberately depicted her earthquake-fear images (Fig. 8-25), the hostile wish to do the same to others (Fig. 8-26), and her split halves in the same picture (Fig. 8-27). Mary began to experience and work with her feelings of yearning for the baby, her grief at giving it up, and her guilt for not

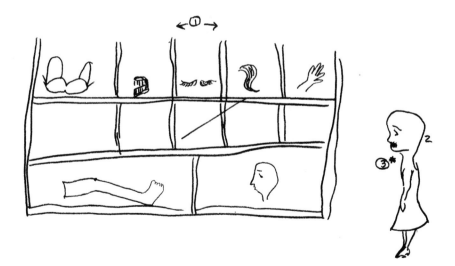

Fig. 8-24. Herself in parts.

Fig. 8-25.   Earthquake.

Fig. 8-26.   Hurting others.

Fig. 8-27.   Her split personality.

keeping it. Some of these feelings were reflected in the interaction drawings of this period (Figs. 8-28, 8-29, and 8-30).

After these therapeutic gains, Mary accepted encouragement to manage her own affairs. She sought work while still in the hospital. For a time she entered a kind of halfway house. Then she "graduated" to outpatient psychotherapy.

Transformation and Disguise.   In the set of images she found most distressing, Mary felt herself empty, damaged, and in danger of disintegration. At an unconscious level she "preferred" to facilitate a cluster of

Fig. 8-28.   The baby theme.

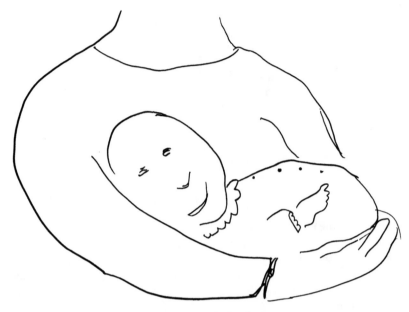

Fig. 8-29.   The baby theme.

Fig. 8-30.   The baby theme.

emotions and self-concepts in which she imaged herself as a bad, dangerous, and angry person. Generation of anger and sadistic revengeful satis-
faction through the destructive images seemed semipurposive; she felt at
least alive and personally intact when angry. Thus, one set of "unbidden
images" seemed to be generated to suppress feelings expressed and aroused
by a still more "unbidden" and intolerable set.

The bad self-concept and world view, while in a sense a defense against
the disintegrative despair, was also defended against; hence the dissocia-
tion of the images from her sense of self, from her thought, and from
verbal communication. The bad identity was too close to painful feelings
of being a bad mother, wishing to hurt her baby, deserting her baby, and
being deserted by men and her parents.

Case Discussion

Both sets of Mary's unbidden images had the same bipolar schema: an
injured person and an injuring person. She could align her sense of self
with either pole: she could be the injured person, as in the "earthquakes,"
or the injuring person, as in the hostile images. The two sets of images
represent layers of the same formulation, which is why one set was labeled
passive, and the other, active.

In the phase in which she aligns herself with the injuring pole, she
forms active images in which she is a destructive aggressor. In terms of
unconscious metaphors, she may feel that she has inside herself, in place
of emptiness, a powerful weapon. In a sense she is strong because she is
full of rage; others are weak victims. In the passive images she aligns
herself with the injured pole. She is in danger of imminent harm or, more
deeply, has been damaged beyond repair.

The dual roles leading to two sets of images demonstrate an important
feature of image formation: image expression allows easy alternation between active and passive self-representations. Usually, in situations of fear
of external persons, the preferred fantasy transformation is from passive
victim to active persecutor (identification with the aggressor, A Freud[1];
see also Perry[9]). For example, a child who has been afraid of his dentist
may, in fantasy, image himself as the man who fixes the teeth of others
(even if it hurts a little). The feared situation is depicted, but the role is
changed from one of helplessness to mastery. This helps in adaptation; in
the new fantasy role, the motives of the feared person may be understood
as benign rather than malignant. Also, the rehearsal in an objective,
external way of how another "victim" behaves and survives may lead to
reduction of fear. On the other hand, when the active role is dreaded—as

when anger, if expressed, would activate guilt—then the passive role may be fantasized. Recall how Isabel visualized the old man "haunting her" to disguise and avoid, and also to expiate in advance, her own assaultive impulses.

Mary's two sets of images, while "uncontrolled," were used by her to regulate feelings. When dangerously enraged, she could "punish" herself or warn herself with the passive images of being injured. When she felt injured, she was able to gratify herself in fantasy retaliation using the active images. When she felt guilty about rejecting or wanting to reject or harm her baby (or her own mother), she was able to inflict the same injury on herself with the passive images. A sample of transformation between active and passive role-structuring of the underlying injured-injurer schema is found in one of her dreams:

> I had a gun and was going to shoot a man. I pulled the trigger, but a hole in my own head occurred. Then I shot a woman in the belly. And there I was, holes in my own head, in my own belly, and no holes in them.

In this dream her rage is turned upon herself by the role reversal. Also, this reversal of roles is important to the stress that preceded her symptoms: she has a baby she will not care for, thus reversing the situation from her own feelings of infantile neglect.

Why did Mary fall ill? She was, of course, engulfed in a life crisis, childbirth after an unwanted pregnancy. But why did she decompensate rather than experience emotional distress and adapt to her situation? Any woman might feel remorse, guilt, depression, and anger. A hypothetical normal woman might undergo a period of psychologic work, consisting of working through a grief reaction with, perhaps, periods of angry, anxious, or depressive moods. Mary required psychiatric hospitalization to work through her emotions. Why? Working through her problem requires thought and emotion. Mary may have a particularly low tolerance for unpleasant emotions and, rather than working through her experience, she avoids memory and feeling by withdrawal, mutism, altered states of consciousness, and suicide attempts. Partly this could be because her childbirth experience gave rise to unusually intense emotions. These would be hard to bear because they activate residues of her childhood deprivations. Rage, depression, and frustration are, by adulthood, "built in" to her character and any situation of rebuff, loss, or need will trigger feelings that the world is totally bad.

A second explanation of her symptom formation concerns her capacity for regulation. She attempts to inhibit ideas but she seems to have a poor inhibitory capacity. It is hard for her to prevent images from entering awareness in the first place: instead, she has to avoid recognition or reaction to images that become conscious. This relatively low inhibitory capacity reduces her ability to "dose" the phases of any psychologic working-through process.

Consider again our hypothetic "normal" woman. In Mary's situation, she might have a grief reaction: she would think over her experience and try different means in thought of appraising it or reacting to it. When emotional responses such as shame or depression reached the level of tolerance, this "normal" woman might be able to inhibit further memories, thus, giving herself only tolerable doses of thinking-through. By repeated doses, within thresholds of tolerance, the working-through is gradually accomplished. If Mary cannot control the entry of memories or thoughts into awareness, she cannot so dose herself: to her, opening up to the experiences means overwhelming floods of painful feelings.

Mary must totally avoid reconsideration of her experience. Total avoidance means that the need to reconsider the experience is not reduced and the predispositions to develop the painful feelings remain at full strength. Mary falls ill, in a sense, because she has poor capacity for inhibition: this means she must totally inhibit rather than periodically "dose herself" with those painful experiences in need of mastery. The poor capacity for inhibition means this total avoidance is doomed to failure: aspects of the experience and her emotions do gain expression, albeit in the disguised form of the unbidden images.

The press toward expression is in conflict with motives of avoidance. This impulse-defense configuration undergoes various transformations as she uses different means of regulating what is represented in conscious thought. The first level of inhibition is repressive: no contents are allowed to "leak out." Her repressive inhibitory capacity is relatively inadequate, and she resorts to another level of inhibition, a form of denial. She describes her unbidden images as alien symptoms and denies to herself their implications. She does not translate their full meaning into words. Thus, she encapsulates the dreaded ideas and feelings as "foreign" images.

There is one additional historic contributant to Mary's tendency to deny, split, and dissociate mental concepts. When she returned home from her grandparents and felt parental neglect, there was a redeeming person, a bachelor friend of the family. He took her to work with him when she was six years old. She worked with him holding tools and was taken by him to enjoyable activities, such as the circus and the ice cream store (the source of the ice cream cones frequently shown in her drawings to depict both longing and gratification). While not directly molesting her sexually, this man used to fondle her, look at her body, and kiss her in a "sloppy, slobbery way." She was frightened and excited by these advances. To maintain the relationship, which she desperately needed, she encapsulated in one mental set the warm parental qualities of the man and held separately his sexual and exploitative qualities.

Like Isabel and Ned, Mary sometimes entered altered states of consciousness in which rational thought in words was diminished, fantasy amplified. Usually, in such states, images increase in vividness. But even if they do not, the loss of the sense of self-willed control over the course of thought lends the images a quality of quasi-reality: the images are not clearly demarcated from perceptions. This blurring of the boundaries between fantasy and reality may make internal images during altered states of consciousness both more gratifying and more terrifying, depending on their contents and on responses to the contents. Mary sometimes entered an altered state on purpose; she accomplished this by staring and repeating patterns of stimulation until they became meaningless. In clouded consciousness she could avoid thinking about unpleasant reality and dwell instead in fantasy. But once in the altered state, she could not necessarily rouse herself to full alertness when the images turned sour or activated too much responsive feeling.

DISCUSSION

The unbidden image is experienced subjectively as a surprise. The thought processes involved in image formation are not available to conscious appraisal, and the more unpleasant forms of unbidden images seem to occur in spite of conscious and deliberate efforts to avoid or dispel them. Nonetheless, clinical investigation of the underlying cognitive dynamics reveals that subjectively "unbidden" images are thought products which result from interactions between impulsive and defensive motives. In the case histories, impulsive motives and the transformations of these motives were described. Now I abstract from such clinical investigations how various defense mechanisms relate to image thinking.

Unbidden images are, first and foremost, a failure in *repression*. Usually dominant inhibitory influences over image formation give way to suddenly stronger facilitory influences. The sudden reversal of regulatory dynamics may be caused by intensification of impulsive motives, or waning of inhibitory capacity. In either event, the sudden entry into awareness lends the experience one aspect of its peremptory quality. When facilitation is relatively strong, the images are likely to be unusually vivid, hence more like perceptions and, therefore, easily regarded as some unpleasant aspect of the outer world rather than a dangerous part of the inner world. (This extrusion of the image contents from the concept of self is a *projective* operation.) Once repression has failed as a total inhibitory defense, then *denial* may be used as a supplement or substitute. In terms of image formation, denial works because of inhibitions that keep the conscious self-observing ego selectively unaware of (1) the image formation process (and hence, the internal origin of the images), (2) the motives for the expression, and (3) the associations that might arise in response to the current image experience (denial of the meaning of the images). Denial of the internal source of images is analogous to the more familiar form of denial in which external perceptions, or their implications, are purposively ignored.

While inhibitory influences may fail to prevent image formation, such influences may still prevent lexical representation. The emerging contents may gain expression as images and yet be blocked from translation into word meanings. This form of *suppression* may contribute to the subjective regard of the images as mysterious and uncanny. In the presence of conflicted motives, the defensive maneuvers of *isolation* or *splitting* might result in one set of contents being expressed in the image system, another set in the lexical system, with avoidance of active conflict by inhibition of translation between the complexes. This would further contribute to the isolation of the images from a sense of meaning.

The revisualization of traumatic perceptions is explained as a particular example of repressive failure. The image records are incompletely mastered and press toward revisualization. This impulsive motive, described in detail in the next chapter, is countered by a motive for repression: the images, like the perceptions, are potentially overwhelming and certainly unpleasant. As with other failures in repression, the emergence of the traumatic images contributes to the sensation of loss of thought control. This adds to whatever emotions are already expressed (or evoked) by the images (usually fear).

Impulsive motives are repressed only when they cause some potential danger: they may seem too strong and, hence, potentially uncontrollable; they may conflict with other motives such as self-preservation, preservation of love by others, or moral standards. If the image contents partially express the impulsive motives, they are appraised as dangerous because the motives are dangerous. Further expression of the impulsive motives is prevented, insofar as possible, by disguise of the ideas and feelings through mechanisms such as *displacement* and *symbolization*. Because of differential abilities to disguise image contents and feeling states some images may appear incongruent to the emotions that accompany them. When present, this incongruity contributes to the subjective strangeness of the unbidden image experience. Bland images may emerge with unpleasant feeling tones; horrible or lurid images may emerge without any accompanying emotion. This latter is a specific form of the defense of *intellectualization*.

If unbidden images were simply repressive breakthroughs they would be easy to explain. But the mind is very complex, even in psychosis, and there is often order in apparent chaos. Defensive motives may take an image, that in terms of content looks like the result of impulsive motives, and use it for defensive purposes. The basic versions of this defensive amplification are as follows:

1. The formation of a particular image may be facilitated to arouse a feeling of danger that in turn is used to motivate further defensive, controlling, or coping efforts. This is a specific form of *signal anxiety*.
2. The formation of a particular image may be facilitated to arouse feelings other than danger for the purpose of transforming more dreaded emotions and urges. This is a form of *reversal*. Fear may be generated to avoid anger as in (1), but anger may also be generated to avoid fear, guilt to avoid anger, and so forth. An important maneuver in this is the use of images to reverse roles from passive to active, or vice versa, so that passive fears become active urges, or active urges become passive fears. Sometimes this is a form of *displacement*, and sometimes it is a form of *undoing*.

Traumatic memories, with their propensity for formation of vivid images, are especially useful to the above defensive motives because they evoke intense fear and a sense of danger. Dormant traumas may be revived for this purpose, or contemporary traumas may remain unresolved, because they both trigger and screen internal conflict. Images that generate feelings such as fear, guilt, and hate, albeit for defensive purposes, will be regarded by the reflective self as unbidden and unwelcome.

Defensive motives tend to repeat trains of thought that end in images that successfully terminate tension states. Repetition results in condensation of the train of thought into the end symbol, the image. When similar tensions arise, the symbol may be activated without the original train of thought and the sudden, seemingly irrelevant, entry will lend the image-symbol a mysterious quality.

In the *defensive use of regression*, a person may deliberately let go of the sense of reflective self-awareness by blurring the boundary between percept and image.[10] Thus, fantasies can be made to seem more real, and perception less real. Fantasy images can, through this defense, seem more gratifying, but they may also become more terrifying. Repressed images may emerge that "traumatize" the person from within. Images in regressive states seem to be unbidden because of the loss of reflective self-awareness and the reduced inhibition of contents and vividness.

The entry into regressive mental states is not always deliberate. A person may enter such a state because he lacks the capacity to organize thought into complex sequences. Even when this is due to an organic incapacity, seemingly unbidden images may be used for defensive purposes: to create emotion or to hold on to content that serves to stabilize cognitive organization and prevent further disintegration into chaos.

REFERENCES

1. Freud A: The Ego and the Mechanisms of Defense. New York, International Univ Press, 1946
2. Freud S: A child is being beaten: a contribution to the study of the origin of sexual perversions. Stand Ed 17, 1955
3. Greenacre P: A contribution to the study of screen memories. Psychoanal Stud Child 3–4:73, 1949
4. Horowitz MJ: Visual imagery: an experimental study of pictorial cognition using the dot-image sequence. J Nerv Ment Dis 141:615, 1966
5. ——— : Graphic communication: a study of interaction painting with schizophrenics. Amer J Psychother 17:230, 1963
6. Jacobson E: Denial and repression. J Amer Psychoanal Assoc 5:61, 1957
7. Jones E: Fear, guilt and hate. Int J Psychoanal 10:383, 1929
8. Klein GS: Peremptory ideation: structure and force in motivated ideas. Psychol Issues 5:80, 1967
9. Perry JW: Emotions and object relations. J Anal Psychol 15:1, 1970
10. Schafer R: Aspects of Internalization. New York, International Univ Press, 1968

Part III

Neurobiologic Influences on Image Formation

9

THE CONTRIBUTION OF THE EYE

Two processes, perception and image formation, occupy to some extent the same channels of consciousness and the same routes of information processing. Of course, some kinds of perceptual input reduce internal image formation by occupying channel capacity and attention. But other kinds of perceptual input augment internal image formation either by triggering motives or by providing a kind of sensory raw material for fantasy. The less definitive, in terms of configuration, the external input, the more likely that something of motivational relevance can be made out of it. The usual form of internal completion of an external stimulus is called an illusion and I shall begin with a general consideration of this phenomenon. Next I will consider in detail a special form of illusion in which the "external" source of perceptual raw material is inside the body, in the optic apparatus itself.

PERCEPTION AND ILLUSION

After considerable psychologic and neurobiologic research, it is now clear that perception is not a passive but an active process. An external signal undergoes many transformations, transportations, interpretations, and recombinations before a person experiences seeing, and any reader interested in image formation will eventually wish to consult texts on perception.*

---

* Excellent resources include texts by Neisser,[59] Haber,[27] Vernon,[84] Gregory,[25] Heaton,[30] Granit,[24] and Broadbent.[15]

We will begin our considerations at a point after perceptual processes have gathered a tremendous array of particulate information, some accurate and some inaccurate in terms of correspondence to external objects, and when cognitive processes strive to reduce and organize this information for meaningful labeling and conscious sampling. One means of organizing bits of perceptual stimuli is to assemble the stimuli according to patterns and forms. These forms may be inherent, part of the visual processing system built in by heredity, or they may be acquired through experience and perceptual learning.[45, 46]

The familiar patterns and forms serve as schemata or templates and those signals that fit the schemata may be facilitated while those that fall outside of its boundaries may be inhibited. A series of trials may establish the best fit of schemata to signal. The signals falling outside the schemata are regarded as "noise" and omissions from the usual pattern or form may be added to the perceptual image from internal rather than external sources. Without such schemata, perception might be, in the words of William James, "a blooming, buzzing confusion."

An example of the need for perceptual schemata is provided by Von Senden,[31] who removed the congenital cataracts that had blinded certain patients from birth. After surgical restoration of sight, these patients could not, at first, interpret with their eyes what they could interpret by touch. To label a block as "a square," a patient might not only have to look at it but count the corners and reason that four corners make a square, not a triangle.

Another example of the need for schemata of interpretation occurs in research on normally sighted persons. Kohler[47] fitted his subjects with mirrors that altered their vision dramatically—the mirrors turned everything upside down. For several days his subjects were perceptually confused, but when their interpretive systems compensated for the altered format of stimuli, they once again used their eyes automatically to label visual stimuli. When the glasses were removed the world resumed its "normal" tilt, the interpretation and labeling systems required a new period of adjustment.

Symmetry is important to schemata, as demonstrated by the completion effect. If a person cannot see part of his visual field, as in partial blindness, a form in the area of intact vision tends to be "seen" in the blind area, completed in a regular way.[87,89]

When a person misapplies old schemata to a new set of stimuli, we call the resulting image an illusion. In consensually valid illusions certain configurations, such as unusual shifts in perspective, "play tricks" on the visual processes. Such illusions are usually geometric and are of interest because they indicate properties of the optical pathways. Like the examples so far, they are, in essence, errors of perception not necessarily bound into a person's feeling state or ideational state. The Müller-Lyer and Herring illusions are classic examples. Lines of equal length appear different because of differences in surrounding forms. These illusions are "consensually valid" because everyone can "see" the illusion.[52]

Idiosyncratic illusions commonly take place within an individual. One example is interpreting a shadow from a tree as a threatening human figure, another, identifying a stranger's face as that of a friend. These illusions are of interest to clinicians because they frequently reflect current motivations and concerns. The schemata for organization of signals into perceptual images are influenced by expectancy. Sometimes an illusion occurs because of wishful expectancy: a person tends to see what he desires. At other times expectancy is influenced more by fear than by wish, and a person may have an illusion of what he dreads. Logical reasoning, conditioning, and incipient conceptualizations also influence expectancy. I use this term, incipient conceptualizations, to indicate the press of certain ideas or feelings toward representation. In Chapter 5, I described how concepts may gain representation in thought through images, words, or anticipatory behaviors. Concepts may also gain representation through perception.

Suppose there is an incipient conceptualization—an idea or feeling not yet clearly represented in thought by words or images—that influences perceptual expectancy. A person may tend to focus selectively on some particular aspect of the environment that expresses the incipient idea. In a sense, the concept is projected onto the environment and "found" rather than "formed" as a thought. The woman who saw the sign "Evangelist's Services," in Chapter 6, is one example. Thus, a prerepresentational thought can be represented through selective perception, and, in the case of defensive avoidance, the opposite process of selective nonperception may take place.

Ordinarily, selective perception does not grossly change the quality of external objects. In some states, however, perception is distorted by the incipient conceptualization, and an illusion occurs. Here is an everyday example:

A young man had broken up with his girlfriend after a fierce fight. He dreaded the thought of running into her on the street because she might continue to recriminate him. He also missed her and wanted to see her again. He was not thinking consciously of such matters, however, as he walked along a main boulevard. He thought he saw her half a block away walking toward him. His heart began to pound as he saw on her face a look of recognition and anger. Then he realized that he was staring at a stranger who was not looking at him and did not even resemble his girlfriend.

In the above illusion, the incipient conceptualization could continue to dominate the conscious perceptual image as long as the signal was relatively indistinct: as long as the real woman was so far away that he could not distinctly see her features. As the distance narrowed, the signals presenting her features became so clear that his conscious image shifted toward presentation of reality, and the girlfriend image was dispelled. This example illustrates the effects of both wishful and fearful expectancy and how they tend to increase the formation of illusions.[3,69]

Illusions also tend to occur in states where signals are unclear because of dimness, brevity, or a low signal-to-noise ratio. Segal[73-75] replicated and extended Perky's[64] demonstration that normal subjects may confuse internal and external images when external signals are dim. In her experiment, a normal subject inserts his face into a partially translucent hood on which the experimenter can project various stimuli. The illumination of projections is started at zero and then slowly increased until the stimuli are barely visible. Subjects can be told to imagine objects, to report any projections, and asked to differentiate the two sources. In this condition, subjects produce a variety of interesting illusionary effects. Sometimes a subject reports as an internal thought image what is actually being projected on the hood. At other times, subjects report as stimuli projected on the hood images that are in reality internally, and not externally, stimulated. A subject may combine the external and internal stimuli to form an illusion. For example, he might be trying to form an image of a red tomato when the experimenter projects, very dimly, an outline of the city skyline. The subject might then report that he sees the skyline of New York with a red sun setting.

Segal[76] also found that when subjects form visual images, they score less correct reports on dim external visual perceptions; when they form internal auditory images, correct visual perception is not as impaired. These data show how image formation influences perception and how perception influences image formation.

Segal's experiments relate, in part, to subliminal perceptions, those registrations not recognized in conscious awareness which, nonetheless, influence subsequent image formation. Pötzl,[67] working early in this century, found that subjects might not recognize certain visual stimuli, and yet evidence for these stimuli might be found in their subsequent internal images. Fisher and Paul[21] replicated and extended this work. They found that very brief perceptions, that could not be consciously deciphered, emerged later in images and dreams and often were elaborated and transformed toward the subject's current motivational needs. Subjects tended to treat supraliminal or conscious perceptions logically, but they tended to absorb subliminal perceptions into fantasy thinking.[2,21,63] Even when supraliminal stimuli are projected at the same time as subliminal stimuli, the impression of the subliminal stimuli is still incorporated into subsequent image formation and fantasy. Eagle[20] found that simple, striking, emotionally charged subliminal stimuli seemed to have greater subsequent effects on image formation and fantasy than well-defined and supraliminal stimuli. When supraliminal stimuli were vague, however, they too seemed to invite fantasy.

To summarize, perceptual events may influence image formation, and internal images may influence the interpretation of perceptual stimuli. People may confuse the two processes, and may interpret or appraise internal images as real perceptions, or real perceptions as internal images.

So far we have only considered stimuli from sources outside of a person's body. Perceptual stimuli may also arise from within the person's body and be formed into an illusion.

THE POSSIBLE INFLUENCE OF EYE MOVEMENTS ON IMAGE FORMATION

The reader may wish to recall, at this point, the possible relationship between eye movements and the formation of dream images described in Chapter 3. What is relevant here is that it has been occasionally possible to relate the direction of the eye movement to depictions of movement in the concurrent dream experience.[71] Are the eyes following the motions of hallucinatory dream objects? Or is it possible that the eye movements contribute stimuli that influence the selection of dream contents? Electroencephalographic data from electrodes placed in various brain locations of animals suggest that the subcortical events may arise first with cortical excitation appearing soon afterwards. It does seem possible, then, that the eye movements are not in pursuit of the already formed dream images but instead may influence or even evoke certain images.

The coincidence of visual hallucinatory dreaming with rapid eye movement sleep led to several speculations and studies concerning the possible coincidence of schizophrenic hallucinations with eye movements. For example, Wallach et al[86] report that there are involuntary eye movements similar to REMs in certain schizophrenics during periods of disturbed behavior.

Recently, as part of an attempt to find physiologic recordings pertinent to studies of subjective experience, there has been an increase in research on the possible correlations between eye movements and waking image formation. Earlier attempts had not found an increase in eye movements with increased vividness or frequency of thought images.[5] But Bakan[12] found that subjects who moved their eyes to the left when shifting into a period of reflective and introspective thought tended to be more imaginative, aesthetic, emotional, and spiritually oriented. Persons who tended to shift to the right tended to be more verbal and logical in the organization of their thought. Meskin and Singer[57] found that subjects who were "inner attentive" were more likely to shift their eyes to the left when thinking of answers to complex questions or recalling early childhood memories. Persons with less frequency of daydreaming were more likely to shift their eyes to the right. Galin and Ornstein[23] gathered similar data. Looking, as it were, to the left even while "looking" inwardly involves seeking relative activation of the right side of the retina, the half that feeds more input into the right hemisphere of the brain. In right-handed persons, this right hemisphere is less associated with language skills, and more associated with visual and spatial skills, as mentioned earlier. Ornstein[61] has suggested that whole life-styles may be centered on modal differences in consciousness based on relative sidedness of brain use and Galin[22] has suggested that such physiologic substrates could account for variances in cognitive styles.

Whatever the role of eye movements, we know that the retina (or the optical pathways from the eye to the brain) provides elementary sensations. The entoptic images are sometimes among the first subjective experiences during an altered state of consciousness that leads to hallucinatory images. For example, after taking LSD a person may have altered perception and entoptic images prior to experiencing hallucinations.[10] A similar series of events occasionally occurs in hypnagogic states.[79] Under certain circumstances, the raw sensory material supplied by an entoptic phenomenon might be elaborated into a hallucinatory experience. As stated earlier, by strict definition the elaboration of an entoptic image into an object-depicting image would be called an illusion. I use the word hallucination, however, because I will be discussing subjective experiences that are usually described by clinicians as hallucinations. Also the "external sensation" component is not external to the body, although it is peripheral to the psyche or mind. The remainder of this chapter considers this possibility.

ENTOPTIC PHENOMENA AS PERCEPTUAL
CONTRIBUTANTS TO IMAGE FORMATION*

As early as 1887, Hoope suggested that the physical eye might furnish the material on which hallucinations are based[42] and Hughlings Jackson[41] described how floaters (muscae volitantes) in the eye might develop into visions of rats. My own clinical experiences suggest the same hypothesis: that some complex image experiences contain a nidus or matrix of simple sensations.

When first questioning patients about their visual experiences, I found it helpful to persist beyond initial verbal descriptions of hallucinations, and to insist that the patient draw exactly what he imaged. For example, verbal description of "vicious snakes" might be drawn as wavy lines; the visual images of moving sets of dots might translate verbally to "two armies struggling over my soul"; "spiders" might reduce to a few radiating lines. Patients could sometimes distinguish a form that they "saw with their eyes" from the more elaborate images described as their hallucinations. If the same hallucination recurred, it might become simpler as their clinical state improved. Below are some case examples.

Case 1. A young man was diagnosed having a borderline and schizoid personality underlying an acute psychotic episode. The first symptom occurred when he had been brooding over the traumatic death of his older brother and staring at the fire in a fireplace. He saw the jagged peaks of the flames as the shape of a menacing dragon and, in spite of efforts to blink it away, the dragon spontaneously reappeared before his eyes several times during the next few days. During the acute state of his illness, he again felt threatened by "heads" which were prominent after-images or double visions of real objects. In Figure 9-1, (a) represents the patient's drawing of the dragon event and (b) the transition of a faucet into a head.

Case 2. A patient having a schizophrenic episode jerked his gaze to one side periodically during an office interview. When asked why, he replied, "You've got bugs over there!" On another occasion he stated that he saw the faces of the Holy Trinity. The drawings from both occasions of what he saw are identical (Fig. 9-2). Ophthalmologic examination recreated "the bugs," and the same floater configuration seemed to provide the signal basis or matrix for the "bugs" and the "Holy Trinity" images.

---

* Portions of the following material were reported in a paper published and copyrighted by the Williams and Wilkins Co. in J Nerv Ment Dis 138:513, 1964. The research was supported by a grant from the Office of Naval Research (NR 105 156).

A.

FLAMES   TO   DRAGON

B.

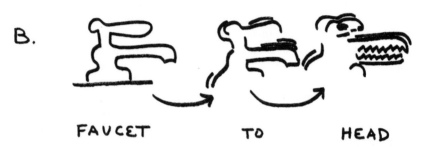

FAUCET   TO   HEAD

Fig. 9-1. From the patient's drawings of his development of hallucinations (Case 1).

Fig. 9-2. From drawings of hallucinations of "bugs" and of "the Holy Trinity" (Case 2).

194

Case 3.   A chronic schizophrenic patient told people that he could see his "eyeball burning." Figure 9-3 represents his drawing; the heavy lines are what he "really saw." As his clinical state improved, he reported that he no longer thought of his eyeball burning and that he saw "just flames" or "just wavy lines."

Case 4.   An 18-year-old enlisted man in the Armed Forces was hospitalized when discovered roaming the streets in a confused and disoriented state. He had "hallucinations" of dots in the corner of his visual field (Fig. 9-4[a])

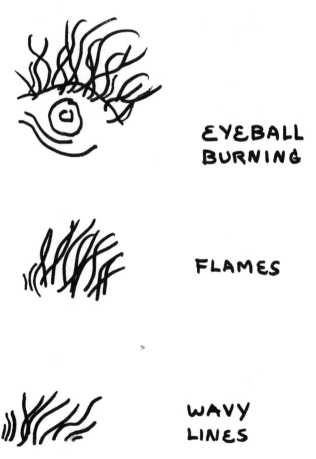

EYEBALL
BURNING

FLAMES

WAVY
LINES

Fig. 9-3.   Excerpts from the patient's drawings showing the transition from the image of "an eyeball burning" to "just wavy lines" (Case 3).

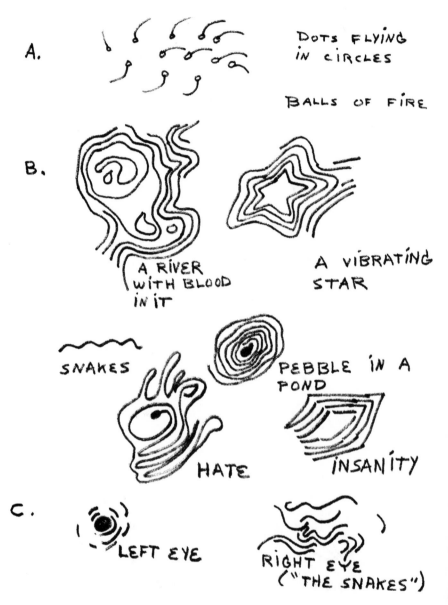

Fig. 9-4. From the drawings of hallucinations (Case 4).

which occurred almost constantly during certain hours of the day, especially if he were not occupied in some distracting activity. During an interview he pointed to them with his finger but, when he attempted to focus them, they drifted to the periphery of his visual fields. At times he was convinced they were "cosmic balls of fire sent to punish me." Treatment was started with chlordiazepoxide (Librium), 20 mg four times daily. He reported a marked worsening of the visual disturbances and made drawings of what he saw (Fig. 9-4[b]). Examination of his visual fields showed a left central scotoma which was confirmed by campimetry (a special study of visual fields) during an ophthalmologic consultation. With the opposite eye closed he could see different figures in each eye (Fig. 9-4[c]). With an exclamation of surprise, he identified the figure in his right eye as "the snakes" he had been "hallucinating." He then reported a psychotic episode, one and a half years previously, which he had kept secret hoping to remain in the service. He stated he had not had visual hallucinations then until he received medication which, by his description of the capsule colors and recognition of the current medication, had been chlordiazepoxide. After chlordiazepoxide was discontinued, the visual phenomena diminished markedly although the dots persisted; the scotoma disappeared subjectively and by campimetry. Later, another dose of chlordiazepoxide caused these particular symptoms to recur, and this medication was permanently discontinued. When the patient was treated with thioridazine, there were no similar effects.

Case 5.   The patient is a 69-year-old woman with a 20-year documented history of Meniere's disease (a disease of the middle ear that includes dizziness as a major symptom). Her first symptom occurred at the age of 40. While she was outside gardening, a shrub seemed to move; then, falling black spots appeared from above; then her vision became obscured by what appeared to be smoke and fog. She experienced a tremendous spinning sensation, characterized by the world moving clockwise. As the "fog" cleared, she saw brilliant herringbone scintillations in the periphery of the right eye's visual field and a bright halo around objects (Fig. 9-5[a]). The attack lasted 20 minutes and recurred two to five times a year thereafter, with some variations. She was intensely frightened, mostly by the herringbone scintillations which she originally interpreted as fire and icicles of metaphysic origin. Occasionally, instead of snowflakes, she would see fiery splashes (Fig. 9-5[b] and [c]).

Case 6.   A 37-year-old man had a syndrome of severe migraine headaches for 15 years. He knew the onset of the headaches because of a visual aura: whatever he was looking at seemed to become pockmarked or rippled. It was as if drops of rain had fallen onto his perceptual image and caused tiny concentric circles of perceptual distortion in many areas. Then, he often

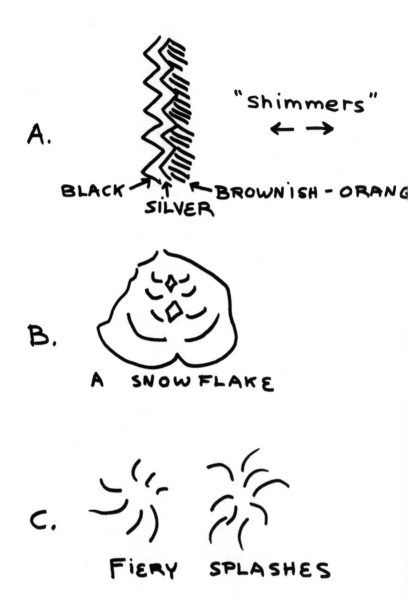

Fig. 9-5.   From the drawings of hallucinations (Case 5).

noted bright, fluorescent, star-like flashes. On occasion he had, with his auras, the visual sensation of looking at six-sided honeycomb figures that could create "an endless wallpaper effect."

REDUNDANT ELEMENTS OF FORM

Clinical descriptions such as those illustrated above suggest that some entoptic event, usually ignored, might provide a nidus around which hallucinations, pseudohallucinations, or (technically) illusions develop, since people commonly experience entoptic phenomena, such as "floaters" or after-images. A questionnaire was distributed to 80 psychiatric staff members in order to obtain drawings of these experiences in normal subjects.

The complete forms and drawings resembled the verbal and graphic descriptions of patients who reported visual hallucinations. The staff tended to interpret visual forms, eg, calling flashes "stars," wavy lines "snakes," or circular figures "marbles," but this was less pronounced than in the descriptions elicited from patients.

Certain words and graphic forms appeared regularly in the data from normals and in interviews with patients having hallucinations. Some redundant words and forms were stars, pinwheels, wheels, marbles, dots, specks, circles, snakes, spiders, worms, bugs, spots, swirls, wavy lines, and filigrees. Many of the descriptions could be categorized as one of Klüver's hallucinatory form constants: spirals, funnels, cobwebs, or lattices. In Figure 9-6, I show the redundant figural elements in their simplest and most common forms; at times they appear as overlapping, combined, or multiplied. These forms also appear frequently in physiologic or biochemical disturbances as in migraine attacks[28,39,70]; chemogenic hallucinations[36,54,55,78]; lesions or stimulation of the brain[38]; retinal stimulation[37]; toxic or starvation deliria[58,88]; and sleep deprivation.[51] Similar figural elements also occur in eidetic imagery[60]; blank screen effects, hypnagogic hallucinations[40]; the visions in sensory deprivation[58,80]; schizophrenic hallucinations[6,14]; artistic imagery[9,35,48]; psychotic art[1,4,82]; and even mystical or "visionary experiences."[81]

Siegel and Jarvik[78] performed careful experiments involving such recurrent forms, and provide excellent illustrations of elaborations upon them. They followed Klüver's form-constant categories and developed the following elaboration:

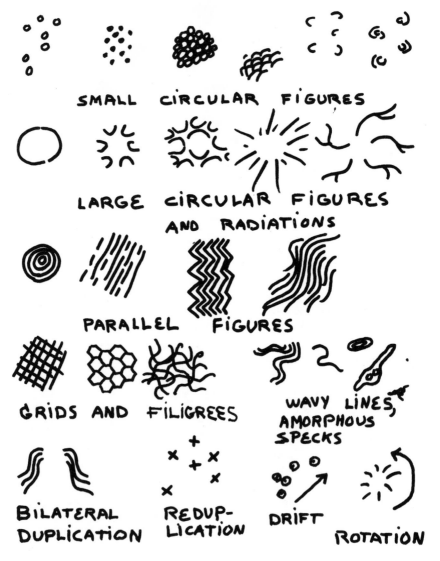

SMALL CIRCULAR FIGURES

LARGE CIRCULAR FIGURES
AND RADIATIONS

PARALLEL FIGURES

GRIDS AND FILIGREES

WAVY LINES,
AMORPHOUS
SPECKS

BILATERAL
DUPLICATION

REDUP-
LICATION

DRIFT

ROTATION

Fig. 9-6. Redundant elements in hallucinations and visual imagery.

- **Random.** Blobs, amorphous shapes, blurry patterns, watery patterns without definite design, etc. (any form that cannot be classified in the categories below)
- **Line.** Herringbone patterns, zig-zags, polygons, all angular figures without curves or rounded corners, crosses, etc.
- **Curve.** Circles, ellipses, parabolas, hyperbolas, sine wave patterns, fingerprint whorls, spheres, balls, scribblings, etc.
- **Web.** Spider webs, nets, unsymmetric lattices and filigrees, veins, etc.
- **Lattice.** Lattices, gratings, grids, screens, fretwork, checkerboards, honeycombs, etc.
- **Tunnel.** Tunnels, funnels, alleys, cones, vessels, pits, corridors, etc.
- **Spiral.** Spirals, pinwheels, springs, etc.
- **Kaleidoscope.** Kaleidoscopes, mandalas, symmetric snowflakes, lacework, mosaics, symmetric flower-like patterns, etc.
- **Complex.** Any recognizable imagery such as faces, people, landscapes, panoramic vistas, animals, inanimate objects, cartoons, etc.*

Siegel and Jarvik trained their subjects to recognize and discriminate these forms to a standard level by projecting slides and obtaining responses before conducting their experiment. Subjects entered drug-induced states in a design in which they were unaware of the particular drug used for a given episode. In the results of the four subjects, the category of random shapes was reported relatively frequently in all states, including baseline and placebo conditions. The web, lattice, and tunnel forms of "hallucinatory constants" were associated most frequently with conditions in which the subjects had ingested hallucinogens: tetrahydrocanabinol (THC), psilocybin, LSD, and mescaline. These forms were rarely reported after ingestion of phenobarbital or amphetamine, or in the placebo and baseline conditions.

DISCUSSION

Clinical material suggests that visual hallucinations and other image experiences may be elaborated from elementary sensations. These elementary sensations might arise either (1) in the retinal ganglionic and postretinal neural network and/or (2) from anatomic bodies within the eyeball.

---

* After Siegel and Jarvik.[78]

Retinal and Postretinal Ganglionic Network

This is the complicated circuitry of interlacing neurons which is fed by stimuli from the rods and cones and, in turn, connects with the optic nerves. Knoll[44] and his coworkers[43] continued the nineteenth century work of Volta, Purkinji, and von Helmholz by studying the subjective visual images which arise on mild electric or mechanical stimulation of the optic system. The drawings and descriptions of their subjects are very similar to those reported earlier and are composed largely of the figures abstracted in Figure 9-6. Knoll suggested that such experiences arise from the effect of the electrical stimulus on the retinal ganglionic network. Similar effects were achieved with flickering light[37] produced by a photostimulator, covered with a sheet of paper. The frequency dial was manipulated slowly back and forth (in a random manner) between 10 and 100 flashes per second. The light appeared steady (flicker fusion) between 75 and 90 flashes per second. Below 15 flashes per second most subjects merely saw the lamp going on and off.

In the intervening ranges all subjects (n = 20) reported visual sensations of various types and to a varying degree. These sensations were probably caused by rapid on-and-off stimuli affecting the more distal circuitry of the retinocortical pathways and consisted of fluorescent colors, myriad parallel lines (both straight and curvilinear), mosaics, reticulated designs, and the other multiplied geometric figures illustrated earlier. Colors were seen as expanding and contracting, and the formed elements were seen as swirling, vibrating, counterrotating, and scintillating. At frequencies of 20 to 40 flashes per second, 8 of 20 subjects experienced a feeling of arousal described as anxiety, fearful expectancy, increased excitement, or joyfulness. In this range, subjects sometimes exclaimed with surprise, they often spoke with a more aroused vocal tone and inflection in reporting, and they occasionally reported visual images of objects rather than patterns, for example, "oh, a hand is coming out at me." "I see faces disappearing," "there is a kitten with a hernia," "a horrible face," and so forth. These idiosyncratic visual images seemed to originate from forms supplied by elementary sensations.

The early view of the optic pathway, as being a kind of telegraphic system with point-to-point retinocortical representations, has been discarded. The retina appears to do more work in terms of codifying information through special receptivity to patterns in the complex tangle of retinal neurons, feedback circuits, and ganglia.[24,49] It is postulated that the basic coding forms include (1) straightness of line, regularity of arc; (2) circularity; (3) parallelisms of straight lines, arcs, and circles; and

(4) congruence of figures, equidistance, and equiangularity (Fig. 9-7).[65,66] These forms resemble, in part, the images abstracted earlier from clinical material, and they also fulfill the Gestalt criteria of figural goodness—the qualities found in figures most readily perceived.[11,33,90] It is conceivable, then, that the images so repetitive in the clinical material may relate to the nature and function of retinal circuitry and to pattern receptivity.

Anatomic Structure of the Eye

The eye usually does not see its own contents, yet most people have visualized one or another of their entoptic elements. These are usually called floaters and are commonly seen while staring at a blank source of

Fig. 9-7. Hypothesized patterns of special retinal receptivity.

illumination such as an overcast sky or a sunlit wall. It seems likely that the figures abstracted earlier (Fig. 9-6) could arise, in part, from anatomic forms. The patterns of the retinal blood vessels affect the light-sensitive rods and cones peripheral to the *macula lutea*, the area of precise vision. The shadows of such vessels could give rise to the wavy, radiating, filigreed elements; the blood cells within them might produce dot-like apparitions. The optic disc, that is, the central scotoma, could give rise to the large circular figures and the layers of rods, cones, and neural bundles to the parallel figures. The fibers of the lens are arranged around six diverging axes, and they cause the rays seen around distant lights (giving them a star-like luster) and can also produce a sense of parallel fibers, swirls, or spots when such defective structures are present in the lens.[32] The *muscae volitantes*, or floaters in the vitreous humor, like the artifacts in the lens, are produced by the invagination of integument during embryonal development of the eye and can give rise to oval or irregular shapes in entoptic visions. The movement of dots could be the flow of formed blood elements. The constant variations in optic movement caused by tremor, flicker, and drift would also impart a sense of movement to the elements. Optic rotation could cause circling effects, and bilateral orbital stimuli could result in the reciprocal duplications. Other features of imagery might be related to such optic phenomena as the production of figural aftereffects.[29,53]

To restate the hypothesis, redundant clinical material of visual images can be abstracted into simple forms, and the origin of such forms may be entoptic—either from the anatomic characteristics of the eye or arising in the bioelectric circuits for pattern receptivity in the retinal ganglionic network.

Why are entoptic images not usually consciously perceived? Images that are stationary on the retina fade out in six seconds. The natural involuntary movements of the eye, especially flicker and tremor, regenerate the image and compensate for drift.[17,68] Certain entoptic elements, especially the optic disc and the retinal blood vessels, would not generate many impulses because of their relatively stable retinal position. Their shadows, however, would shift under certain circumstances of moving illumination. In addition to fadeout, then, there must be other ways of limiting the penetration of such stimuli.

There is continuous retinal activity, even with the eye at rest, and there are continuous forces of inhibition and facilitation which alter receptivity to various stimuli and patterns.[13,24] It is known that the visual field varies with the deployment of attention and that receptivity to visual messages depends on the state of visual pathway excitability.[16,50,62,89] With the evidence for centrifugal control, ie, for optic nerve impulses moving toward the retina, comes the realization that inhibition and facilitation may operate at a peripheral locus as well as in the brain.[24,65] Cortical responses to stimulation of the retina show (1) a topographic, organized process and (2) a slower, more diffuse process, partially intraretinal, which activates major portions of the visual cortex.[19] Vision is a complex transactional process with the eye telling the brain what it sees and the brain telling the eye what it should look for, and what it should not look for. Stimuli originating within the eyeball would register at the retinal level but could be kept from being perceived, under normal circumstances, by active inhibition or lack of facilitation. The play of such regulatory processes would account for the perceived fragmentation of forms low in meaning even though gaze continues.[85] Such inhibition and facilitation probably occur at both the retinal and higher levels of the nervous system and represent the somatic equivalents of the deployment of attention. Under conditions of increased need to see, as in sensory deprivation, entoptic imagery would be facilitated or "tuned up." The somatic purpose would be to prevent optically dependent areas of the brain from being lulled by insufficient afferent stimulation.

What might happen when entoptic images or vague "noisy" perceptions are disinhibited or especially facilitated? This raw material would then impinge on higher centers for image representation and undergo a variety of secondary elaborations leading to the final conscious image. The nature of the secondary elaborations would depend on current motivational states and also on current regulatory capacity. In persons with a relatively well-functioning ego, simple and momentary illusions or hypnagogic images of pleasing lights and patterns might result. With further regression of regulatory function (or intensification of motives) the images might become illusions or pseudohallucinations of current wishes, needs, or fears. In states of impaired control (as described in Chapter 7) hallucinations might be elaborated out of the entoptic raw material. I tentatively suggest, also, the possibility that entoptic sensations contribute sensory quality to dream images. Some subjects, awakened from dreaming sleep, have reported to me an increase in entoptic sensations as they look with open eyes into the darkness of their room.

Entoptic phenomena may, as illustrated in several of the case vignettes, contribute a vivid raw material that is elaborated into a waking hallucination in certain schizophrenic patients. This phenomenon could be explained in two ways: one way suggests impairment of control capacity, the second suggests a purposive regression to primitive levels of regulation of perception and image formation.

Perhaps some schizophrenic syndromes contain an impairment of inhibitory capacity. Many patients do describe being swamped by an incoming tide of sensations, especially during the early phases by decompensation.[23,56] In this state they seem either unable or unwilling to screen out meaningless stimuli to focus their visual attention on meaningful stimuli. Also, their labeling, interpretation, and elaboration of incoming signals follow regressive lines, approximating the rules of the "primary process" (as described in Chapter 6).[23a]

The second possibility is that there is a regression of regulatory capacity for defensive purposes. Thus, to avoid an environment perceived as hostile or empty, to avoid an environment that triggers dangerous motives within, the schizophrenic person may regress to a style of diffuse perception and image formation with blurring of the distinction between what is within and what is without. Entoptic images, for example, might be used as a focus of interest to defensively withdraw from external perceptions.[8] Once facilitated or disinhibited, these images might undergo the archaic elaborations just mentioned. These two possibilities are not contradictory and follow the outlines of schizophrenic thought postulated by von Domarus[18] and Arieti.[7] They also correspond with ideas concerning other, nonvisual, modalities of representation. Luby et al[51] suggested that disrupted body input mechanisms, such as in audition, are responsible for some of the disturbances of schizophrenia. Hoffer and Osmond[34] accounted for olfactory hallucinations by a hypothesis of lowered olfactory threshold.

Sullivan postulated a loss of inhibitory ability as the cause of schizophrenic language. When inhibition is lowered, language regresses to its primal purpose—the establishment of a sense of security with others rather than the transmission of information. Such a process, he continued, goes on at all times but is screened out as unreasonable as long as one is alert. Should a person fall asleep while talking, however, he may awaken to find himself talking schizophrenic language.[83] Shakow summarized the disorganization in schizophrenia as the inability to maintain a major or generalized set in conjunction with a trend to establish minor sets—to segmentalize both the external and internal environments. Thus, "there is an increased awareness of, and preoccupation with, the ordinarily disregarded details of existence—the details which normal people spontaneously forget, train themselves, or get trained rigorously to disregard."[77] To summarize, schizophrenic persons may selectively "adapt-in" entoptic visions as an environmental avoidance defense (ie, perceptual withdrawal) or they may be physiologically unable to "adapt-out" entoptic visions as can normal persons.

None of the above comments are, of course, specific to schizophrenic syndromes. Any type of regression or impairment of regulatory capacity might lead to both increased visual "noise" and a greater propensity to elaborate the sensory material into vivid images. Normal persons may experience identical phenomena in altered states of consciousness. Of interest, a very similar line of reasoning has been advanced for auditory hallucinations. Gross et al[26] and Saravay and Pardes[72] postulate that elementary auditory sensations such as buzzing or popping noises may contribute to the auditory hallucinations seen in alcohol withdrawal psychoses.

It is wise for clinicians to be alert for the redundant visual forms described in this chapter. Sometimes these pinwheels, hexagons, or wavy lines in the description of an animated hallucination indicate a physical basis for the hallucinatory syndrome. Also, some patients are reassured and relieved of disorganizing degrees of anxiety when the "spots in front of their eyes" are explained as actual physical bodies within the eyes. The following vignette is illustrative:

A middle-aged woman rushed to see her minister whom she consulted intermittently for recurrent anxiety and depression. When she told him she was "seeing the blood of Christ" and seemed very distraught, he sent her for a psychiatric consultation, for he feared this was the onset of a hallucinatory psychosis. The psychiatric resident recognized her distress but wondered about possible organic contributions to the reddish color she described as "the blood of Christ," which began with a shower of sparks and a sensation of darkness. Her eyes were examined, and she was found to have a retinal hemorrhage and partial retinal detachment which needed immediate treatment. When this was explained to her she was, of course, realistically apprehensive, but she was also very relieved that she was not losing her mind.

REFERENCES

1. Adler G: Studies in Analytic Psychology. London, Routledge & Kegan Paul, 1948
2. Allers R, Teller J: On the utilization of unnoticed impressions in associations. Psychol Issues Monogr 7(2):121–155, 1960
3. Allport FH: Theories of Perception and the Concept of Structure. New York, Wiley, 1955
4. Anastasi A, Foley JP: An experimental study of the drawing behavior of adult psychotics in comparison with that of a normal control group. J Exp Psychol 34:169, 1944

5. Antrobus JS, Singer JL: Eye movements accompanying daydreaming, visual imagery and thought suppression. J Abnorm Soc Psychol 69:244, 1964

6. Arieti S: The microgenesis of thought and perception. Arch Gen Psychiat 6:454, 1962

7. ———: The loss of reality. Psychoanalysis 48:3, 1961

8. Arlow JA, Brenner C: Psychoanalytic Concepts and the Structural Theory. New York, International Univ Press, 1964

9. Arnheim R: Art and Visual Perception: A Psychology of the Creative Eye. Berkeley, Univ California Press, 1954

10. Asher H: Experiment with LSD: they split my personality. Saturday Review 39–43, June 1, 1963

11. Attneave F: Symmetry, information, and memory for patterns. Amer J Psychol 68:209, 1955

12. Bakan P: The eyes have it. Psychol Today 4:64, 1971

13. Bartley SH: Some facts and concepts regarding the neurophysiology of the optic pathway. Arch Ophthalmol 60:775, 1959

14. Bleuler E: Dementia Praecox (trans J Zinkin). New York, International Univ Press, 1950

15. Broadbent DE: Decision and Stress. London, Academic Press, 1971

16. Callaway E: Factors influencing the relationship between alpha activity and visual reaction time. Electroenceph Clin Neurophysiol 14:674, 1962

17. Ditchburn RW, Fender DH, Mayne S: Vision with controlled movements of the retinal image. J Physiol 145:98, 1959

18. Domarus E von: The specific laws of logic in schizophrenia. In Kasanin JS (ed): Language and Thought in Schizophrenia. Berkeley, Univ California Press, 1944

19. Doty RW: Functional significance of the topographic aspects of the retino-cortical projection. In Report of Symposium: The Vision System: Neurophysiology and Psychophysics. Freiburg, Germany, 1960

20. Eagle M: Personality correlates of sensitivity to subliminal stimulation. J Nerv Ment Dis 134:1, 1962

21. Fisher C, Paul IH: The effect of subliminal visual stimulation on images and dreams: a validation study. J Amer Psychoanal Assoc 7:35, 1959

22. Galin D: Hemispheric specialization: implications for psychiatry. In Grenell RG, Gabay S (eds): Biological Foundations of Psychiatry. New York, Raven, 1976

23. Galin D, Ornstein R: Individual differences in cognitive style. I. Reflective eye movements. Neuropsychologia 12:367, 1974

23a. Goldstein K: A methodological approach to the study of schizophrenic thought disorder. In Kasanin JW (ed): Language and Thought in Schizophrenia. Berkeley, Univ California Press, 1944

24. Granit R: Receptors and Sensory Perception. New Haven, Yale Univ Press, 1955

25. Gregory RL: Eye and Brain: The Psychology of Seeing. New York, McGraw-Hill, 1966

26. Gross MM, et al: Hearing disturbances and auditory hallucinations in the acute alcoholic psychoses. I. Tinnitus: incidence and significance. J Nerv Ment Dis 137:445, 1963

27. Haber RN: Contemporary Theory and Research in Visual Perception. New York, Holt, 1968

28. Hachinski VC, Porchawka J, Steele JC: Visual symptoms in migraine syndrome. Neurology 23:570, 1973

29. Hanawalt NG: Recurrent images: new instances and a summary of older ones. Amer J Psychol 67:170, 1954

30. Heaton JM: The Eye: Phenomenology and Psychology of Function and Disorder. Philadelphia, Lippincott, 1968

31. Hebb DO: A neuropsychological theory. In Koch S (ed): Psychology: A Study of a Science, vol. 1. New York, McGraw-Hill, 1959

32. Helmholtz H von: Popular Scientific Lectures. New York, Dover, 1962

33. Hochberg J, McAlister EA: A quantitative approach to figural "goodness." J Exp Psychol 46:361, 1953

34. Hoffer A, Osmond H: Olfactory changes in schizophrenia. Amer J Psychiat 119:72, 1962

35. Holstijn AJ: The psychological development of Vincent van Gogh. Translated by H.P. Winzen. Amer Imago 8:239, 1951

36. Holt RR: On the nature and generality of mental imagery. In Sheehan PW (ed): The Function and Nature of Imagery. New York, Academic Press, 1972

37. Horowitz MJ: Visual imagery and cognitive organization. Amer J Psychiat 123:938, 1967

38. ——, Adams JE, Rutkin BB: Visual imagery on brain stimulation. Arch Gen Psychiat 19:469, 1968

39. ——, Adams JE, Rutkin BB: Dream scintillations. Psychosom Med 29: 284, 1967

40. Isakower OA: A contribution to the patho-psychology of phenomena associated with falling asleep. Int J Psychoanal 19:331, 1938

41. Jackson JH: In Taylor J (ed): Selected Writings of John Hughlings Jackson, vol. 2. New York, Basic, 1958

42. Klüver H: Mechanisms of hallucinations. In McNemar Q, Merrill MA (eds): Studies in Personality. New York, McGraw-Hill, 1942

43. Knoll M, et al: Effects of chemical stimulation of electrically induced phosphenes on their bandwidth, shape, number, and intensity. Confin Neurol 23:201, 1963

44. ——, et al: Note on the spectroscopy of subjective light patterns. J Anal Psychol 7:55, 1962

45. Koffka K: Principles of Gestalt Psychology. London, Routledge, 1935

46. Kohler W: The Task of Gestalt Psychology. Princeton, NJ, Princeton Univ Press, 1969

47. ——: The formation and transformation of the perceptual world. Psychol Issues Monogr 12:3:1, 1964

48. Langui E: Fifty Years of Modern Art. New York, Praeger, 1959

49. Letvin JY, et al: What the frog's eye tells the frog's brain. Proc Inst Radio Engin 47:1940, 1959
50. Lindsley DB: Basic perceptual processes and the electroencephalogram. Psychol Res Rep 6:161, 1956
51. Luby ED, et al: Model psychoses and schizophrenia. Amer J Psychiat 119:61, 1962
52. Luckiesh M: Visual Illusions. New York, Dover, 1965
53. MacKay DM: Interactive processes in visual perception. In Rosenblith N (ed): Sensory Communication. Cambridge, Mass, MIT Press, 1961
54. Maclay WS, Guttmann E: Mescaline hallucinations in artists. Arch Neurol Psychiat 45:130, 1941
55. Malitz S, Wilkins B, Escover H: A comparison of drug induced hallucinations with those seen in spontaneously occurring psychoses. In West LJ (ed): Hallucinations. New York, Grune & Stratton, 1962
56. McGhie A, Chapman J: Disorders of attention and perception in early schizophrenia. Brit J Med Psychol 34:103, 1961
57. Meskin B, Singer JL: Daydreaming, reflective thought, and laterality of eye movements. J Pers Soc Psychol 30:64, 1974
58. Miller SC: Ego autonomy in sensory deprivation, isolation, and stress. Int J Psychoanal 43:1, 1962
59. Neisser U: Cognitive Psychology. New York, Appleton, 1967
60. Nickols J: Eidetic imagery synthesis. Amer J Psychother 16:76, 1962
61. Ornstein RE: The Psychology of Consciousness. San Francisco, Freeman, 1972
62. Oswald I: Sleeping and Waking: Physiology and Psychology. New York, Elsevier, 1963
63. Paul IH, Fisher C: Subliminal visual stimulation: a study of its influence on subsequent images and dreams. J Nerv Ment Dis 129:315, 1959
64. Perky CW: An experimental study of imagination. Amer J Psychol 21:422, 1910
65. Pitts W, McCullock WS: How we know universals: the perception of auditory and visual forms. Bull Math Biophys 9:127, 1947
66. Platt JF: How we see straight lines. Sci Amer 202:121, 1960
67. Pötzl O: The relationship between experimentally induced dream images and indirect vision. Psychol Issues Monogr 7(2):41, 1960
68. Pritchard RM: Stabilized images on the retina. Sci Amer 204:72, 1961
69. Rapaport D: Emotions and Memory. Baltimore, Williams & Wilkins, 1942
70. Richards W: The fortification illusions of migraines. Sci Amer 224:88, 1971
71. Roffwarg HP, et al: Dream imagery: relationship to rapid eye movement of sleep. Arch Gen Psychiat 7:235, 1962
72. Saravay SM, Pardes H: Auditory elementary hallucinations in alcohol withdrawal psychosis. Arch Gen Psychiat 16:652, 1967
73. Segal SJ: Imagery; Current Cognitive Approaches. New York, Academic Press, 1971

74. ———: Patterns of response to thirst in an imaging task (Perky technique) as a function of cognitive style. J Pers 36:574, 1968
75. ———: The Perky effect: changes in reality judgments with changing methods of inquiry. Psychonom Sci 12:393, 1968
76. ———: Imagery and reality: can they be distinguished? In Keup W (ed): Origin and Mechanisms of Hallucinations. New York, Plenum, 1970
77. Shakow D: Segmental set. Arch Gen Psychiat 6:1, 1962
78. Siegel RK, Jarvik ME: Drug induced hallucinations in animals and man. In Siegel RK, West LJ (eds): Hallucinations: Behavior, Experience, and Theory. New York, Wiley, 1975
79. Silberer H: Report on a method of eliciting and observing certain symbolic hallucination phenomena. In Rapaport D (ed): Organization and Pathology of Thought. New York, Columbia Univ Press, 1951
80. Solomon P, et al: Sensory Deprivation. Cambridge, Mass, Harvard Univ Press, 1961
81. Stace WT: The Teachings of the Mystics. New York, New American, 1960
82. Stern M: Free painting as an auxiliary technique in psychoanalysis. In Bychowski G, Despert JL (eds): Specialized Techniques in Psychotherapy. New York, Basic, 1952
83. Sullivan HS: The language of schizophrenia. In Kasanin JS (ed): Language and Thought in Schizophrenia. Berkeley, Univ California Press, 1946
84. Vernon M: The Psychology of Perception. Boston, Penguin, 1962
85. Walker P: The perceptual fragmentation of unstabilized images. J Exp Psychol 28:35, 1976
86. Wallach S, Wallach M, Yessin G: Observations of involuntary eye movements in certain schizophrenics: a preliminary report. J Hillside Hosp 9:224, 1960
87. Warrington EK: The completion of visual forms across hemianopic field defects. J Neurol Neurosurg Psychiat 25:208, 1962
88. West LJ, et al: The psychosis of sleep deprivation. Ann NY Acad Sci 96:66, 1961
89. Williams D, Gassel M: Visual function in patients with homonymous hemianopia. I. The visual fields. Brain 185:175, 1962
90. Woodworth PS: Dynamics of Behavior. New York, Holt, 1958

10

INFLUENCE OF THE BRAIN

We know that the neurobiology of the brain influences image formation, but the precise nature of these influences is as yet unknown. Regulation of image formation is a complex process that probably requires mass action of nets of nerve tissue in many parts of the brain. When some aspect of the brain's structure or function is abnormal, then a person may experience a large range of visual images and perceptual distortions, or he may experience a loss of certain image-forming capacities.

We can use two approaches to study the relationship between brain function and structure, and image formation. One approach would be to alter image formation and observe what happens to brain functions. The second approach would be to alter brain functions and then to observe image formation.

RELATIONSHIP BETWEEN CHANGES
IN IMAGE FORMATION
AND THE ELECTROENCEPHALOGRAM

While at rest, with their eyes closed, many persons have an electro-encephalographic pattern known as the alpha rhythm, a brain wave with eight to twelve peaks per second. Investigators have noted a relationship between the alpha rhythm and image formation. Lehmann et al[24] find that as images disappear alpha rhythm appears and vice versa. Costello and MacGregor[6] report that the alpha rhythm is suppressed as image experiences increase in vividness. Kamiya and Zeitlan[22] found that subjects could increase alpha by avoiding images and decrease alpha by forming images and focusing attention on them.

Some researchers have tried to type individuals as verbalizers or visualizers on the basis of the relative frequency of alpha waves on their resting EEG and on the degree to which this alpha wave is blocked when subjects follow instructions to form mental images.[16,38] Slatter[39] finds that his visualizer subjects are likely to block alpha on image formation, while verbalizer subjects do not show this effect as readily.

Most researchers agree that as awareness of images increases, the alpha rhythm of the EEG tends to decrease. The alpha rhythm does not correlate directly with image formation, but with some relevant variable such as perceptual alertness or mental effort.[27] For example, the alpha rhythm might be produced by synchronous activity of large masses of resting cells. An effort of perception, of forming images, or of thinking may disrupt the synchronous activity that produces the alpha rhythm. Galin and Ornstein[14] have found higher alpha amplitude over the right hemisphere when subjects engage in verbal tasks and more alpha over the left hemisphere when subjects (who are all right handed) perform spatial tasks. Since alpha amplitude is thought to indicate relative idling in terms of information processing, this is a further suggestion that the right brain specializes in visual and spatial imagery.[13]

CLINICAL OBSERVATIONS OF ALTERED STRUCTURE AND FUNCTION: ORGANIC BRAIN DISEASE

Organic brain disease includes either permanent or transient changes in structure or function. These changes may arise from many causes including physical trauma, atrophy, infection, inflammation, intoxication, vascular disturbances, tumors, degenerations, or metabolic shifts such as vitamin, oxygen, or blood sugar deficiencies. In general, pathology in the nondominant hemisphere impairs the visual and spatial tasks that require image formation. Although a disturbance that alters or destroys nerve tissue in any anatomic site may influence control of image formation, the *site* and *nature* of the pathology determine (with wide variations and exceptions) the changes that occur.

For example, the geniculocalcarine pathway goes from the input of the optic tracts into the midbrain to the cortical receptive areas in the occipital lobe. Pathology anywhere along this pathway, or in the calcarine cortex, results in blindness or visual symptoms that correlate highly with the size and exact location of the lesion.[2,4,10] Irritative lesions usually give rise to elementary sensations, similar to the entoptic-type experiences reported in the previous chapter. About one-quarter of patients with tumors along the geniculocalcarine pathway report such elementary sensations.[1,44] Such patients usually report the sensations as occurring on the side of their vision opposite to the site of pathology, although sometimes the sensations are straight ahead or even on the same side as the pathology. At one time it was believed that this pathway supplied all of the visual information available to the brain and was wired like a telegraph system, ie, one point on the retina corresponded with one point in the calcarine cortex. Recent work suggests, instead, that there are multiple areas for registering information from the retina. For example, Sprague[41] reported that removal of one side of the occipitotemporal neocortex results, as is well known, in total blindness in the opposite visual field (a contralateral hemianopia). Sprague demonstrated this effect in cats but then, in a second operation, he removed the opposite sided superior colliculus, a structure in the midbrain involved in visual perception. Remarkably, there appeared to be a return of vision in the blind field! Apparently, the initial blindness is due to inhibition of function rather than total loss of function.

From the calcarine cortex there extend nerve bundles to various cortical areas considered to be visual association areas. These extend into the temporal lobe of the brain. Pathology centered in or near the temporal lobe commonly gives rise to complex hallucinations of persons, places, or things. A temporal lobe epileptic seizure, for example, may consist of a hallucinatory experience.[37]

Epileptic or migraine seizures may be preceded by an aura that can include perceptual distortions, intrusive images, elementary sensations, or hallucinations. The cause may be transient impairment of brain function, or the resultant altered state of consciousness.[43] Like the images in a recurrent dream, the images of the aura in successive seizures may always be similar. Sometimes the images are simple and discrete; sometimes they are miniature fantasies or "microdreams"; or sometimes they take the form of "dream scintillations," in which images seem to pass through consciousness in rapid succession but escape recollection.

Frequently noted varieties of perceptual auras include illusions, micropsia, macropsia, change in brightness of color, movement, shimmering, distortion, and alterations in body image. Jackson[20] described these phenomena in the nineteenth century and noted the occasional occurrence of a sequential elaboration progressing from crude sensations, such as sensations of color, to formed images, such as fearsome faces.

Hallucinatory states can also be caused by shifts in metabolism, such as low blood sugar, low blood oxygen, excessive hormone levels, vitamin deficiencies, fevers, poisonings, or withdrawal from habitually used sedatives or narcotics. Delirium tremens (DTs) and acute alcoholic hallucinosis are prime examples: the pink elephants and the numerous small carnivorous animals of the DTs are part of our cultural lore. Visual hallucinations are more common than auditory hallucinations in delirium tremens, and include themes of dismemberment, being devoured, small animals, and castration. Auditory hallucinations are more common in acute alcoholic psychosis.[5]

The above examples demonstrate general tendencies for what frequently happens with specific brain pathology. But there are many exceptions, and each case should be carefully reviewed for its individual idiosyncrasies. For example, transient impairment of brain function leading to hallucinations may require both neurobiologic and psychologic levels of explanation. Hallucinations of sparks and flashes to the right of the person's visual field may suggest pathology somewhere in the left optical-cortical pathway. But such hallucinations could also arise without brain pathology. A hallucination of a pink elephant might arise because of a particular set of psychologic motives, but it also might indicate the presence of acutely impaired neurophysiologic functions in centers that regulate and control image formation.

Usually, with organic brain disease, impaired image formation is associated with other symptoms, such as loss of memory; orientation for time, place, and person; intellectual deficiencies; and emotional lability.[42] Sometimes, however, there may be a discrete loss of image formation.[4] Such syndromes, though rare, support the notion that image formation can be regarded as a separable system from lexical representation. The following clinical example shows a case that began with the loss of the ability to form visual images:

A 42-year-old man had a brain tumor that destroyed cortical tissues in the ventral-parietal and dorsal-temporal regions of his right cerebral hemisphere. His earliest symptom was loss of ability to visualize memories or to form visual thought images. He also reported a reduction in visual dreaming. As the disease advanced, he developed a spatial disorientation, later followed by loss of memory, speech impairment, partial deafness, and progressive dementia. In the early stages, the patient could not recognize his own children, but relied on hearing them speak to identify them by their tone and inflection of voice. Later he required a guide whenever he left his home, as he could not retain spatial relationships and would get lost immediately.

Another type of brain pathology is that produced by certain medical treatments, such as surgical cleavage of the fiber tracts that connect the two cerebral hemispheres. This treatment is used rarely and only as a last resort in cases of severe epilepsy in a procedure called cerebral commissurotomy.[3] The result hoped for is reduction or cessation of disabling seizures, but a side effect is a loss of communication of information between the cerebral hemispheres.

It has long been known that unilateral lesions to one or another hemisphere produce results differently if the injury is to the dominant or nondominant side of the brain. Study of commissurotomy patients expands knowledge of specialization of the right and left brains. Sperry[40] devised ingenious ways of presenting visual stimuli to the right or left visual fields of the eye discretely, and hence to the right or left brain. He demonstrated that the commissurotomy limited information so that, in effect, the right hand knew what the left brain knew, but the left hand, with its connections to the right brain, did not. The reason for the right-left pairings between brain and hand is that the motor pathways cross over. More importantly, these patients could describe objects well verbally when the item was placed in their right hand, but when the item was placed in their left hand they could not label it well with language, but could show its use or select a picture that resembled it. They could also draw well with their left hand, guided as it is by the right brain, but do poor tracings with their right hand: a result contrary to what their previous handedness skills would predict.[3] This is further evidence for the hypothesis that the right brain, in right-handed persons, tends to specialize more in image formation than in lexical representation.

IMAGES ON BRAIN STIMULATION

Penfield and his associates[28, 30,31] found that stimulation of the calcarine cortex produced simple visual sensations in the contralateral visual field. One type of report included simple visual sensations: stars, balls, disks, wheels, wavy lines, honeycombs, outlines, black forms, flashes, and colors which were either stationary, moving, or rotating. These forms are common in various hallucinations and deliria and have been discussed in Chapter 9. Stimulation of the extracalcarine cortex of the occipital lobe produced similar sensory experiences. Stimulation of the superior and lateral cortical surfaces of either the right or left temporal lobe produced more complex visual hallucinations of objects, faces, persons, or scenes.

Penfield was impressed by what he labeled "experiential hallucinations," which sometimes simultaneously combined vivid sensations of several modalities. Of 453 patients who had electrical exploration of the temporal lobe cortex, 38 (8.4 percent) reported very vivid and life-like flashbacks of their past lives. When the same point was restimulated after a few seconds, the same experience was usually repeated. After more time had elapsed, another experience appeared on restimulation. Other electrical stimulations at times produced distortions of actual perception. An object viewed might appear to have unusual alterations in distance, size, shape, movement, or clarity, or change in its reality-sense. It might appear either uncannily familiar, or very strange, even unreal.

Although Penfield speculated that these perceptual-cognitive experiences might be due to the hallucinatory evocation of memories by stimulus activation of their neurophysiologic substrates, he did not presume that the electrode was necessarily placed on the specific site of memory storage: "The psychical or interpretive areas of the temporal cortex produced recall of past experiences, or illusions of interpretation by conduction to some distant zone, such as the hippocampus."[29] He believed that some memory storage site was activated and that an actual perceptual memory was then rerun.

In addition, he postulated a "scanning mechanism," at least partially resident in the temporal lobes, that compared present experiences with past similar experiences.[32] This scanning of past experiences would usually be at a level subliminal to subjective consciousness. However, during the alteration in function provoked by the electrical stimulations, the past experiences might reach hallucinatory vividness. Penfield and his associates carefully emphasized that hallucinations of prior experience were evoked from persons with temporal lobe epilepsy who had long histories of brain malfunction.

The postulate that these experiences were reruns of memory engrams is attractive, but it does not explain all of the phenomena. For example, some of Penfield's subjects saw themselves in the visual images they reported. Other than memories of self-perceptions in a mirror or photograph, this could not be derived from an actual perception that was laid down directly as an engram. Rather, it was derived from a reconstruction of various actual perceptions into imaginative images. The imagination can use such bits and pieces of prior perceptions.[34, 35]

The occasional progression from simple sensations to complex hallucinations reported by Penfield, and noted by Hughlings Jackson for auras, suggests that some of the animated imagery is elaborated out of a matrix provided by the elemental sensations of colors and of geometric forms.

Jasper and Rasmussen[21] inserted electrodes in structures deep within the temporal lobes in persons with temporal lobe epilepsy. They reported that stimulations of the amygdaloid regions sometimes produced confusion, diminished awareness, amnesia, and/or automatic behavior. Some hallucinations or illusions were produced from stimulations deep in the Sylvian area and the periinsular regions, as well as from surface stimulations. Amygdala stimulations of 46 patients rarely produced visual events. One patient reported a visual distortion; one patient seemed to have a visual hallucination, but his report was vague and uncertain. No visual effects were reported for hippocampal stimulation.

Mahl and his coworkers[26] reported the results in a single patient who underwent psychologic interviews during stimulation sessions. This patient reported auditory hallucinatory experiences when deep structures of the temporal lobe were stimulated using a needle electrode. While no visual experiences were reported, we are interested in Mahl's data because he was led to modify Penfield's hypothesis that stimulations activated memory traces in the neural record. The hallucinatory experiences could often be shown to relate to the patient's mental content before the stimulation. Repeated stimulation at short time intervals tended to elicit responses with related content. If the time intervals were long, then thematic content was unrelated. Also, the relationship between the prestimulation mental content and the sensory experience resembled the processes of dream construction: displacement, distortion, and condensation were prominent, and ideas were translated into sensory images.[11] Mahl concluded from these observations that

> . . . electrical stimulation of the temporal lobe does not directly activate memory traces in the ganglionic record. Instead it induces a state of consciousness which makes it more probable that primary-process modes of functioning will prevail. If there is a background of subliminally excited memory traces in the ganglionic record at the time of stimulation, then all the conditions exist for the occurrence of hallucinatory experiences, and the content of these experiences would necessarily be related to the prestimulation mental events, for it would be determined partly by them. (p. 361)

All of the studies cited so far have concerned patients with temporal lobe epilepsy. Each group of investigators carefully pointed out the danger of considering their results from stimulation of an abnormally functioning brain to be equivalent to the results of stimulating a non-epileptic brain. However, a group in Japan has reported the results of stimulation of both the temporal cortex and deep structures of the nondominant temporal lobe in persons with chronic schizophrenia and hallucinatory symptoms, in order "to treat the auditory hallucinations."[19] Visual hallucinations were reported in five of 17 cases (29 percent). Elementary visual hallucinations—those of color or simple geometric forms—did not result from surface stimulation but did arise from stimulation of the depth structures. Only one of their cases showed clearly clouded consciousness.

To summarize, electrical stimulation to the temporal lobe cortex may give rise to formed and meaningful visual hallucinations. The temporal lobe is apparently the primary portion of the cortex where stimulation may evoke such phenomena. Stimulation of the deep structures of the temporal lobe gives rise to conflicting findings: some investigators report evoked hallucinations; others do not.

Two major theoretical explanations of the phenomena have been offered. One theory suggests that a memory "engram" from an actual past experience is activated by the stimulations and is rerun with perceptual vividness. The second theory suggests that stimulation produces an altered state of consciousness with a concomitant shift toward primary process thinking. In work previously reported in association with Adams and Rutkin[17] we hoped to see which theoretical explanation seemed most correct.

Method

Depth electrodes were implanted in patients with long-term intractable temporal lobe epilepsy for diagnostic and therapeutic reasons. This afforded the invaluable opportunity for research into the behavioral and experiential effects of stimulations. We hoped particularly to derive answers to the following questions.

1. Would stimulation of the deeper limbic system structures such as the hippocampus, hippocampal gyrus, and amygdala of persons with temporal lobe epilepsy (a) produce visual events similar to those elicited by Penfield on his stimulation of the surface of the temporal lobes; (b) resemble the results of Jasper and Rasmussen whose stimulations of depth structures were fairly negative for visual events; or (c) follow the results of those groups who reported both simple and complex visual hallucinations on depth stimulation?
2. If fully formed hallucinatory events were reported by the patient subjects, would the contents and the dynamics of the formation of the hallucination support the memory trace hypothesis of Penfield or the

motivational construction and altered state of consciousness hypotheses of Mahl?

The subjects were 16 patients with intractable temporal lobe epilepsy who (after appropriate clinical study) underwent implantation of depth electrodes in order to obtain data about possible focal sites of epileptogenesis.

The patients were fully conscious and seated semiupright in hospital beds during recording and stimulation sessions. Their responses to stimulation were recorded on magnetic and synchronized video tape. Thus it was possible to record simultaneously electroencephalogram and vocal and behavioral responses. These taped records were reviewed subsequently. Each sensory event was recorded and categorized.

A stimulation was delivered at a moment when the interviewer had an idea of what to expect from the patient in terms of continuous behavior. Thus the effect of a stimulation could be judged from changes in behavior as well as from introspective reports. Most of the performance tasks were verbal, ranging from nondirective psychiatric interviews to counting and remembering situations. Occasionally, perceptual-motor tasks were used.

Most stimulations were given without specific warning. The patient knew that stimulations might occur at any time during a session, but he did not know precisely when they would occur. At times after a given site had already been stimulated without the patient's foreknowledge, the patient would be told exactly when stimulation was on and off. This was done (1) to increase the patient's awareness of his experiences and (2) to see if the patient would report differently when he knew he was receiving a stimulation.

Visual sensations that subjects reported during or after stimulations were categorized as "A," "B," "C," or "D." We classified events "A" if visual hallucinations were described by the patient as externally placed with contents related to formed objects. We classified events as "B" if visual imagery experiences were reported with formed, object-related content in which the images were not clearly projected onto the external environment. The differentiation of "A" and "B" events depended on the quality of description given by subjects. If a sensation was not described as having apparent reality or external spatial location, it was classified as a "B" event. We classified events as "C" if they consisted of elementary sensations such as colored lights, geometric forms, and amorphous shapes —that is, visual sensations that did not represent objects or scenes. The fourth classification, "D," was used for visual distortions of actual perceptions.

Results

Patients described many varieties of sensory, motor, and emotional experiences as a consequence of electrical stimulations. Here, only the visual events are reported.

Ten percent of 1,509 stimulations in all subjects resulted in some type of visual event. Most of the events were elementary sensations ("C" events). Less than 1 percent of the stimulations resulted in events that could be categorized as formed hallucinations of an object or scene ("A"). Less than 1 percent of the stimulations led to reports of vivid visual thought images ("B"). While we attempted an impartial survey of all electrode points, we did tend to repeat stimulations of sites where previous stimulations resulted in reports of a visual sensation. This increased the percentages of reports of visual events beyond the percentages likely to occur from random and equal frequent stimulations of each anatomic site.

Anatomic Correlates of Events

The anatomic sites that were thought to have received stimulations were the anterior (pes) hippocampus, the posterior hippocampus, the hippocampal gyrus, the amygdala, the globus pallidus, the anterior commissure, the optic radiation, the corpus collusum, the caudate nucleus, the putamen, the cingulum bundle, and occasionally the anterior thalamus and the temporal lobe cortex. The number of visual events in each category and the number of patients reporting such events are shown as related to the presumed site of stimulation in Figure 10-1. The optic radiation stimulations produced many "C" events but did not produce any "A" (hallucinatory) or "B" (image) events in any subject. The posterior hippocampus was the site of greatest interest in terms of visual events. Stimulations of the posterior hippocampus led to eight of the 13 "A" events in addition to many "C" events. Five of the 13 "B" events were from stimulation of the posterior hippocampal site. Thus, 13 of 26 (50 percent) of the fully formed imagery events ("A" and "B") occurred from stimulations of the posterior hippocampus while only 4 (15 percent) occurred from stimulation of the amygdala, the second most productive site.

In scattered instances the visual imagery occurred in conjunction with an electrically evoked aura or seizure, but usually the visual events had no observable relationship to suspected areas of focal epileptogeneses. Nor did the frequency of visual events have any consistent relationship to the side of the brain stimulated or to the presence or absence of visual events in the aura.

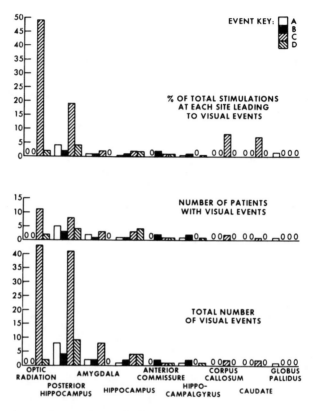

Fig. 10-1. Anatomic correlates of visual events (from Horowitz, Adams, and Rutkin[17]).

Electrographic Correlates of Subjective Visual Sensations

Recordings from the site of a stimulation frequently showed a high-voltage, rapid, "spiking" afterdischarge which lasted from several seconds to a minute or more after the end of the stimulus train. Such afterdischarges were frequent, but they did not always occur after a stimulation had evoked a visual event. Afterdischarges accompanied subjective visual phenomena 33 to 100 percent of the time in the 16 patients, and the median patient had a 75 percent likelihood of an afterdischarge.

Afterdischarges were not restricted to the site of stimulation but spread at times to other areas of the same hemisphere or crossed over to the limbic system of the opposite hemisphere. Since many of the visual events arose from stimulation of the posterior hippocampus, we assessed stimulation of other sites for spread of afterdischarge to the posterior hippocampus. Of 81 visual events produced by stimulation in sites other than the posterior hippocampus, 18 (22 percent) were accompanied by an afterdischarge recorded from posterior hippocampus electrodes.

Certain visual events were very brief and occurred only during the period of stimulation. Others persisted during the period of the afterdischarge. Several patients reported that subjective visual experience ceased at a time coincident with the observed cessation of the afterdischarge.

Subjective Experiences

We anticipated that some brain stimulations would lead to hallucinatory experiences. We hoped to relate the hallucinatory content to the patient's prestimulation stream of thought. Constant verbalization in a nondirective interview was our goal. Organic brain damage, psychopathology, and situational stress interfered, and directive questioning was frequently necessary.

In spite of many communication difficulties, we felt that reports were reasonably reliable and that errors, when present, were on the side of omission (false negatives). False positives, that is, reports of imagery in the absence of brain stimulation, occurred twice to our knowledge and may have been due to a hypnagogic or regressive mental state.

Not all stimulations led to some sort of subjective or behavioral effect. Some stimulations led to subjective experiences that patients did not report immediately: instead, the patient might finish a sentence he had started before telling his experience. We instructed patients to report always and immediately any sensation, but "rules" of courtesy and grammar sometimes prevailed. Frequently, stimulations that resulted in some subjective experience also led to speech interruption. If the patient became unresponsive, he was asked firmly what he was experiencing, and if he was still unresponsive, he was asked to give some body movement signal—for example, raising a hand to show that he could hear us. We then obtained the patient's introspective report as soon as possible. In spite of persistent questioning, one out of four instances of visual experience was impossible to locate in time. Additional communication difficulties were created by the psychomotor retardation, increased speech pathology, perseveration, and loosened associations that followed some stimulations, especially those stimulations followed by an afterdischarge.

A striking finding concerned memory for the hallucinatory experience. Several of the "A" (hallucination) events were forgotten by patients from

10 to 15 minutes after occurrence. When questioned the next day, patients still could not recall the experience. If, however, they were given partial contents as clues and if they were encouraged repeatedly to remember, then they sometimes reconstructed other portions of the experience.

The same object-related visual event ("A" or "B") was never repeated in our sample by subsequent stimulation of the same site with the same parameters of stimulation. As mentioned above, we tried to reproduce events by repeated stimulation of the same site later the same day or during subsequent sessions. Sometimes nothing was reported, while at other times another type of visual event was reported. Sometimes the same category of event was repeated but with a shift in content.

The following sections briefly review perceptual distortions and elementary sensations and then describe the formed imagery.

"D" Events—Perceptual Distortions

The perceptual distortions reported during brain stimulation resemble certain apparently psychogenic visual disturbances and perceptual distortions occurring during auras and regressive experiences. Stationary objects appeared to move or to bend, reduplicate (eg, double vision), or to develop a halo. Occasionally micropsia or tunnel vision was reported. (Macropsia was not reported.) Sometimes a portion of the visual field was lost: one patient reported a spotty, "here and there" loss of his visual field during a stimulation. Such perceptual distortions arose most frequently on stimulation of the optic radiation, the hippocampus, or the posterior hippocampus.

"C" Events—Elementary Sensations

As indicated earlier, most "C" events were elicited from the optic radiation and appeared usually in the contralateral visual field. Flashes of blue or white light, described as splashes or starbursts, were common. Colors of gold, red, green, and orange were reported less often. At times, the lights, "splashes," or "balls" were reduplicated so that two, three, or even a dozen lights were seen. Klüver has noted that reduplication is one of the "constancies" of hallucinatory experiences of any origin.[23] Flickering and moving lights were common. One subject reported a "rolling X," another, "vibrating, wavy lines." Several subjects saw "lines" or "circles."

"B" Events—Pseudohallucinations

A gross idea of the types of images reported can be obtained from a brief list of the "B" events. For brevity and clarity, the patient's words are condensed.

1. An elephant, something on its back, associated with the world of crime.
2. A doctor, name forgotten, but you find him over there (Dr.H.). I recognized him as a radio signal.
3. An animal, maybe a monkey; it has something to do with my spells. (The patient stated that he saw this regularly as part of his aura although previously he had never mentioned it.)
4. A series of numbers—"30," "40"—moving and changing size. (Previously the patient had performed a counting task.)
5. My sons.
6. Walking in the park, I see a park.
7. I see myself having a spell in the hospital corridor and hitting my head.
8. Flashes—mother talking on phone with doctor, next, people from school—waxes and wanes; now it flashes.
9. My sons flying.
10. A symptom, a base plate, mountains like triangles.
11. An upright pig, talking. (This was reported also as an aura. See elaboration below.)
12. A closet, familiar, not empty.
13. A room, familiar.

Whether or not a person reported a visual event did not have any observable relationship to his prestimulation reports of the phenomena of his auras and seizures. On the other hand, precipitation of an aura-like sensation by electrical stimulation led some patients to say, "This is what I have all the time." They then proceeded to tell us of phenomena they had not described previously in spite of repeated, careful questioning during the preimplantation work-ups. This may be attributed to the poor memory for events occurring during auras and seizures.

Example of a "B" Event. A few seconds after stimulation of the right anterior commissure, a young woman reported she felt as she did before her typical seizure. Then she said she had seen "pigs walking upright like people" and that she saw such images frequently during her auras. Further questioning clearly revealed that the pigs were not hallucinations, since she did not project them into external reality or think that they were real perceptions. Yet, the pigs were very vivid visually, more so than her usual pictorial ideation. Her association to the pigs was:

> They called me a pig a lot; it got me upset. I'd seen the image of a pig— standing on two legs—dressed in clothes—staring at me—as if it were

saying to me, "You're not a pig. You don't belong with us even if they call you a pig."—Like myself talking to myself. The pig was me, but telling me I wasn't a pig—but I see it all the time before spells.

The content of the vivid thought image, apparently initiated by the electrical stimulation, is not derived directly from a perceptual experience. Even if she had seen pigs in storybook illustrations, any perceptual source was reworked in the construction of the imagery that the patient reported. This alone does not indicate that the experience could not be a rerun of a memory. The patient might have been reexperiencing a memory of an imaginary experience. She might have developed a specific fantasy image that compounded various ideas and affects, and this fantasy image might have become a symbolic substitute for a more extended train of thought—a condensation of various ideas, affects, defensive attitudes, and so forth. The symbol might then have been rerun into visual imagery when the systems of visualization were activated, when the underlying affects or ideas were activated, or when the substrates of that particular symbol were activated.

This incident of the pigs was reported only once during the stimulations and recording sessions, although the same site was stimulated twice more with similar stimulus parameters.

"A" Events—Hallucinations

A condensed list of the visual hallucinations reported will give an overview.

1. Round room off to the side, remembered from when a little girl.
2. A dog and a man.
3. Self sitting, giving sister a "sickle cell" treatment (injection).
4. A man wearing a brown sports outfit, sitting in a chair. Seemed to be Dr. A.
5. A cherry grove, familiar—near home, changing into a single tree, then into a wire (attached to the TV camera at which the patient had been staring).
6. Three boys playing on a swing in the yard. One was the patient's youngest son. (Patient did not recall ever seeing this.)
7. A white number moving. (Patient had performed a counting task previously.)
8. Flashes of light becoming a doorway, then becoming flashing light again.
9. A "No Smoking" sign. (There was such a sign on the surgery room door.)

10. Gold color becoming an invitation—then a boy and girl—then Dr. H. and someone else getting papers.
11. Orange color—becoming people.
12. A spinning phantom, assuming the shape of the overhead light fixture.
13. Lady with a pink dummy.

Example of an "A" Event—Two Hallucinations Evoked by Repeated Stimulation of the Same Site. The patient was an 18-year-old man who received a stimulation of the left posterior hippocampus. At the onset of stimulation, the patient's facial expression changed, and he began to look and turn his head to the right. He said that he saw the investigator's glasses turning an orange color that changed shape "every split second" and continued to "travel" to the right. Approximately a minute later he reported seeing people he knew "50 years ago," one of them a boy standing on a street. This was associated with unusually prolonged left limbic afterdischarge that lasted 4 minutes and 30 seconds while the patient responded to questions in a more obtunded manner than prior to the stimulation. He seemed to comprehend some of the meaning of the questions, but his verbal contents and tonal inflections resembled those found in aphasia, sleep-talking, or hypnagogic speech.

During the following day, the same electrode within the left posterior hippocampus was stimulated.

The following notes are taken from the transcript.

Stimulus on. Patient looks and turns his head gradually to the right, gazing intently at blank spaces on the wall. He stopped talking with the onset of stimulation: "Do you see anything now?"

"I see, uh, up against that canvas there, there's, uh—" (*points toward the wall*).

"What do you see?"

"What's that?"

"What do you see?"

"A gold drovoil (*sic*)—you see, it's moving."

"What's moving?"

"The sign—it's—"

"It's moving?"

"Yeah."

"It's a gold sign?"

"Yeach, goldvoy (*sic*). It's still moving."

"And what does the sign say?"

"Uh, it's, uh—seems like—uh—(*unclear word*) invit—invitation for, uh—for, uh—"

"What?"

"I can't even describe it right now—a thing—invi—initation."

The sign (or invitation) then became "some guy" and the images apparently persisted when he shut his eyes: "Is it anybody you know?"

"Yeah, but I can't recall the name. That's just the funny thing about it."

"It's a boy?"

"Yeah."

"Where is he?"

"He's going, uh, I—"

"Shut your eyes. Do you still see him?"

(Eyes shut) "Uh—yeah, I can still see it."

"The boy?"

"Uh, yeah—"

The patient was then asked to open his eyes. He reported a boy and girl "traveling a lot together." "They're traveling a lot together?"

"Yeah."

"And?"

"This is all it" *(sic).*

"You see two of them?"

"Yeah. . . . Kind wonder if, uh—the dear, the idea about them, ya-know. . . ."

"Well, was it a boy and another boy, or a boy and a girl?"

"It was a boy and a girl."

"How old were they?"

"Uh—really couldn't say."

"Were they wearing clothes?"

"Yeah—"

"Can you describe them?"

"Uh, no, not really. I can't describe it. I don't—really pay much attention to what they're wearing. I do know they didn't come here naked or nothing."

The patient drifted off into a semistuporous but wakeful state in which he continued to respond to questions with replies such as "I'm completely lost. I don't know how many, nary a thing, I feel real weird right now. I can't stray" (he meant "say") and "feel like I'm—feel all like I'm ready to go to sleep." He apparently continued to form visual images for, after a pause, he continued: "I mean this picture—uh, you and somebody else—picking up papers" *(an unclear, mumbled phrase).*

"Me and someone else getting papers?"

"Yeah—I don't even know if I'm—uh saying anything that makes sense or not—"

"It seems funny to you, your thinking?"

"Yeah."

The initial visual events seemed to be of hallucinatory intensity and projected into the external environment; the latter event of picturing "you and somebody else" is more likely a visual thought image than a hallucination.

The depth EEG showed high-voltage, rapid spiking activity in both the left inferior and posterior hippocampus and the left hippocampal gyrus. Fifteen minutes after this visual event, the subject was asked if he remembered seeing anything. He replied, "I did remember seeing it, but I can't remember what it was."

The two preceding episodes are illustrative of a frequent occurrence: an initially unformed, geometric, or colored visual sensation occurred, probably because of excitation in some section of the visual pathways, then was elaborated into "what it looks like." The elaboration followed the form of the initial elementary impression but was also guided by other psychologic processes. The afterdischarge continued throughout the period of elaboration of the images. Both visual hallucinations were forgotten about 15 minutes after occurrence.

As mentioned, the hallucinatory quality of thought seems to have, at times, a crude coincidence with the intense afterdischarge that often follows stimulation. This afterdischarge may be followed in turn by a period of low-voltage, irregular EEG activity. The patient mentioned above continued to be responsive during this period of relatively quiescent EEG activity. He answered questions in a rational manner, but the quantity of mental contents seemed to be reduced. Some patients reported the experience of a haunting sensation—"trying to grab hold of my memory but can't"—or the flickering of images through consciousness that has been labeled "dream scintillations."[12,18,36] In short, there is at times a quality suggestive of a regressive state of consciousness following electrical stimulation of structures deep within the temporal lobe.

Example of an "A" Event with Psychomotor Seizure. The patient was a 40-year-old man who received an electrical stimulation of the left posterior hippocampal gyrus. As an immediate consequence, both a generalized electrical spiking discharge and a psychomotor seizure developed for a period of 1 minute, in which the patient looked about with a startled expression, saying, "who, who, who," and fumbled with his clothes. Following this he returned to the coherent, alert, and communicative mental state that preceded the stimulation. He reported having seen an attractive woman, whom he identified as a hospital worker, enter the room carrying a pink, plaster dummy in the form of a woman. She appeared to be smoothing over the plaster just as the doctor had done when applying his cast "to mend his arm." While telling this, the patient patted the plaster cast of his broken arm, saying, "like this." He stated that the woman was going to "fix things up." The dummy he associated with the manikins he worked with in a department store. He lost his job because of a psychomotor seizure in the company cafeteria, but it was the best job he had ever had and he wished he had one like it now.

Just prior to the stimulation, the patient had been looking carefully at his broken arm and talking of his inability to work because of it. Just after the seizure, he asked if he was going to be cured of his spells. He also reached absently for the arm of a nurse with whom he had been indulging in a mild flirtation during intervals before the stimulation. He seemed to provide a cover for this gesture by looking at her watch. The content of the hallucination seemed to be a highly condensed pictorialization of his motivational state at the time of the stimulation.

Comment

In our study, stimulation of deep structures of the limbic system produced a variety of visual events that resembled in phenomenology the events reported as a consequence of surface stimulations. Psychologically, we were most interested in those visual events that depicted formed objects. Penfield had found that stimulation of the temporal cortex of epileptics occasionally evokes hallucinations.[29] He suggested that experiential hallucinations might be activations of the engrams of perceptual memories. He was careful to point out that such activation of mnemonic engrams might be true only of epileptics since normative data were not available. In the foregoing description of our clinical results, I made several comments on the relationship of the events to current percepts and motives. In this discussion, I would like to speculate further into the processes involved in the formation of images and hallucinations and into the ingredients that supply the content.

The Processes of Image Formation

According to the memory-"engram" model, perceived events are stored as memories in some sort of neuronal or molecular site. Activation of the storage site evokes the memories and may lead to hallucinatory reenactments of the perceptions. The subject reports these perceptual reruns as reliving a past experience.

Several of our observations have led us to believe that this model is too simple.

1. No two stimulations at the same anatomic point produced the same images or hallucinations. This in itself, however, does not necessarily contradict the memory-"engram" model since the same site is never in the same state of excitation and since, as Penfield[28] pointed out, it is doubtful that stimulations are of the memory sites directly.

2. Images and hallucinations were reported that probably were never actually seen in prior experience. Sometimes the self was seen in a way which would not be possible by self-perception: sometimes imaginary scenes were depicted. Again, this in itself does not necessarily refute the memory-"engram" model, for to retain a memory of a previous fantasy or dream is possible. Such a memory of an imaginary product could conceivably be aroused by stimulations.

3. Many of the images were related to recent perceptions, active ideas, or current motives. Of course, perceptions, ideas, emotions, and motives may all "prime" certain memories subliminally, thus rendering such engrams more likely to be selected for further activation into psychic representation. Many of the visual events were also produced in association with an altered state of awareness. In such states, image formation is enhanced and increased influence of primary process prevails.

4. At times the image or hallucination seemed to be elaborated out of a matrix provided by elementary sensations such as light, color, or amorphous shape. Such progressive elaborations (and simplifications in some instances) are very similar to the descriptions in the previous chapter.

To summarize, the relatively few hallucinations and pseudohallucinations found in our study could be due simply to a loss of inhibition over image formation and to, in some instances, the elaboration of elementary sensations evoked by irritation of the optic radiations. Our results support the hypothesis of Mahl et al[26] that brain stimulations may lead to regressive alteration of the state of consciousness and regressive alteration of the organization of thought.

The Hippocampus

We found that a relative preponderance of reports of formal visual sensations occurred after stimulation of the posterior hippocampal gyrus in comparison with other limbic sites of stimulation. MacLean and his coworkers, using microelectrodes in waking animals, found that the cortex above and below the calcarine fissure was found to "fire" into the posterior hippocampal gyrus and this gyrus in turn was found to "fire" into the hippocampus.[33] In squirrel monkeys, photostimulation evoked discharge in the posterior hippocampal gyrus and the adjoining lingual cortex.[7] A class of cells in the posterior hippocampal gyrus that responded to slowly adapting "on" cells of the retina was also identified.[25] The findings of our empiric study and the neurophysiologic work of MacLean et al suggest that there are visual pathways to the posterior hippocampal gyrus or that this area is, in some way, involved in the regulation of image formation.

What possible role does the posterior hippocampus structure play in image formation processes? Douglas[8] reviewed the literature on hippocampus function in man. Four theories survive his analysis.

1. The hippocampus appears to be involved in working memory in relating present situations to previous ones. In terms of the model of image formation advanced in Chapter 7, the process would involve holding an image of a perception, forming images based on similar schemata, and comparing and modifying the external and internal images until a match occurs, and the current situation is deciphered according to relevance and similarity to past memories and perceptual schemata.

2. The hippocampus appears essential to internal and external inhibitory processes. In terms of image formation this process would involve preserving the autonomy of images of internal and external origin. That is, when the image formation apparatus was in perceptual use, internal images would be inhibited. When daydream images were the content of attention, then perceptual images might be inhibited.

3. The hippocampus is believed to be involved with suppression of conditioned responses. Suppression of conditioned responses in image formation would involve the capacity to preserve the independence of images of perception from schemata of prior sensory memory. This suppression capacity makes it possible to recognize a *novel* perceptual image and avoids an imperative or erroneous transformation of a novel image into a false correspondent to a memory image or traditional schemata.

4. The hippocampus may exert inhibitory control over attention, possibly by means of inhibitory control over incoming sensations.[9,15] In image formation, this inhibitory control would allow a flexible shift between fantasy and assessment of external reality without confusion between the two or excessive centering on one activity.

In summary, the hippocampus apparently serves a regulatory role. Possibly the posterior areas of the hippocampal formation are relatively devoted to the regulation of image formation. Disrupting the function of this area, as by electrical stimulation, might alter controls. Images of perceptions might be confused with images of memory resulting in poorly differentiated composites or illusions (failure of Function 1 above). In a sequence of thought in images there might be failure to connect together and keep separate those images derived from sequential perception from those in a fantasy (failure of Function 2). Similarly, the person would be unable to suppress the peremptory interpretation of external signals according to currently active internal schemata (Function 3) and would lose the power to shift at will from perception to fantasy and back (Function 4). The results could be the perceptual distortions, elementary sensations, illusions, pseudohallucinations, and hallucinations reported by our patients.

Conclusion

Examination of the content of the imagery and hallucinatory-type events indicates that object-related contents are sometimes evolved from a matrix or gestalt provided by elemental sensations. These images and hallucinations may also relate to current motivational dynamics. They cannot be explained entirely by Penfield's theory that stimulation activates memory "engrams" that are then rerun. The stimulations, at least at times, produced an altered state of consciousness in which lexical cognition was reduced and image formation was enhanced or disinhibited.

The contents of the last two chapters illustrate the usefulness and necessity of the concept of regulatory controls. The inhibition and facilitation of image formation can be influenced by psychologic motives, and these motives involve changes in neurophysiologic variables. The inhibition and facilitation of image formation is influenced by neurophysiologic factors, and these factors change the current state of psychologic motives. In sum, then, whether we can figure it out or not, any given image experience is a result of both psychologic and neurobiologic influences and their interrelationship.

REFERENCES

1. Bailey P: Intracranial Tumors. Springfield, Ill, Thomas, 1948
2. Bender MB: Neuroophthalmology. In Baker AB (ed): Clinical Neurology, 3rd ed. New York, Harper & Row, 1965
3. Bogen JE: The other side of the brain. I. Dysgraphia and dyscopia following cerebral commissurotomy. Bull Los Angeles Neurol Soc 34:73, 1969
4. Brain R: Loss of visualization. Proc Roy Soc Med 47:288, 1954
5. Bromberg W, Schilder P: Psychologic considerations in alcoholic hallucinosis —castration and dismembering motives. Int J Psychoanal 14:206, 1933
6. Costello CG, MacGregor P: The relationships between some aspects of visual imagery and the alpha rhythm. J Ment Sci 103:786, 1957

7. Cuenod M, Casey KL, MacLean PD: Unit analysis of visual input to posterior limbic cortex. I. Photic stimulation. J Neurophysiol 28:1101, 1965

8. Douglas RJ: The hippocampus and behavior. Psychol Bull 67:416, 1967

9. ———, Pribram KH: Learning and limbic lesions. Neuropsychologia 4:197, 1966

10. Feldman M, Bender M: Hallucinations and illusions of parietooccipital lobe origin. In Keup W (ed): Origin and Mechanisms of Hallucinations. New York, Plenum, 1970

11. Fisher C, Paul IH: The effect of subliminal visual stimulation on images and dreams: a validation study. J Amer Psychoanal Assoc 7:35, 1959

12. Forbes A: Dream scintillations. Psychosom Med 11:160, 1949

13. Galin D: Hemispheric specialization: implications for psychiatry. In Grenell RG, Gabay S (eds): Biological Foundations of Psychiatry. New York, Raven, 1976

14. ———, Ornstein R: Individual differences in cognitive style. I. Reflective eye movement. Neuropsychologia 12:367, 1974

15. Gerbrandt LK: Generalizations from the distinction of passive and active avoidance. Psychol Rep 15:11, 1964

16. Golla FL, Hutton EL, Walter WG: The objective study of mental imagery. I. Physiological concomitants. J Ment Sci 89:216, 1943

17. Horowitz MJ, Adams JE, Rutkin BB: Visual imagery on brain stimulation. Arch Gen Psychiat 19:469, 1968

18. ———, Adams JE, Rutkin BB: Dream scintillations. Psychosom Med 29:284, 1967

19. Ishibashi T, et al: Hallucinations produced by electrical stimulation of the temporal lobes in schizophrenic patients. Tohoku J Exp Med 82:124, 1964

20. Jackson JH: Taylor J (ed): Selected Writings of John Hughlings Jackson, vol. 1. New York, Basic, 1958

21. Jasper HH, Rasmussen T: Studies of clinical and electrical responses to deep temporal stimulation in men with some considerations of functional anatomy: the brain and behavior. Res Publ Assoc Res Nerv Ment Dis 35:316, 1958

22. Kamiya J, Zeitlin D: Learned EEG alpha wave control by humans. Report 182, Dept Mental Hygiene, Research Div, Sacramento, California, 1963

23. Klüver H: Mechanisms of hallucinations. In McNemar Q, Merrill MA (eds): Studies in Personality. New York, McGraw-Hill, 1942

24. Lehmann D, et al: Changes in patterns of the human electroencephalogram during fluctuations of perception of stabilized retinal images. Electroenceph Clin Neurophysiol 19:336, 1965

25. MacLean PD: The limbic and visual cortex in phylogeny: further insights from anatomic and microelectrode studies. In Hassler R, Stephan H (eds): Evolution of the Forebrain. Stuttgart, Thieme Verlag, 1966

26. Mahl GF, et al: Psychologic responses in the human to intracerebral electrical stimulation. Psychosom Med 26:337, 1964

27. Oswald I: The EEG: visual imagery and attention. Q J Exp Psychol 9:113, 1957
28. Penfield W: Speech, perception and the cortex. In Eceles JC (ed): Brain and Conscious Experience. New York, Springer-Verlag, 1966
29. ———: The excitable cortex in conscious man. In Baldwin M, Bailey P (eds): Temporal Lobe Epilepsy. Springfield, Ill, Thomas, 1958
30. ———, Jasper H: Epilepsy and the Functional Anatomy of the Human Brain. Boston, Little, Brown, 1954
31. ———, Rasmussen T: The Cerebral Cortex of Man. New York, MacMillan, 1950
32. Perot P, Penfield W: Hallucinations of past experience and experimental responses to stimulation of temporal cortex. Trans Amer Neurol Assoc 85:80, 1960
33. Pribram KH, MacLean PD: Neuronographic analysis of medial and basal cerebral cortex: monkey. J Neurophysiol 16:324, 1953
34. Rapaport D: The theory of attention cathexis: an economic and structural attempt at the explanation of cognitive processes. In Gill M (ed): The Collected Papers of David Rapaport. New York, Basic, 1967
35. ———: Emotions and Memory. Baltimore, Williams & Wilkins, 1942
36. Saul LJ: Dream scintillations. Psychosom Med 27:286, 1965
37. Sedman G: Being an epileptic. Psychiat Neurol 152:1, 1966
38. Short O: The objective study of mental imagery. Brit J Psychol 44:38, 1953
39. Slatter KH: Alpha rhythms and mental imagery. Electroenceph Clin Neurophysiol 12:851, 1961-62
40. Sperry RW: Lateral specialization of cerebral function in the surgically separated hemispheres. In McGuigan FJ, Schoonover RA (eds): The Psychophysiology of Thinking. New York, Academic Press, 1973
41. Sprague JM: Interaction of cortex and superior colliculus in mediation of visually guided behavior in the cat. Science 153:1544, 1966
42. Stepien L, Sierpinski S: Impairment of recent memory after temporal lesions in man. Neuropsychologia 2:291, 1964
43. Whitten JR: Psychical seizures. Amer J Psychiat 126:560, 1969
44. Williams D, Gassel M: Visual function in patients with homonymous hemianopia. I. The visual fields. Brain 185:175, 1962

11

PSYCHEDELIC IMAGES
AND FLASHBACKS

Psychedelic agents evoke many unusual experiences, but none as dazzling as visual images which reach hallucinatory proportions. Even before any increase in images, the psychedelic experience alters perception. Colors may take on a new vividness or meaning; illusions are common, so that the outline of objects may appear haloed, or telephone wires may look like snakes. Images often contain reduplication of figural elements as illustrated in Figures 11-1 and 11-2. At the height of the experience, images flow effortlessly, often into complicated and bizarre stories, and seemingly without voluntary control. Reality testing is often lost so that it becomes difficult to distinguish fictive images from perceptions. Factors such as mood, current motivational states, expectancy, and environment largely determine image contents. Indeed, environment may be crucial; persons taking LSD in laboratory experiments report much different imagery than those in a candle-lit room with friends, music, and incense. Because a person loses his sense of volitional direction of thought, he may be amazed at the content of his images, but in spite of this nonvolitional sensation, images can be altered to some degree by voluntary effort. This "march of experience" from perceptual distortion, through perception and image fusion, to hallucination occurs in many organic conditions, intoxications, and in certain brain stimulation experiences. The resemblance of the phenomena in these conditions suggests that drug action affects the organic substrates of control of image formation and perception.

Frequently, as volition decreases, people report ideas and feelings that are usually repressed. Under benign conditions, a person may "trip" on

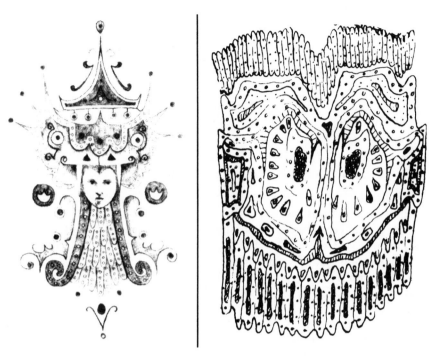

Figs. 11-1 (left) and 11-2 (right). An artist's drawing of two of his images under the influence of LSD.

pleasantly gratifying wish fulfillments (as in a dream), accompanied by distortions of memory and time. Afterwards, a person may remember that he had unusual visions of great personal relevance, but forget the details. Sometimes the release of normally inhibited ideas leads to new symbol formations which work to resolve defensive and impulsive conflicts (again, as with a good dream).[13] On the other side of the coin, the release of what has been dormant or buried can result in a "bad trip," and, instead of a successful compromise among previously irreconcilable motives, there may be an excessive eruption of fear, hatred, or guilt.

After a trip, some persons increase their sensitivity to internal and external sensations. They may become more observant of their mental life (particularly images) or notice new sounds in music or new forms or colors in nature. Usually most of the contents from a trip are forgotten except for fragmentary memories. But sometimes people have intrusive returns of sensations which they first experienced during the drug state.

DESCRIPTION

Flashbacks (flashes, flashing) may persist for weeks or months after the last drug experience. The most common and clearest content of the flashbacks seems to involve the visual sensory system, but flashbacks have been reported in every sensory modality: taste, smell, touch, kinesthetics, vestibular changes, auditory images. In addition, distortions of time sense, self-image, or reality sense may occur.

Spontaneous Return of Perceptual Distortions

Distortions of perception experienced during the drug experience may recur long afterwards, as previously reported.[3,12] Subjective experiences include halo effects, blurred vision, shimmering, reduplication of percepts, distortion of spatial planes, and changes in normal coloration. Micropsia, macropsia, and tunnel vision may also appear during the period "off" drugs. Examples of such perceptual distortions and elementary sensations are:

> Now I often see a bright shiny halo around people, especially at the dark edges—sometimes it's rainbow colors—like during the trip.

> Sometimes the sidewalk seems to bend as if it's going downwards—even when I'm not on anything—or it just kinda vibrates back and forth.

Increased Susceptibility to Spontaneous Imagery

Some persons report that after repeated use of hallucinogens they find visual imagery occupies a greater proportion of their thinking than formerly. As in the following example, they also state that their imagery now has a different quality: it is more vivid, seems to spring from some nonvolitional source, and is less readily suppressed than formerly. The incidence of this type of flashback appears related to total dose over time.

> Now I see things—walls, and faces, and caves—probably imprinted on my thalamus from the prehistoric past. Sometimes as clear as on a trip, but mostly not. My dreams sometimes are really spectacular now.

RECURRENT UNBIDDEN IMAGES

Three examples clarify the recurrent and unbidden imagery of the flashbacks:

A 17-year-old boy had taken marijuana, DMT, methedrine, LSD, and LSD with arsenic ("for that special kick"). Although his behavior was noted by his friends to be "freaky when he was flashing," he was able to deliver his thoughts in a rational manner. He described his theme song as "LSD and speed are all that there is for me" and spent most of his time drawing morbid and bizarre references to death. His costume was black with steel link chains. During a recent "trip" he hallucinated a dark scorpion on the back of his hand and experienced terror: "It had many legs, and I was worried it might sting me." In the five weeks after the "trip" he claimed to have ingested no drugs, but the scorpion continued as "flashings," sometimes in a changed position, but always brown or black in color.

A 21-year-old man had had numerous trips on LSD and other drugs. He described himself as preoccupied with life and death. After taking STP for the first time he had repeated visual and kinesthetic images of himself crashing through the window of his car. He had never had such an accident in reality, yet during the flashbacks he felt fear at the vividness of the experience. He was sensitive about his flashback and said it was *not* a symptom but a "release of the within" from the drug. The image appeared symbolic of repressed fears of losing control and of self-destructiveness.

A 16-year-old boy reported an estimated 10 LSD trips and 100 marijuana smokings. He denied use of other drugs. Generally, during LSD trips he experienced interesting, wild, intense, and usually pleasant visual imagery. Recently, however, he had had a "bad trip" with images of a human figure being sucked into the vortex of a whirlpool. Returns of this image began three weeks after the LSD trip and persisted for about three additional weeks. Five to ten times a day the vivid, black-and-white images interrupted whatever he was thinking. These images were more pressing when he was "high" on marijuana. Whenever he had the flashback he felt frightened and unsuccessfully tried to get rid of it. Although the time seemed very long, he knew that after approximately 15 to 20 seconds the image would leave of its own accord.

Since leaving home a year previously, he had stayed in various places, having incidental sexual and drug experiences without forming emotional attachments. However, where he had been staying most recently he had formed a close relationship with a particular boy and girl. Further discussion revealed that he had recently been asked to leave. While denying that this had any emotional impact on him, his tone of voice and facial expression indicated his sadness.

Later he began to talk of his loneliness and feelings of rejection with considerable feeling. Thereafter, he reported no more flashbacks. Possibly this symptom relief was due to working through his feelings and having a positive (substitute) relationship with the psychotherapist. The flashback seemed to symbolize three trends of his feelings: (1) loneliness, despair, and helplessness on being removed from a situation that had been home-like for him; (2) his feelings of being sucked down by drugs and lack of plans or structure in life; and (3) his dread of being overwhelmingly incorporated by getting too close to others.

INCIDENCE OF FLASHBACKS

In their 1967 review of the literature, Smart and Bateman[14] reported only 11 cases of spontaneous recurrence of LSD effects. In contrast, a questionnaire survey of professionals revealed a very high rate of reports of "flashbacks" in patients who had used LSD.[15] Robbins et al[11] found that 11 of 34 patients admitted to a psychiatric ward because of LSD ingestion had some kind of reappearance of LSD effects after the drug had worn off. Keeler et al[7] state that spontaneous recurrence of marijuana effects are relatively common and, when associated with severe anxiety, constitute a psychiatric emergency.

In 1971, McGlothlin and Arnold[9] reported a follow-up study of 247 persons who had received LSD in an experimental or psychotherapeutic setting. In a structured interview, subjects were asked if they experienced any uncontrolled LSD-like experiences without using the drug. If they answered yes, they were asked to describe their experiences. Thirty-six of the respondents answered affirmatively, which was about 15 percent of the sample. Of these, seven reported minor imagery experiences such as flashes, and five reported major changes such as hallucinations or unbidden image repetitions of frightening scenes experienced during the original drug experience. Respondents with ten or more LSD exposures were somewhat more likely to report these recurrences than those with less than ten exposures.

Investigators in San Francisco conducted an extensive investigation of street drug users in the Haight-Ashbury district, during the climax of the "drug scene."* Lengthy questionnaires were filled out by 177 subjects, and interviews about drug experiences were conducted. In the questionnaire, 43 percent of subjects replied affirmatively to the global question, "Do you experience flashbacks?" This proportion was subsequently reduced on interview to 30 percent who had some evidence for such experiences. Only 34 subjects (19 percent) had any type of visual flashback; this is

---

* Supported by NIMH grant 15737, Drs. R. Wallerstein and S. Pittel, principal investigators. Peter Armetta helped collect the data on flashback occurrences.

detailed in Table 11-1. Six subjects are listed more than once because they had multiple types of experience.

McGlothlin and Arnold reported a similar nonsignificant tendency for subjects with more hallucinatory trips to have more flashback experiences.[4] This does not indicate a major size of effect. These data on the global incidence of flashbacks are similar to those reported by Moskowitz,[10] who found that 33 percent of persons in a population of about 4,000 drug abusers entering a naval prison reported flashbacks after LSD use.

Usage of any of the major hallucinogens may be followed by flashbacks. The phenomenon may also occur after marijuana use.[6,7] Marijuana, seconal, physical fatigue, or stress may produce a state in which flashbacks from previous LSD "trips" are more likely to recur. I have only two reports of such recurrence with alcohol intoxication.

Persons with flashbacks insist that the imagery of the flashback has a different quality from thought images experienced prior to drug use. Usually the content of the flashbacks is derived from frightening imagery experiences during drug intoxication; less commonly, new images may be produced.

EXPLANATORY THEORIES

Several theories can be put forward to explain why recurrent unbidden images, often of identical content, may intrude into awareness for an extended period after the immediate effects of drugs have worn off.

The Release Theory

The release theory suggests that psychedelic agents may produce changes at the neurophysiologic level in the processes that regulate image

Table 11-1
Incidence of Flashbacks in 177 Users
of Street Drugs

Type of Experience	Number	Percent
Hallucinations	3	2
Vivid thought images	8	4
Lights, geometric designs	7	4
Perceptual distortions	22	12

formation.[2] Repeated toxic effects may lead to enduring changes in such processes although blood levels of LSD rapidly diminish.[1] The neurophysiologic changes, just as in brain stimulations, may create a situation in which image formation is disinhibited.

The content of the flashbacks lends some support to the release theory. Hallucinatory constants are common (the spiral shapes of the whirlpool, the radiating lines of the scorpion, and the broken windshield).[8] Elementary sensations, such as these forms, and perceptual distortions, such as those of the first examples, are also reported during the auras of epilepsy or migraine and on electrical stimulation of the eye or brain, as described in the previous chapters.

Psychodynamic Theory

In some flashbacks, the image content seems to be a symbolic depiction of an affect state or situational crisis (eg, despair and hopelessness). In some flashbacks, the recurrent images seem to be a return of traumatic perceptions—images of the drug experience that were overwhelmingly frightening at the time they were hallucinated.

Recurrent flashbacks bear some resemblance to other clinical phenomena such as peremptory ideation, obsessive rumination, and repetitive visual pseudohallucinations (as in hysteric psychosis). The experience is felt as a loss of volitional control over the contents of awareness, and this sensation of loss of control contributes to the attendant anxiety or loss of reality sense. As with unbidden images, the contents seem to be returns of traumatic perceptions, breakthroughs of repressed ideas or affects, or screen images to symbolize but conceal emotional conflicts. In particular, many of the images reported symbolized feelings of disintegration or impending doom, fears characteristic of persons undergoing an identity diffusion.

The Mystic Theory

Some members of the drug subculture believe that the mind has imprinted upon it memories of all ages past and possibly projections of the future as well. These prehistoric and archetypic perceptions are released, it is thought, by psychedelic experience. Once the images have learned the route to awareness, they press for remembrance. Perhaps, if we substitute "childhood" or "unconscious fantasy" for "prehistoric," "archetypic," and "ages past," this mystic theory is not as incompatible with psychologic theories as it might seem.[5]

CONCLUSION

Flashbacks are returns of images for extended periods *after* hallucinogens have worn off. The most symptomatic form consists of recurrent intrusions of the same frightening image into awareness without volitional control of this event. Like the imagery of the "trip" and imagery on brain stimulation, the image experience may arise because of alteration of the neurobiologic capacity to use various regulatory controls over image formation. The image contents, however, and the secondary usage of the experience relate to psychodynamic motives for expression and control of expression. While chemotherapy, as with phenothiazine medication, may terminate the immediate experience of peremptory images, psychotherapy seems helpful for flashbacks, especially if there is a focus on traumatic and screening aspects of the imagery.

REFERENCES

1. Aghajanian GK, Bing OH: Persistence of lysergic acid diethylamide in the plasma of human subjects. Clin Pharmacol Ther 5:611, 1964
2. Freedman DX: On the use and abuse of LSD. Arch Gen Psychiat 18:330, 1968
3. Horowitz MJ: The imagery of visual hallucination. J Nerv Ment Dis 138:513, 1964
4. ———: Flashbacks: Intrusive images after the use of LSD. Amer J Psychiat 126:565, 1969
5. Jung CG: The Archetypes and the Collective Unconscious. New York, Pantheon, 1959
6. Keeler MH, Ewing JA, Rouse BS: Hallucinogenic effects of marijuana as currently used. Amer J Psychiat 128:2, 1971
7. ———, Reifler CB, Liptzin MB: Spontaneous recurrence of marijuana effect. Amer J Psychiat 125:384, 1968
8. Klüver H: Mescal and Mechanisms of Hallucination. Chicago, Univ Chicago Press, 1966
9. McGlothlin WH, Arnold DO: LSD re-visited. A ten-year follow-up of medical LSD use. Arch Gen Psychiat 24(1):35–49, 1971
10. Moskowitz D: Use of haloperidol to reduce LSD flashback. Milit Med 136(9): 754–756, 1971
11. Robbins E, Frosch WA, Stern M: Further observations on untoward reactions to LSD. Amer J Psychiat 124:149, 1967
12. Rosenthal SH: Persistent hallucinosis following repeated administration of hallucinogenic drugs. Amer J Psychiat 121:238, 1964
13. Schilder P: Mind: Perception and Thought in Their Constructive Aspects. New York, Columbia Univ Press, 1942

14. Smart RG, Bateman K: Unfavorable reactions to LSD. Canad Med Assoc J 97:1214, 1967
15. Ungerleider JT, Fisher DD, Fuller M, Caldwell A: The "bad trip": The etiology of the adverse LSD reaction. Am J Psychiatry 124(11):352, 1968

12

HALLUCINATIONS RECONSIDERED

In previous chapters, various psychologic and biologic factors involved in image formation were considered, and mention of hallucinations was frequent. In this chapter, hallucinations are again discussed as a way of reviewing theoretical principles and of testing their explanatory power. There is a wide range of experience encompassed in the term hallucinations, for different properties are present to varying degrees in any given episode. As described in Chapter 2, four properties characterize the hallucinatory experience: (1) hallucinations are mental experiences that occur in image form; (2) they are derived from internal sources of information; (3) they are appraised incorrectly as if from external sources of information; and (4) they usually occur intrusively. Each of these properties will be reviewed below.

ACTIVATION OF THE IMAGE SYSTEM

Any system, whether enactive, image, or lexical, can be activated by physiologic and psychologic changes. As discussed in Chapter 5, the everyday thought of average persons is usually a blend of all three modes, without excessive dominance of any one form. High activation of an image system relative to the levels of the enactive or lexical systems would be one way to predispose a person toward hallucinations. This may occur when there is altered activity anywhere along the neural pathways from the eye to the brain, as when electrical stimulations of the eye or brain produce the conscious experience of colored lights, geometric forms, or faces and figures as described in the last three chapters. The heightening of one representational system over the others might give a quasi-perceptual quality to the resulting mental content and thus contribute to the several constructs that as a whole are labeled hallucinations.

The biologic factors that activate image systems might at the same time interfere with the translation of images into words or with the sequential processing capacity necessary for coherent organization of information in the lexical system. Image representations would then be experienced as estranged from the usual "orchestration" of thought in multiple modes of representation. The "isolated" quality would resemble that of unlabeled percepts.

Such shifts to a preponderance of image representation can also occur due to psychologic motivation, as outlined in Chapters 6 and 7. When the image system is accentuated for biologic and/or psychologic reasons, emergent but warded-off ideas and feelings may gain expression as unbidden images. The translation of these images into word meanings may be impeded as a defensive operation. This is especially useful to avoid labeling either person in a two-party image as the self. For example, if an intrusive, conflictual image depicts a victim being harmed by an aggressor, the image experience itself may be so vague that it precludes recognition of which role is fulfilled by the self. Avoidance of self-designation as victim or aggressor is possible only when words are not added to the experience, since lexical organization requires designation of the self and other as object or subject.

The degree to which images are habitually experienced will relate to the degree of "strangeness" of an isolated image experience. Not all persons have the same usual conscious experience of thought: some have vivid imagery, while others seldom experience images, as described earlier. When persons unfamiliar with mental imagery actually have a vivid image experience, they may react to it or describe it in such a dramatic manner that they or others label it as hallucinatory.[10]

To recapitulate, one determinant of a holistic experience that is labeled hallucinatory is the accentuated use of an image system of representation. Such increased use may result from alterations in the relationship between systems of representation and may be due to either biologic or psychologic factors.

INTENSIFICATIONS OF INTERNAL INPUT

Dual Input in Image Formation

As shown in Chapter 7, nearly every interested investigator of imagery has suggested the existence of some sort of dual input model in which information from external sources can be blended with internal information to form a composite image. Illusions are a perfect example of such composites. The internal and external sources not only blend but cause reciprocal inhibition by, in effect, occupying the image system channels available for information processing.

Another compelling example of dual input into composite image experience is the transition from nonhallucinatory to hallucinatory states, as described in Chapter 7. To recapitulate briefly, these transitions commonly are of two types. In one, there is a gradual distortion of perception, then an increase in illusion formation, and finally hallucination, first of abstract forms and then of personalizations. This transition is most common in response to hallucinogenic drugs. The second form, which is more common in the onset of schizophrenic syndromes, progresses from intrusive images, through intensification of frequency and vividness of such images, to the erroneous estimate of inner images as perceptions. Both types of transition have periods in which inner and outer elements are combined into single holistic experiences.

Image Processing

In Chapters 5 and 7 a model of image formation was suggested which considered a multiple matrix system. These matrices could be considered as stages of information processing. Multiple representations would be created by optic stimuli and internal schemata. Comparisons and revisions of information to obtain good matchings between "external" and "internal" matrices would be made. With good matches there would be reduplication of information over a number of matrices or some type of enlargement of the "right image."[11]

The dual inputs to these matrices, the transitions between them, and the matrices themselves would be interrelated with feedback processes, and the outcome, known as checking, reality testing, or revision of information, could be achieved.

These regulatory processes would provide for matching perceived images with inner schemata of memory, fantasy, and expectancy. Information in the image matrices would also be interrelated with information in sensorimotor control systems, especially those involving schemata for eye movement, binocular focus, head position, and vestibular sensation. The regulatory operations would include means for facilitation, inhibition, preservation, short-term storage, and extension of short-term storage of images until conflicts or ambiguities were resolved.

In such a model, relative intensification of internal sources of information could occur under divergent circumstances, as follows:

1. A relative reduction of external input with no relative lowering of activity (receptivity) of the representational system (eg, sensory deprivation hallucinations).
2. An increase in the activity of the representational system without an increase in the availability of external signals (eg, hallucinations due to brain stimulation).
3. Augmentation of internal input due to arousal of ideas and feelings secondary to wishes, needs, and fear states (eg, hallucinations of the lost spouse in widows or widowers).
4. A reduction of the usual levels of inhibition over the internal inputs (eg, dream and hypnagogic hallucinations).
5. An alteration in the transition between matrices so that internal inputs might gain more representation on matrices oriented to and more often associated with perception. Ambiguous external signals ("high noise-to-signal ratio") might allow the internal schemata greater access to these more "perceptual" matrices. That is, the ambiguous perceptual stimuli might activate these matrices but allow patterns of internal origin to serve as organizers. The resulting reduplication or enlargement would lend the image an intensity in conscious experience, as well as an association with "out-thereness." According to this model, then, an unclear perceptual nidus might provide subsequent vividness for internal elaborations.

As reviewed by Neisser[9] and Arnheim,[2] perception is a constructive process governed essentially by two needs: the need for accurate knowledge of reality and the need to find what is hoped or feared *may* be "out there." The latter purpose directs perception and is called expectancy, a priming of certain schemata for matching with potential patterns. Suppose there is a highly "tonic" schemata, the result of an intense need state. Because of dual input, the internal schemata might be matched with the perceptual nidus and the composite image would yield a perception-like experience.

In intense need states, no perceptual nidus is necessary. Thus a hallucination may fulfill some aspects of needs, however temporarily, and these satisfactions would reinforce whatever changes in controls made hallucinations possible in the first place.

ERRONEOUS APPRAISALS OF INFORMATION

Construction of a conscious image does not complete an information-processing cycle. If the image episode is important, it must be interpreted to a point of completion. Disruption of such information processing, after formation of what I will call the baseline image, but before meaningful completion of appraisal, will lead to conceptual isolation of the baseline image, and a quasi-perceptual rather than thought-like quality will be associated with the experience. This is what McKeller[8] aptly calls "loss of the 'as-if' experience."

Impaired Information Processing

Suppose a person forms a baseline image composed of an entoptic nidus of blue jagged lines and an internally derived form "like a dragon." If immediate information processing of "the blue dragon" does not categorize that image as a familiar event, then secondary appraisals continue the analysis ("Are there dragons?" "Could it be real?" "What is really experienced?" "Can effort alter the image?" "Is it there if I blink or turn away or pinch myself?"). If the image is threatening or seems important but defies immediate explanation, then the memory of the image episode would tend to remain active in terms of access to consciousness. It remains unusual, weird, and alien to past experience. These qualities are more frequently associated with perceptual input, and hence the intensified internal information will tend to be labeled as if it were perceptual.

Imagine, now, two separate episodes of conscious experience, both of visual images and both of identical vividness, clarity, and conceptual "space." Suppose these episodes occur to two identical persons who differ in only one respect. To one, the image content is familiar, while to the other it is novel. The first person rapidly processes and is done with the image. The second person retains the novel image in active memory; it is isolated conceptually from cross-modal translation and is difficult to appraise. The latter image would be more likely to be labeled "hallucinatory."

The novelty of a stimulus contributes to such doubts, but so do brevity and ambiguity. Hallucinations are usually considered to be dramatically intense images, but many of them are dim and brief episodes of awareness. When the episode is brief, there is insufficient time for appraisal as well as poor memory encoding. These conditions foster misinterpretation, especially during states of cognitive impairment, psychologic conflict, and high need or drive.

Causes of Impairment

The impairment in information processing alluded to earlier could occur under a variety of circumstances. As mentioned previously, translation into word representations is probably important to many kinds of logical appraisal. For such appraisal, the lexical system requires sequential organizational capacities. These capacities are among the first cognitive processes to be disrupted during impaired brain function.[7] An episode of image experience that was easier to process in a state of "higher" functional capacity would be harder to process in a state in which sequential organization, or the lexical system in general, was operating at reduced capacity. A "lit-up" image system and a "tuned-down" lexical system could result in more images than could be processed for meaning and hence contribute "strangeness" to the experiences.

Defensive maneuvers may interfere with processing, even when adequate capacity exists in terms of biologic substrates. That is, one way that defense mechanisms may operate is by controlling information transformation at the interfaces between representational systems, as discussed in Chapters 5 and 7. These defensive operations may interfere with "ideal" cross-modal translation of information and the sequential matchings and appraisals necessary to establish complete integration with already ordered information.

The result is the conceptual isolation of some representations in the image system, as mentioned earlier. This sort of isolation lends a strange, alien, unwelcome, and even "out-there" quality to the episode of image experience. Controls operating at the boundary of the transformation of internal codings into images may contribute to the "strangeness" of the image.

The strangeness of an initial image may be maintained in the phases of appraisal *after* the initial image episode, phases that may relate to a memory of the image episode, which is itself subject to continuous revision. This kind of information processing follows certain rules or plans. One set of rules corresponds to the reality principle, particularly to the differentiation of reality from fantasy. But what is most adaptational may be to discard ordinary rules and accept fabrications as if they were real. In conditions such as states of intense need, the reality principle would be derailed in favor of the pleasure principle.[3] Such derailment would contribute to the acceptance of image experiences as if they were real. Restitutional hallucinations in schizophrenia might be a case in point.[1]

One point needs further elaboration. As the baseline image episode occurs and as the appraisal processes continue over time, the attempts at appraisal may involve matchings with a *memory* of the baseline image experience rather than the baseline image itself. Loss of sequential short-term memory, as in many states induced by mind-altering drugs and other altered states of consciousness, leads to poor reconstructive capacity. This inability to reconceptualize may contribute to erroneous retrospective appraisals, and thus to mislabeling an internal event as a perception. The following example illustrates this phenomenon.[4] It is a reconstruction of a hashish-induced image as experienced by a man at different moments in time. The image experienced was of the hand of a woman companion reaching to touch his face.

> *Moment 1.* The man is relaxed and random thoughts about his companion enter awareness. He would like to be touched, and he has a visual thought image of her hand touching his face. This baseline image is more lucid or clear than his ordinary visual thought images but not "hallucinatory" in quality.
>
> *Moments 2 and 3.* His thought moves to other topics.
>
> *Moment 4.* He tries to recall what has been happening over Moments 1 to 3. He remembers and reproduces an image of the hand touching his face. He cannot recall whether it just happened, because he has lost memory for the sequence of mental contents from Moments 1, 2, and 3. If he were touched, what happened before and after? If not, what fantasy was he having before and after what thoughts? Because he cannot reconstruct sequences (a drug-induced impairment of short-term memory), he also cannot recall whether the image he *now* reexperiences was *then* (at baseline) a perceptual or conceptual image.
>
> As he reviews his memory now in Moment 4, it seems to him that the baseline image was experienced as a perception rather than as a thought. *He has developed, then, what could be called a retrospective hallucination.* The baseline image during Moment 1 was *not* hallucinatory, but is now, in Moment 4, appraised erroneously as a real past happening. If he believed in the real occurrence of the episode and told his companion in Moment 5, she might label his experience a hallucination. This revision of belief might of course go on. In Moment 6, he could use her new information and reappraise the memory on the baseline image as a fantasy.

A nonbizarre image was deliberately used as illustration to make the point that impaired cognitive appraisal—in this instance loss of sequential short-term memory, hence poor reconstructive capacity—may contribute "hallucinatory" quality to an experience.

Suppose the image is bizarre. In the rechecking of Moments 4 and 5, a "normal-minded" subject might "reality-test." If the image were a blue dragon, he might conclude that the experience was unreal on the grounds that he has no evidence for the existence of blue dragons and he has heard that persons have weird images on drugs. But suppose he is in a paranoid state and has a delusional system that requires belief in the existence of blue dragons to maintain internal consistency. He will more likely accept the idea of the image episode as real. Thus aspects of hallucinatory quality are determined by the nature of information processing after the episode of awareness has occurred.

INTRUSION INTO CONSCIOUS AWARENESS

The preceding section included discussion of defensive *overcontrol* that might so impede cognitive appraisal of images as to leave them strangely isolated from other concepts. This section describes *undercontrol* that results in intrusive image experiences. The unplanned emergence of images also contributes a sense of their estrangement from thought-like domains of meaning and gives them a quasi-perceptual quality. As described in detail in Chapter 7, the following three instances are predominant: (1) unbidden images occurring as sequels to stressful perceptions, (2) unbidden images occurring as eruptive representations of usually warded-off ideas and feelings, and (3) unbidden images occurring as the result of defensive operations aimed at transformation of affective states.

Whenever a stress-related content proceeds from coding in active memory to image representation, cognitive appraisal will be resumed, although the current image is incongruent with enduring concepts (in a qualitative or quantitative sense—otherwise it would not be stressful). Emotional responses occur in reaction to the discrepancy between current meanings and schematic memories of attitudes, and these emotional responses are themselves represented. Intolerable levels of guilt, shame, and fear may occur. The threat of unbearable emotional responses motivates inhibition of transfer of the information from active memory to experienced representations.[5]

As Klein[6] has reconceptualized, such repression wards off but also preserves memories in original form. The cognitive process remains incomplete. The repressed memory retains the potential for activity and may return to consciousness with any stimulus or shift of the impulse-defense configuration in favor of impulse. The result would be an unexpected episode of the warded-off images. This intrusion might then become a hallucinatory experience, depending on other factors already discussed, such as the kind of cognitive appraisal of the episode, the intensity of the images, the degree of shift in representational mode, the labeling tendencies, and the degree of general disorganization in the regulation of thought.

There are many other determinants of psychologic function, such as tendencies to reduce threat by denial, projection, or externalization and tendencies toward self-punishment by repetitious reminders of personal guilt. These tendencies, which are too complex for full discussion here, contribute an "alien" or "not-of-the-self" quality to such images and thus lend a quasi-perceptual or "out-there" quality to either the image experiences or subsequent interpretation and description.

Intrusive images can also be eruptive representations of usually warded-off ideas and feelings without external stress events as precursors. The emergence of threatening, conflicted ideas and feelings can be conceptualized as an internal stress event. An analogy to the active memory hypothesis outlined earlier would be the following: Ordinarily, inactive memories or fantasies are activated by current motivational states, resulting in a baseline image experience. This representation and the processing that it initiates activate strong, unpleasant emotional responses. To avoid a continuation of or an increase in emotional disruptions, emergent representations are inhibited. As these inhibitions weaken relative to motives for representation, intense unbidden images recur, leading to effects similar to those described earlier.

Another example of the internal origin of the "stress event image" is the flashback phenomenon as described in the preceding chapter. During a hallucinatory experience evoked by drugs such as LSD, symbolic images of great personal impact may emerge and may have stressful implications that are impossible to process at the time. These images may be stored in active memory and have an impulsive tendency toward repeated representation; each episode would then have the intrusive quality under discussion. The drug-induced state may also lead to prolonged reduction of functional inhibition of internal inputs to image formation.

As any form of thought, hallucinations may directly or symbolically represent current emotional states. A person who is fearful of others may hallucinate monsters or attackers. A person fearful of himself may concretize vague ideas of disintegration into fragmented or diseased body images. A person who feels guilty or ashamed may hallucinate accusatory voices or faces; an angry person will tend to hallucinate destructive scenes. But, as other kinds of thought, hallucination formation may occur not only to express an emotional state but also to alter one. A bereaved and despairing person may try to relieve sadness by hallucinating the deceased relative.

Perhaps the most interesting episodes of hallucination to alter affective states occur in persons who are threatened by loss of control over their own destructive rage. At times such persons seem to hallucinate not only destructive themes but also images that tend to generate feelings of guilt or fear. It appears that activation of these affects can reciprocally inhibit anger. The fear-generating image (such as an accusatory face or monster, or a prior traumatic perception) will enter awareness intrusively because the processes and purposes of its formation are not conscious. In addition, the affect reversal is "aided" if reflective self-awareness is set aside and the image is regarded as being really perceptual.

Thus various types of relative undercontrol of internal input to image-forming systems may lead to sudden intrusive experiences. This *relative* undercontrol may be secondary to the motivational power of active memory, warded-off ideas, or a need to transform affective states. It may be due to a deficiency of self-regulatory capacity in general or at the moment because of regression. These would be psychologic factors. Relative undercontrol can also be a loss of biologic regulatory capacity leading to a release of usually inhibited visual systems.[12,13] Psychologic factors alone are seldom sufficient to yield an image experience of perceptual quality during a state of fully alert, waking, rational, problem-solving thought. The addition of an altered biologic state, as in the altered states of consciousness described in Chapter 3, is often necessary for the advance from pseudohallucinatory to hallucinatory experience.

CONCLUSION

Four constructs combine to form the holistic experience sometimes labeled as hallucination. The analysis of each construct as a dimension of the cognitive process provides a model of hallucination formation. The first construct, activation of image representation, was discussed in terms of isolation of information in this mode from other modes of representation. The second construct, internal input into the image system of representation, was illustrated by the elaboration of a perceptual nidus into forms determined by wishes and fears.

The third construct, impaired information processing, probably accounts for experiencing or labeling some quite dim and fleeting images as hallucinations. States of general cognitive impairment, high conflict, stress, or need for fantasy gratification will increase the likelihood of such episodes. Disruption in short-term memory can lead to a retrospective hallucination, that is, a misjudgment about a remembered image. The fourth construct involves sudden lapses in control over internal input-to-image systems. These lapses occur after stressful perceptions, when warded-off ideas and feelings gain eruptive intensity, when motivated by defensive operations aimed at transformation of emotional states, or they may be due to a variety of physiologic factors. The resulting episodes of experience seem unrelated to the immediate context of ongoing thought. Such impairments in regulatory function lend an intrusive quality to an experience, and this contributes to labeling an image as hallucinatory.

Hallucinations are a final common pathway entered because of various determinants. By variation of the four constructs described, one could evolve the myriad forms of hallucinatory experience that add to the awesome range of human consciousness. Psychotherapy and, when indicated, chemotherapy should be directed at modifying these underlying determinants. Understanding the formative process is a precursor to the highly individualized approaches that would be involved.

REFERENCES

1. Arlow J, Brenner C: Psychoanalytic Concepts and the Structural Theory. New York, International Univ Press, 1964
2. Arnheim R: Visual Thinking. London, Farber, 1969
3. Freud S: Formulations on the two principles of mental functioning. Stand Ed 12, 1958
4. Horowitz MJ: Hallucinations: an information processing approach. In Siegel RK, West LJ (eds): Hallucinations: Behavior, Experience, and Theory. New York, Wiley, 1975
5. ———: Stress Response Syndromes. New York, Aronson, 1976
6. Klein GS: Peremptory ideation: structure and force in motivated ideas. Psychol Issues 5:80, 1967
7. Luria AR: Higher Cortical Functions in Man. New York, Basic, 1966
8. McKellar P: Imagination and Thinking. New York, Basic, 1957
9. Neisser U: Cognitive Psychology. New York, Appleton, 1967
10. Sarbin TR, Juhasz JB: The social context of hallucinations. In Siegel RK,

West LJ (eds): Hallucinations: Behavior, Experience, and Theory. New York, Wiley, 1975

11. Tomkins S: Affect, Imagery, and Consciousness. New York, Sprirger, 1962
12. West LJ: A general theory of hallucinations and dreams. In West LJ (ed): Hallucinations. New York, Grune & Stratton, 1962
13. West LJ: A clinical and theoretical overview of hallucinatory phenomena. In Siegel RK, West LJ (eds): Hallucinations: Behavior, Experience, and Theory. New York, Wiley, 1975

Part IV

The Use of Images in Psychotherapy

13

ART THERAPY

Painting or drawing furthers expression of emotional ideas by allowing participation of the motor and perceptual systems. The construction of an external picture modifies the internal image; the external picture may stimulate further internal image formation which is then used to elaborate the external picture.

Some patients communicate graphically better than verbally. A mute person may draw or paint, incoherent patients may make understandable pictures. A patient who does not respond to words may acknowledge a picture drawn by a therapist. Thus, graphic productions may offer a meaningful alternative to distrusted verbal interactions.

Some concepts are poorly labeled with words and yet may be well depicted graphically. Take for example the body image. Sometimes a drawing of a person's body may convey to the observer an impression that is hard to describe in words, either by the patient or the observer—note the eerie effect of Figure 13-1. The same patient on the same day also made the drawing in Figure 13-2. While the style is different, both figures have a floating and unstable quality characterizing this patient's bizarre and unstable self-representation.

GRAPHIC PRODUCTIONS

While pictures can be useful tools for the communication of internal images, they do not necessarily depict such images accurately. Several filtering processes distort or elaborate the experience between image

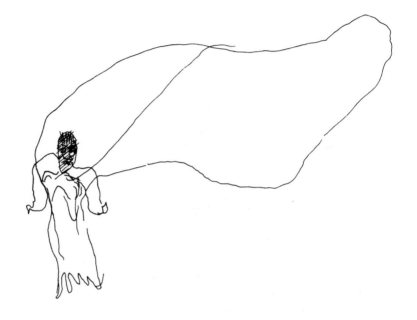

Fig. 13-1. A person drawn by a schizophrenic man.

Fig. 13-2. Another person drawn by the same patient that drew Figure 13-1.

formation and graphic production. As Gombrich[13] notes, drawing skills require not only accurate perception but also the acquisition of conventional graphic schemata. Thus, many persons draw not the flower they see but the one they were taught to draw by their kindergarten teacher: a stalk, a blob, two leaves.

In addition to the requirement of graphic schemata, a person must be able to use his hand and eye to make the representation. An alcoholic trying to draw his hallucinatory experience may have learned enough drawing schemata to produce his image yet make a drawing far from his intention because of his trembling hands.

Figure 13-3 shows the minimal complexity of processes required to produce a drawing of an image. Motivation is included as an important

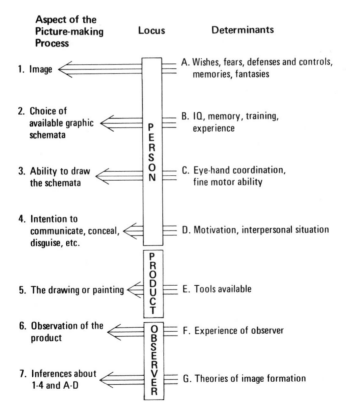

Fig. 13-3.   Minimal complexity of process required to form, communicate, and interpret a graphic production.

factor. Many persons are reluctant to draw because they anticipate ridicule. They defend themselves by resorting to stereotypes as shown in Figure 13-4. Because of wide variation in filter processes, graphic productions are useful in the hands of experienced clinicians who interpret them in the light of other information about the patient. On the other hand, in research studies where only judgments of the graphic productions are made, the results are often unreliable. A prime example is the figure-

Fig. 13-4. Stereotypes used defensively in compliance with a request to draw.

drawing or draw-a-person test, which has generated a large literature of advocates and critics.[32,35]

PSYCHOTIC ART*

Before modern psychiatric hospitals were available, some patients made pictures on their walls with food, blood, or feces. More advanced institutions supplied patients with proper materials. The superintendents of these early asylums collected the resultant art works as curios and sometimes studied them in search of clues to the nature of the mental disorder. More recently, efforts have been made to see if psychotic persons produce consistently different forms or contents than do normal persons. In terms of diagnostic use, other than deepened understanding of a single individual or separation of large groups, the results are disappointing.

Expert judges can sometimes reliably separate drawings by schizophrenic persons from drawings or paintings by normal persons.[1-5,9,24] But there are too many false positives and negatives: some schizophrenic drawings appear normal, some normal drawings contain elements common in schizophrenic drawings.[10,11,15,16]

Form

Persons undergoing a schizophrenic episode usually behave with greater variation than normal persons. While they are more impulsive, they are also more inhibited. This general tendency is reflected in their graphic productions.

Impulsive modes of production are revealed in harsh angular lines, scribbling, marking over, abrupt erasures, violent color combinations, and disregard for the conventional use of materials. Usually, impulsiveness in drawing or painting correlates with impulsiveness in general behavior or speech. Sometimes, however, a patient may be subdued in all other respects and only permit intense displays of emotional ideas in painting or drawing. Occasionally, pictures may be a useful barometer and this is one advantage of obtaining and retaining a series of graphic productions.[30] For example,

---

* The reader interested in the psychology of creative art is advised to consult Kris,[23] Arnheim,[8] Gombrich,[13] or Freud.[12] Kiell[21] provides a bibliography of over 7,000 citations on the psychology of art, esthetics, and psychopathology and art. Corman et al,[11] Caligor,[10] and Horowitz[15,16] have provided information on the genesis of images in series using graphic products.

Fig. 13-5.   This drawing preceded a violent episode. Note the overdrawing of the "M" in harm.

Figure 13-5 was done by a patient during a period in which he was overtly quiet on a psychiatric ward. Internally, there was build-up of paranoid rage, and an episode of violent behavior occurred the next day.

At the other end of the spectrum, overorganization and elaboration are also frequent in the graphic productions of schizophrenics. Sometimes, intricate filigrees are produced as shown in Figures 13-6 and 13-7. A psychotic woman painted her initials very carefully with many tiny lines in Figure 13-6. On the same day, she did the figure shown in Figure 13-7, which also is based on her initials. The elaboration is so great that they would be unrecognizable without the previous graphic production. The "E" has collapsed and, as if in restitution, it is ornamentalized endlessly. The reader is reminded again of the nonspecific quality of such over-elaboration: many a doodler fills telephone pads with similar drawings.

Content

Bizarre contents characterize many drawings by schizophrenics. Occasionally, the contents of hallucinatory experiences are depicted.[18] In

Fig. 13-6. First painting during a psychotic episode. The patient depicted her initials clearly.

Fig. 13-7. Second painting during a psychotic episode. The patient has disguised and elaborated her initials. They are at once collapsed and ornamentalized.

schizophrenic episodes there seems to be a special tendency to decompose or distort the body.[6] Drawings may contain anatomic deformities, transparencies, impossible positions, fragmentations, and depictions of sexual or aggressive assault to humans, animals, or things. Scenes of desolation and loneliness also appear (as they do commonly in depressive illnesses). Figures 13-8 through 13-13 show an image sequence from a young schizophrenic man. Each picture was elaborated from 6 blank sheets of paper containing a central dot as an image evocation device.[15] The dot is located by an arrow in the illustration. The series depicts story-like content. Relationship with a girl is threatening, the male face changes from happy to unhappy in Figure 13-8. The mouth has both expressions in Figure 13-9— the girl, although she looks coquettish in the drawing, is turned away from

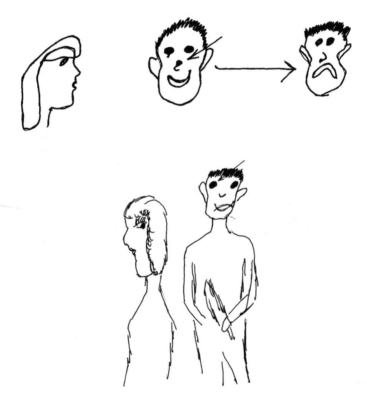

Fig. 13-8 (top) and 13-9 (bottom).   The first two drawings from a series done by a schizophrenic patient.

Fig. 13-10 (upper left), 13-11 (upper right), 13-12 (lower left), and 13-13 (lower right). The third to the sixth picture of the series begun in Figure 13-8.

his sexual arousal. The next four drawings show permutations of the idea of harsh or dangerous women. Figure 13-10 is an evil-looking woman drawn with very hard and angular lines. Figures 13-11 and 13-12, his fourth and fifth drawings of the series, are less evil looking, but there are still aggressive aspects in the harshness of the hair lines and possibly the mouth (Fig. 13-12). In Figure 13-13 the face is drawn violently with scribbling and hard lines.

Themes of disintegration are common in schizophrenic graphic productions, but it is important to note the frequency of an opposing content: themes of reconstruction and integration. They may consist of inscription of the alphabet, the series of numerals, all the states of the union, addresses, names, or mathematical figures. Of larger proportion, entire cosmologies may be drawn, or systems involving religious figures, metaphysical symbols, or fantastic machines. I believe these all may be grouped as symbolic efforts at integration, control, organization, and reconstitution of the self. Figure 13-14 may combine both disintegrative and reconstructive aspects in simple form: the human figure has a detached and bizarrely constructed penis and testis. Note also the asymmetry between right and left limbs. Various abstract symbols are added: a cylinder, a square, a plus, and the sign for infinity. It seems likely these symbols are added to give a feeling of definitiveness and labeling, a sense of mastery as when one first learned the multiplication table or how to draw a square in school.

The extreme variation in form and content, from impulsivity and disaster to control and reconstruction, may reflect the psychologic struggle of a person in the midst of a schizophrenic psychosis. At the onset of the break with reality, the person is dimly aware of, and alarmed about, the dissolution of his mental capacities. To express this sense of psychologic disintegration he may use concrete symbols such as the body. Instead of thinking "my mind is coming apart," the person may draw his body, or the world, coming apart. Such drawings may represent subjective feelings, hypochondriac delusions, or bodily hallucinations. The danger may be projected outward onto other persons or things which are shown in states of destruction. These destructive themes may also be motivated by intense and primitive hostile impulses that are poorly controlled.

In a similar manner, the feeling of despair and isolation leads to pictures such as lonely broken trees in desolated landscapes or figures lost in space. Again, such themes occur at some time in the lives of all persons. Every amateur picture gallery will show paintings of the lonely tree (perhaps at sunset on a lonely mountain) and the sad clown who makes everyone else laugh while his heart is breaking.

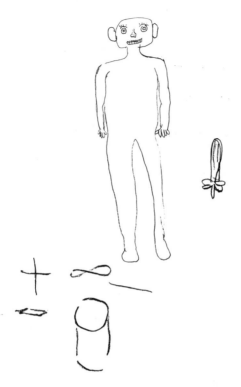

Fig. 13-14.   A picture combining bodily fragmentation—separation of the penis
—with abstract symbols. The symbols may serve as a pseudoexplanation for the
loss.

The response to feelings of coming apart, to fears of destroying the
world because of primitive inner rage, and to despair is to attempt
reparation or restitution.[7,34] This restitutional desire leads to the creative
strivings in psychosis and couples with efforts to control impulses. The
result is the spiritual, metaphysical, idealized contents and the careful,
overdrawn, and excessively ornamental forms. In the process of drawing
curlicues everywhere in a picture, a person may gain feelings of organization and productivity that counteract his dread of chaos. The metaphysical
symbols serve to heal the world a patient feels he menaces with his
destructive impulses. Symbolically, the careful construction makes his own
body and ideational structure intact and secure.

ART THERAPY

Early in the development of psychoanalytic psychotherapy the reliving of traumatic experiences and intense expression of feelings (abreaction and catharsis) were regarded as powerful ingredients of therapy. Art therapy began as an effort to provide an avenue of such discharge and expression.

The use of art therapy in the United States was pioneered by Margaret Naumberg.[25-27] She encouraged the patient to paint at home and in her office and regarded the pictorial productions as equivalent to the free associative method of psychoanalytic treatment. The trusting relationship with the therapist, the development of expressive clarity, the interpretation of the meaning of symbols, and the working through of troubled emotions and painful memories were regarded as the therapeutic agents (see also Stern[31] and Pickford[29]).

Other art therapists, such as Elinor Ulman,[33] focused on art therapy as a means of fostering growth and maturation. The effort to produce clear pictorial symbols was believed to help the patient gain a sense of identity, self-esteem, esthetic pleasure, and creativity.

In adults, as in children,[20,22,28] art therapy may also foster a sense of mastery and control. To some extent, impulses, unclear but dreaded urges, and disquieting fears can be tamed by actively drawing or painting them.

Most art therapists encourage patients to use various modes of graphic depiction. They may suggest what medium to use, what subject matter to attempt, or give advice on technique. Art therapists more experienced in psychodynamics and trained in psychotherapy may encourage associations and offer interpretive remarks that seek to clarify further the meaning of the patient's expressions.

Interaction Painting and Drawing

Sometimes it may be of value to communicate with a patient in the same graphic mode of expression. Early in my psychiatric career I attempted such interaction with two series of patients with chronic catatonic forms of schizophrenic disorders.[19] The patient and I usually sat side by side and used the same media, either paints or felt-tipped pens or pencils. I encouraged the patient to begin, then tried to respond. Most of the time we took turns, sometimes we both worked at once. When we finished the activity, we discussed the productions or separated until the next session. These sessions lasted 15 to 30 minutes and were generally repeated three to five times each week.

One example of this technique was included in Chapter 8 (Mary). Here is another.

The patient, a late adolescent male, was originally placed in a psychiatric inpatient treatment unit because of bizarre behavior, seeming disintegration of thought processes, preoccupation with his body, and withdrawal from his usual activities and interpersonal relations. Once on the ward he was unable to speak coherently, avoided the gaze of other persons, and turned his body away from them when approached. Periodically he stared at the ceiling or wall and moved his lips wordlessly—we wondered if he was hallucinating, but he was so verbally unresponsive that we could not tell. Interviews with his family indicated that periodically he had been verbally abusive and had kicked furniture; what he said at such times was unclear as his speech was incoherent or severely fragmented into unrelated phrases. He did not speak in group meetings or in individual interviews. When spoken to he sometimes looked up and stared for a long time at the other person with a suspicious and sour expression. On occasion he would say yes or no or make a tangential statement, usually with reference to the diseased state of his body.

At this point verbal communication was a one-way channel, and we were uncertain even as to the clarity of his reception of what was said to him. He did not reply. Even his nonverbal communications were reduced; he maintained a wooden face and a rigid, protective, and withdrawn type of posture. He made few gestures. Staff received the message that he wished to keep his distance from us and, if we were to get close, that he wished to repel us. We knew little else about what went on in his mind and, since this was not a satisfactory situation for therapeutic interventions, since neither milieu nor drugs seemed to be altering the picture, another form of communication was attempted. Instead of words, visual symbols, colors, and lines were used. The patient was asked to sit down and paint with me.

At first it seemed that this, too, would fail to establish a network of give-and-take communications. With a certain forcefulness of approach, on my part, he was willing to enter the office, but sitting side by side was apparently too threatening for him. He sat at another table and watched me paint. I made a few abstract dabbings of colors. He watched with apparent interest when my gaze was on what I was doing, and looked away when I glanced at him.

We did this for two sessions. On the third he was willing to paint too—although separately from me. He used only a corner of the painting paper, at times ignoring the boundary and extending a line onto the desk top. After some time at this level of activity he let me approach closer to him, and we began to paint on the same panel. He painted on his side of the paper, and I got the message that I was to paint on my side. Generally, he copied what I did, but whenever he added something different I copied that.

This developed into a kind of game. The feeling of cooperating was my main indicator; I tried anything that maintained contact between us and avoided things that increased his apparent tension or withdrawal. From an esthetic point of view our paintings were nothing to look at—just lines and dots of color at two sides of the paper.

After this had gone on for awhile and I thought I had his confidence—at least a little bit of trust—I allowed one of my lines to advance into what had become his territory. He withdrew his hand from that area. By now we were painting in sequence one after the other. At this point he stopped. But the next day his first stroke was a heavy black line down the middle of the paper. For a few sessions I resumed painting on "my" side, but as soon as it seemed permissible I painted something adjacent to his last effort. He added a series of dashes surrounding it as if it were a foreign body, and this began a new kind of game. He painted in my half of the paper, I approached it, then he jumped back to his side. If I followed, he circled my line. At times he got so involved that he grunted or laughed. Occasionally I tried verbal communication: "That was interesting," and at times he answered, "Yes."

In the next phase we were building up complex abstract structures of shape and color. We worked together and even talked a little bit before and after. When he seemed comfortable with this activity, I took an opportunity to paint over an area that he had done. He was shocked and stopped, peering at me suspiciously. I smiled a little and nodded. I hoped this communicated that he was to go on. He did and painted over something I had done. He looked at me intently. I went on painting. Then he demolished parts of the construction with great gusto. I made no verbal interpretations.

In subsequent phases we made stick figures. I started this and he copied. In time we began talking more, and eventually he was able to tell me some of his current concerns.

I have presented this illustration because the communicative process clearly proceeds in graphic form with minimal content. The paintings were composed of areas of color with various shapes, primarily just dots and lines. They became more complex and appeared to be more integrated when the patient and I began working together. Florid content and bizarre symbols were not present. What was recorded in the series of pictures was the working through of an early phase in a therapeutic relationship. What was communicated was interpersonal intentions: I intended to work with him, to avoid threat situations, but to push against his withdrawal. I tried to indicate I was trustworthy. He tested me and then gradually expressed some of the feelings he had so tightly inhibited.

Of course, in many other patients this kind of work takes place using recognizable graphic forms, especially depictions of human figures in various types of relationships. In such instances the therapist and the patient gradually progress through phases. The first phase almost invariably seems to be a testing phase.

Testing Phase

During this phase the communication networks of territory, time, symbols, and modes are used guardedly until they are anxiety free and successful in transmitting messages. My efforts center around demonstrating the possibilities, encouraging the patient to be free in his expression, and establishing interaction. During initial encounters many patients resist interaction. At first they prefer to paint independently; then they may copy or tolerate being copied. Later, play and cooperative interactions emerge.

During the testing phase, spatial considerations are also important as indicated in the foregoing example by the patient's reluctance to sit at the same table with the therapist and also his concern for territories during the joint efforts. Interpersonal distances that seem natural and comfortable for the therapist may seem threateningly close to some schizophrenic patients: this spatial sensitivity applies both to interpersonal distance and to the use of space on the drawing or painting. Therapists should be alert to this spatial aspect of nonverbal behavior, and avoid infringing prematurely on the patient's "body-buffer zone."[14,17]

Expressive Phase

Establishing a safe relationship with another human being protects patients from their conflicts and troubled feelings to the extent that they allow themselves a greater range of expression. The expressive phase varies from patient to patient. The patterns that emerge in a series of paintings with any one patient are naturally related to my reactions and interventions as well as to the patient's psychologic and psychopathologic characteristics. Nevertheless, each patient often develops a characteristic theme that emerges in a series of pictures related to his life style, conflicts, or clinical state. Some patients paint symbolic reparations of lost objects. Some draw their fears or traumas. Others concentrate more on the relationship with the therapist.

Phase of Therapeutic Interventions

When the therapist has sufficient insight into the problems of the patient, he may attempt to help the patient clarify his expression. This may involve confrontation with the patient's defensive operations. For example, a patient may block his own expression by repetition of just a few symbols. The therapist may attempt to develop the range of available symbols by drawing different elements. Here is one illustration.

In a series of interaction paintings, a young adolescent patient had gradually increased his openness so that he and the therapist now mutually executed pictures. Landscapes were the repetitive theme. These landscapes consisted of green meadows, trees, blue skies, the sun, and mountains. The patient showed no indication to express anything further. The therapist began to introduce animals into the pictures. At first the patient merely watched the therapist's activities. After a while he also drew animals. When the patient was comfortable with this, the therapist began to add human figures. The patient seemed uneasy. Then he drew in not a single figure but an army complete with spears, bows and arrows, and machine guns. A series of "fighting" pictures developed: airplanes were shot down in flames, tanks and ships were blown up, people were killed. The patient seemed alternately uneasy and excited about these pictures, but gradually seemed to experience a sense of control over his hostile impulses. Only then did he begin to discuss his intense rage toward his parents.

Therapeutic interventions in art therapy are not very different from those in conventional verbal psychotherapy. The therapist tries to understand the current situation. In general he tries to work on the surface first and to avoid excessively "deep" interpretive thrusts. He seeks to effect a more effective and adaptive use of the patient's control and defense capacity. When he thinks the patient can tolerate it, he may encourage him to consider troublesome topics. Suggestions for adaptive attitudes toward other people and work functions may then be made. In art therapy he can introduce these topics gradually through pictorial symbols. Some of the methods for guiding image formation, to be discussed in the next chapter, will clarify the other options of the art therapist.

CONCLUSION

Drawings or paintings offer to the therapist a wide range of useful information for clinical interpretation. The information contained in graphic productions has a different mode of communication and representation than the face-to-face verbal interview. Contents may be expressed in pictures that go unmentioned verbally.

The patient may record his ideas and feelings while alone or in a group with other patients. He does not have to be there when the communication is "received." This indirectness of communication may allow increased message sending in patients who are regressed, withdrawn, frightened, or overly aroused during contact. It is possible to use art therapy in a great number of interpersonal settings ranging from a kind of meditative self-communicative process, while alone, to the interaction drawing or painting described in the latter half of the chapter. The method seems especially useful in mute, withdrawn, or very blocked patients.

REFERENCES

1. Anastasi A, Foley J: An analysis of spontaneous artistic productions by the abnormal. J Gen Psychol 28:297, 1943
2. ———, Foley J: An experimental study of the drawing behavior of adult psychotics in comparison with that of a normal control group. J Exp Psychol 34:169, 1944
3. ———, Foley J: A survey of literature on artistic behavior in the abnormal. I. Historical and theoretical background. J Gen Psychol 25:111, 1941; II. Approaches and interrelationships. Ann NY Acad Sci 42:1, 1941
4. ———, Foley J: A survey of literature on artistic behavior in the abnormal. IV. Experimental investigations. J Gen Psychol 25:187, 1941
5. ———, Foley J: A survey of literature on artistic behavior in the abnormal. III. Spontaneous productions. Psychol Monogr 52(6), 1940
6. Arieti S: Interpretation of Schizophrenia. New York, Brunner, 1955
7. Arlow J, Brenner C: Psychoanalytic Concepts and the Structural Theory. New York, International Univ Press, 1964
8. Arnheim R: Toward a Psychology of Art. Los Angeles, Univ California Press, 1966
9. Burton A, Sjöberg B: The diagnostic validity of human figure drawings in schizophrenia. J Psychol 57:3, 1964
10. Caligor L: A New Approach to Figure Drawing. Springfield, Ill, Thomas, 1957
11. Corman HH, et al: Visual imagery and preconscious thought processes. Arch Gen Psychiat 10:160, 1964
12. Freud S: Leonardo Da Vinci and a memory of his childhood. Stand Ed 11, 1962
13. Gombrich EH: Art and Illusion: A Study in the Psychology of Pictorial Representation. New York, Pantheon, 1969
14. Horowitz MJ: Spatial behavior and psychopathology. J Nerv Ment Dis 164:24, 1968
15. ———: Visual imagery: an experimental study of pictorial cognition using the dot-image sequence. J Nerv Ment Dis 141:615, 1966
16. ———: Notes on art therapy media and techniques. Bull Art Ther 4:70, 1965
17. ———: Body-buffer zone. Arch Gen Psychiat 11:651, 1964

18. ———: The imagery of visual hallucinations. J Nerv Ment Dis 138:513, 1964
19. ———: Graphic communication: a study of interaction painting with schizophrenics. Amer J Psychother 17:230, 1963
20. Kellog R: Understanding children's art. Psychol Today 1(1):16, 1967
21. Kiell N: Psychiatry and Psychology in the Visual Arts and Aesthetics. Madison, Univ Wisconsin Press, 1965
22. Kramer E: Art therapy and the severely disturbed gifted child. Bull Art Ther 3:3, 1965
23. Kris E: Psychoanalytic Explorations in Art. New York, International Univ Press, 1965
24. Levy B, Ulman E: Judging psychopathology from paintings. J Abnorm Psychol 72:182, 1967
25. Naumberg M: Dynamically Oriented Art Therapy: Its Principle and Practice. New York, Grune & Stratton, 1966
26. ———: Psychoneurotic Art: Its Function in Psychotherapy. New York, Grune & Stratton, 1953
27. ———: Schizophrenic Art: Its Meaning in Psychotherapy. New York, Grune & Stratton, 1950
28. ———: Studies of the "free" art expression of behavior problem children and adolescents as a means of diagnosis and therapy. J Nerv Ment Dis Monogr 71, 1947
29. Pickford RW: Studies in Psychiatric Art. Springfield, Ill, Thomas, 1967
30. Plokker JH: Art From the Mentally Disturbed. Boston, Little, Brown, 1965
31. Stern M: Free painting as an auxiliary technique in psychoanalysis. In Bychowski G (ed): Specialized Techniques in Psychotherapy. New York, Basic, 1952
32. Swenson CH Jr: Empirical evaluations of human figure drawings. In Murstein BI (ed): Handbook of Projective Techniques. New York, Basic, 1965
33. Ulman E: Art therapy at an outpatient clinic. Psychiatry 16:55, 1953
34. Whitmont EC: The Symbolic Quest. New York, Putman, 1969
35. Witkin HA, et al (eds): Psychological Differentiation: Studies of Development. New York, Wiley, 1962

14

VISUALIZING TECHNIQUES

Psychotherapy is communication about ideas and feelings aimed toward modification of maladaptive patterns. By his actions, the therapist influences the patient's deployment of attention as well as the themes the patient chooses to elaborate or set aside. Communication, like the modes of representation discussed in Chapter 5, takes place in lexical, image, and enactive forms. The patient is informed by the therapist of how and why each of these systems is used within the therapeutic context. This information ranges from interpretation about the patient's spontaneous use of expressive forms, to suggestions of a shift to one mode or another, and what themes to think about in given modes.

Because image formation is a means of expressive communication as well as an emotionally rich and free form of thought, it is used in nearly every kind of psychotherapy. Psychoanalysis and dynamic psychotherapies involve free association, fantasy elaboration, and dream interpretation. The latter intervention is described in the Old Testament stories on Joseph in Egypt and it was even used in the healing temples of Greek medicine, where stimuli for dreams were suggested to the sleeping patients by priests. More directive uses are found in the suggestion of themes in gestalt therapy and guided imagery techniques, and in the detailed prescription of specific image contents in behavioral and cognitive therapies.

This chapter is concerned with the aims and purposes of interventions that increase the use of image formation as compared with lexical or enactive thought and communication. It begins with a discussion of what therapists hope to accomplish when they ask patients to form and communicate image experiences, and then deals with some advantages and disadvantages of specific kinds of techniques for this purpose.

AIMS AND PURPOSES OF INTERVENTIONS

Images can be used in psychotherapy to (1) yield information, (2) establish empathic understanding, (3) evoke expression of and working through of usually warded-off themes of conflict or unintegrated themes, and (4) transform mood by modification of which attitudes are dominantly organizing current thinking, feeling, and acting.

Obtaining Useful Information for Case Formulation

Within his own mind the therapist constructs a model of the patient's inner assumptions and styles of relating to the surrounding world. Reported images are especially useful for providing the therapist with quick information about self-concepts and internalized relationship patterns. The manner or style of evolving and reporting the images provides further information on expressive capacity and defensive styles. Thus, the therapist looks at both form and content.

In evaluation sessions especially, the therapist may seek additional data by asking about dreams, fantasies, or early childhood memories (the latter are usually recalled in visual images). In addition to recollection, active image formation during the interview may yield useful impressions, as in this example.

A teenage girl with vague medical complaints was referred for psychiatric consultation. Her responses during a nondirective psychiatric interview were desultory. When specific questions were asked, she was not evasive, but still gave meager information. For example, when asked about her mother she said, "She's OK." When asked about their relationship, she said, "Pretty good." When asked to form an image of herself together with her mother, she reported a detailed image of her mother and herself in the kitchen, with her mother's face angry and yelling at her and her own face downcast and sullen.

Similarly, when asked about her father, she gave nonspecific information of a general, socially acceptable type: "He's OK, we get along so-so," et cetera. When asked for an image of herself with her father, she described herself walking down a stairway, blushing, as her father made a lewd comment about her tight sweater.

Later, when asked to form an image of her school friends, whom she had described verbally as "just a bunch of girls," she cried and said she was always left out of the group at lunchtime and stood apart, watching the laughter of the group.

In this example, the request for images released information. The effect, of course, was not solely due to the power of images to evoke emotion and information about object relationships. For this girl, discourse in words was a superficially useful social convention. Her rich inner fantasy life was contained in images. The therapist's request for images meant to her that he was interested in her inner life rather than in surface socialization. The release of information was due not only to her transition from words to images; it indicated her understanding that the therapist's interest was in developing a therapeutic rather than social alliance. His request for images meant "OK, now, let's really talk about what's on your mind." The request might not have the same meaning to a different patient, who might hear it as an invitation to a social rather than therapeutic alliance ("let's do image tricks now"), or to a transference relationship ("submit to my powerful techniques").

In diagnostic sessions, although the therapist may wish to gather maximal information, the patient may not have developed a therapeutic alliance and may wish, consciously or unconsciously, to withhold some information. Censorship over images is often less meticulous, and the patient may convey information without acknowledgment or without having to recognize officially the implications of the images. In the previous example of the patient describing the scene with her father when she wore a tight sweater, she did not have to acknowledge her feelings of excitement, shame, and anger.

Because of the lower threshold of censorship of images in some patients, the therapist may ask the patient to use image formation to learn about the deeper levels of a patient's mental life. Knapp[29] distinguishes conceptual schematizations at each of the conscious, preconscious, and unconscious levels. The easiest to distinguish is the conscious layer, which consists of the person's overt images of himself and others. Behind this is a preconscious layer, one partially emergent and partially hidden. From this fringe, or background layer, daydreams of being a super-spy or movie heroine may enter consciousness periodically, or be readily formed with volitional effort. The third layer of unconscious conceptual potentials Knapp later called the "schemactive core" to emphasize its dynamic potential in influencing the content and sequence of conscious experiences. These inferred unconscious patterns express primitive urges and fears, mythic self- and object concepts, and are estimated by pattern repetitions in reported images.

Fully conscious images usually can be translated readily into verbal metaphors. Preconscious and inferred unconscious schematizations may be approachable by description of the image contents, but the patient may remain unaware of the implications of these images.

Empathy

As a therapist listens to his patient describe the images of a dream or fantasy, the therapist may internally form an image like the one described which serves to generate empathic understanding. When a therapist is accustomed to using such images in his work and encounters a situation in which he feels blocked in responsive imaging or finds his images are not congruent with a patient's descriptions, he may suspect that empathic understanding is not present.[20] When the images of the therapist seem incongruent with experiences reported by the patient, the therapist may ask himself whether the patient is being clear, whether there is some resistance within the patient or some difficulty in the relationship, or whether the therapist is having some personal conflict or countertransference reaction.[45]

The therapist will generally scan his own images but seldom report them to the patient directly. At times, however, the therapist's internal image response may contain the kernel of an interpretation that is not only correct but phrased with a useful degree of simple, concrete clarity. Sometimes this concrete metaphoric or symbolic casting of information is more convincing to the patient than an abstract generalization.

Expression and Working Through

Image formation is closely linked with emotion. This linkage has been dissolved in some people, and images are produced without associated feeling. Generally, however, image formation may propel a patient toward expression of previously restrained emotions.

Once conflicted feelings are clearly labeled and expressed, the useful tool of rational thought is available for resolving as much of the conflict as possible, and for accepting realistic limitations. Unfortunately, we do not have a clear map of the optimal pathways for a given personality to follow in working through conflicts, traumas, and losses. But we do recognize clinically the importance of many-faceted expression. In this way, previously vague ideas and feelings are labeled in words as well as images, and in images as well as words. When the patient has the security of clear labels, a powerful constellation of feelings and ideas can be examined and conceptually reworked. Once there is a breakdown into tolerable components, he or she can separate reality from fantasy and make new plans for action or routes of expression, or develop higher tolerance for frustration.

Isolation, intellectualization, and denial are defense mechanisms that interfere with many-faceted expression. In intellectualization, ideas emerge without continuity with other ideas and feelings. Using this defensive maneuver, some persons can contemplate a recent loss or a traumatic experience without emotion. Their numbness is not the consequence of mastery, but a defense against potentially powerful emotions or out-of-control states of mind. Because of their defenses against expression of grief or fear, such patients may repeatedly describe important experiences without any adaptive change. Sometimes a visualization of the experience, when the patient is ready to tolerate unpleasant feelings because of a therapeutic alliance, may release emotions and permit progressive change to take place.

Image formation can circumvent a defense such as denial, isolation, or repression, as in this example.

A young woman had an argument with her husband about whether he should go out late in the evening to obtain medicine recently prescribed for their sick daughter. He left angrily to do her bidding but was killed in his car in a head-on collision. She refused to believe he was dead when she was informed. She even denied his death during his funeral. She claimed the body was not his because it did not look like him: his face had been badly shattered by the accident and was reconstructed by a mortician.

She developed a delusion that she was pregnant following the accident and was afraid people would accuse her of being a whore because she had no husband. This delusion was partly restitutional: her husband lived on inside of her, and she would have the second baby she had wanted within the marriage. She had no menstrual periods, although she had negative pregnancy tests on several occasions. A gynecologist did a diagnostic procedure which showed only normal, nonpregnant uterine tissue. She then reported suicidal thoughts and was referred to a psychiatrist.

She seemed bland and flagrantly denied any depressive feelings, although she described sleeplessness and suicidal impulses. The psychiatrist prescribed an anti-anxiety agent. She took all of this medication in a suicidal effort and was admitted to a psychiatric inpatient unit.

During the drug-induced deliria, she had visual hallucinations of her husband's face talking to her, telling her to come with him "to the land of the dead." These apparitions persisted after the toxic effects of the anti-anxiety agent had worn off.

She continued to deny her husband's death and asked the psychiatric staff not to mention such unpleasant topics, because her husband would only visit her when she was not feeling depressed or planning suicide. After several days she was told firmly that her husband had died, that this was so painful to her that she was trying to ignore it, but that she would have to accept it and begin to talk about her emotional reactions. She did not acknowledge the intervention directly. Yet the next time she experienced the visual hallucination of her husband's face, according to her description, she screamed, "Go away! I'm not going with you!"

Thereafter she reported no further hallucinations but continued to deny that he was dead. She was then asked to visualize her husband as she had last seen him but burst into tears and could not describe her image. Later she drew a picture of him in his coffin (Fig. 14-1). (A flag is present because he had a military funeral.) She described the argument before the crash and her feelings that if she had not been so vehement he would have stayed home and remained alive. Her guilt, sadness, and delayed grief response to her tragic loss could then begin to be worked through in psychotherapy.

Transformation of Feelings or Attitudes

The power of images to evoke emotion may be used to alter emotional states. Indeed, the counsel of friends often takes this form: a despondent person is told to "buck up" and to imagine some pleasant time in the past or future to change his mood. The bigot, in order to diminish his biases, is told to "imagine yourself in the other person's shoes." This imagining is a kind of internal drama that allows one to experience the difficulties of others and, therefore, feel greater understanding and tolerance of their apparent shortcomings.

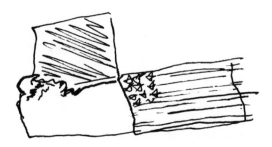

Fig. 14-1.   The acknowledgment and acceptance of loss in a patient with a delayed grief reaction.

In a similar manner, patients may imagine future courses of events on their own or following suggestion by the therapist. In psychodynamic psychotherapies this has been called "trial action." The technique was reinvented by behaviorists and cognitive therapists who call it "rehearsal." These advance planning trials may range from the worst possible outcomes, to realistic probabilities, to playing with the possibilities of very good solutions to current dilemmas. The freedom of image formation allows the "unthinkable" depiction of both the patient's most idealized hopes and most catastrophic fears.

The patient may experience negative emotions while imagining a disastrous outcome, but at the same time be appraising the actual likelihood of the results he has depicted. When fears are based on irrational expectations, this exercise may improve the patient's mood after a tolerable passage of painful feelings. Similarly, a good outcome, seen as a realistic possibility, may calm an anxious or despairing patient. These exercises of imagination may lead to alterations of defensive avoidances, based on preconscious or unconscious attitudes and hopeless appraisals, and replace the assumptions with new coping efforts, based on conscious contemplations and decisions.

As mentioned earlier, feelings may also be transformed by remembering past experiences or by daydreaming. This too may usefully take positive or negative directions. A pleasant memory or story in which a competent self-image is prominent can restore a sense of well-being or hopefulness. The purpose of evoking a painful or traumatic memory is not to experience the negative emotions, although this may be necessary in order to accomplish the aim, but to establish the continuity of the event within a life story and to revise unrealistic attitudes, such as assumptions of omnipotent responsibility.

TECHNIQUES

Singer has provided a scholarly review[50] of a variety of therapeutic techniques. There is a spectrum of approaches to altering the patient's regulation of image formation.[53] Two major aspects are the degree to which the therapist draws attention to what the patient is doing (interpretation and clarification) and the degree to which the therapist tells the patient what to do as an alternative (suggestion and redirection).

I do not think that image techniques have intrinsic curative properties. They are tools to be selected within a larger array of potential therapist actions. Choice from this array is organized by formulation of the case and consensual goals for change.

Sometimes these goals are to work through inhibitions used to avoid certain irrationally feared emotional states or interpersonal actions. Sometimes the aim is to complete a specific train of thought that has been wastefully and intrusively repetitive, to reach closure on a particular line of interpersonal transaction, or to resume a developmental line that has been arrested or distorted. There are times when the goals are to change styles of self-regulation, such as modifying habitual defensive distortions or deficits of information processing. Specific techniques are selected in relation to the patient's habitual styles of expression and defense, as described in detail elsewhere.[25,26]

The technical maneuvers now to be considered begin with the least suggestive—empathic interest and inquiry about what the patient has been experiencing—and move toward the opposite pole, where the therapist takes directive control of the themes of visual imagination.

The Shift from Lexical Ideation to Image Formation

Inquiry about images conveys to the patient that the therapist is interested in this mode. If the patient believes the therapist is expert in how to proceed, or if the patient wants to please the therapist, shifts to image formation will occur.

The therapist asks the patient to disclose subjective experiences fully. Some patients interpret this as a request to describe lexical thought, not images which may occur in a parallel system. When the therapist observes this separation of trains of thought, it is generally helpful for him to ask about imagery experiences. As noted in earlier chapters, patients vary in style of thinking; some are less aware of imagery than others. To them, such inquiry is surprising because they have not thought in terms of images or regard them as peripheral and irrelevant.

This inquiry may address different kinds of visual images in different contexts, such as daydreams, sexual intercourse fantasies, masturbation fantasies, fantasies during ruminations after insults from other persons, or good and bad dreams. Inquiries should also include attention to hallucinations, pseudohallucinations, and recurrent illusions when these are present. A complete inquiry asks after form and content; not only what is hallucinated, for example, but how and when it forms, how it changes, when it stops. The information is then related to overall states of mind, and to cycles of entry into and exit from these states.

Inquiry into images may allow patients to express ideas and feelings that they have been unable to share with others, or to reexamine them in the contemplative matrix of the therapeutic alliance. A pertinent example is found in the psychotherapy of the post-traumatic stress disorders,[25] in which a frequent symptom is unbidden images. In many evaluations of such patients it has been found that the patient will not fully express the experience and contents of such intrusive images until explicitly asked.

The meaning of the images should be explored. Some patients are afraid that unusual image experiences may mean they are losing control of their minds. Once inquiry has led to revelation of the experiences, a sense of control may be gained. This is possible in the first place because the patient has learned to label experiences for which he has not had language, and is able thus to socialize the experience by communicating it to the therapist. In addition, the patient gains from the therapist's realistic response. For example, the patient who is having repetitive intrusive images of a deceased relative may be informed that this is not an uncommon experience during bereavement, and that it may go on for some months and does not indicate an impending psychotic state, as the patient may have feared.[25]

Similar differentiations of real experiences from unreal ones may occur when patients reveal hypnagogic or hypnopompic experiences, recurrent nightmares, or sexual fantasies they regard as perverse. This is true also when image experiences occur in the context of altered biological substrates. A patient with a brain lesion or disturbed neurotransmitters may have unusually vivid imagery. He reacts to these forms and their content according to his individual psychology. Realistic explanation by the therapist of the imagery experiences and their substrates may reduce the patient's irrational interpretations of them and consequently improve his mood and coping capacities. Such explanations do require knowledge by the therapist of aspects of the biological substrates of image formation, as discussed in Chapter 9.

Relating the usually private and concealed world of imagery to the therapist tests the communicative safety of the relationship. The therapist's neutral and supportive response reduces fear of criticism and estrangement. The habitual defensive postures of the patient are revealed and modified, as the situation becomes less threatening.

Suggestion of Shift to Image Formation

In a more directive technique, the therapist may suggest that the patient allow himself to form images and to describe them. Breuer and Freud[10] used this method to explore repressed memories during a period of transition in Freud's technique from hypnosis to free association. Freud found that some patients were difficult to hypnotize and, to unravel the meaning of a hysteric symptom, he would simply ask a patient to form an image relevant to the time when the symptom first began. He enforced his request with the power of suggestion. The patient reclined on a couch, and Freud placed his hand on the patient's forehead and pressed firmly. He then told the patient that when he lifted his hand a memory would form as a visual image. The patient was instructed to report all the details of the image and the associated emotions. When associational connections were made, followed by a period of abreaction, catharsis, and interpretation, the symptoms were expected to disappear.

While contemporary psychotherapists do not customarily suggest a deliberate shift from words to image formation, they do usually pay attention to such shifts when they spontaneously occur, and an effort is made to understand the motivation for the shift and the meanings of the images. Image contents are analyzed in terms of underlying defensive motives as well as current conflicts and developmental implications.[19] Thus the therapist may be interested in (1) the reasons for use of an image at that point in treatment; (2) the sources of content in memories and fantasies; (3) the meanings represented in the images; (4) the defensive or cognitive style manifested in the sequential process; and (5) the organizational structure or pattern of the image in terms of object relations (how primitive versus how differentiated, how human versus inanimate, how close versus distant, and the characteristic role depiction of self, other, and surroundings).

Jung, in 1916,[28] developed a means of focusing on image formation that he called *active imagination*. The purpose of Jung's active imagination was to encourage a patient to get in touch with his "unconscious" and to establish a continuity between conscious and unconscious mental contents. In active imagination the therapist instructs the patient to allow a deliberate dimming of conscious mental activity and to concentrate passively on the "unconscious background to mental life." The technique involves a kind of active passivity, a setting aside of organized thought, as in free association. In this state, warded-off contents may emerge, often with intense emotion, and often in the form of visual images. Then the conscious mind again assumes control and cooperates in the analysis of the images. This may even include a colloquy in which the self as onlooker to the fantasy engages one of the fantasy characters in a dialogue.[22] Through such inner conversation, previously unconscious interpersonal fantasies can be integrated with other aspects of conceptualization of self, others, and relationships. G. Adler[3] states that the products of images produced by this Jungian technique carry a quality of inner conviction that differs subjectively from reactions to ordinary daydreams.

In such Jungian therapy, *archetypal images* tend to emerge as a consequence of active imagination: witches, devils, tempters, sorcerers, magicians, princes, heroes, wise men. According to Jung, archetypal images are ones that take similar forms in many patients because they emerge from an unconscious memory shared by all people.

I agree with the prevalence of archetypes in fantasy images, but trace this symbolic similarity to the basic patterns of the human life situation rather than to a collective unconscious. That is, these dramatic role labels are general schematizations because they depict the intrinsic properties of human nature and social bonds. For example, almost every child is raised in a family where there are dominant figures who are perceived at times to be good and at other times as bad. The child may permit himself to think dangerous thoughts about such persons by using the guise of displacement to imaginary figures, either his own or those supplied by myths and fairy tales. Thus, a bad parent may become a witch in fantasy, a powerful parent a magician, and a yearned-for ideal parent a fairy godmother. The active imagination technique, coupled with a style of interpretation that labels roles in terms of archetypes, has a propelling quality: the patient is encouraged to develop the images further and, in essence, to "lure out" all the hidden characters of a core story schematization.

Kubie[32] suggested that induced *hypnagogic reverie* might enhance image formation. He found his technique valuable with patients who had not revealed the roots of their neurosis in an analysis that seemed too prolonged. Kubie used suggestion and the Jacobson[27] method of progressive muscular relaxation to induce the reverie state, and he then asked the patient to allow and report a free and spontaneous flow of images. Kubie found that the emergent fantasies were often clearer, in terms of apparent meaning of the latent contents, than the dreams reported by the patient.

Other therapists such as Reyher[43] report the usefulness of requesting image formation within the first few interviews to discover hidden motives and memories. In a technique he calls *emergent uncovering psychotherapy*, Reyher describes a typical sequence within the psychotherapeutic situation.[44] The therapist and the patient are seated face to face. The patient talks until he runs out of topics. The therapist then instructs the patient to relax and close his eyes, and to say whatever comes to mind. Typically, the patient becomes anxious and reports sensations of psychosomatic responses. The therapist focuses on these feelings and interprets them as insecurity responses to the immediate interpersonal context.

As the patient relaxes in response to these interpretations, the therapist instructs him to form visual images in addition to the previous general association suggestion. The typical patient usually reports everyday images, followed by more idiosyncratic images, until he manifests resistance to this process. The patient will often proceed to have more psychosomatic responses or anxiety symptoms and to eventually develop images symbolic of typical conflicts. The therapist interprets these conflicts in terms of word meanings and helps the patient work out solutions to the problem.

Reyher may also employ a technique of revisualization of "hot images" —episodes that evoke emotional responses. As the patient revisualizes such episodes, he gains insight into the symptoms, images, and resistances produced. The inability to form images also indicates an area of conflict, and the therapist may try to help the patient to develop images which are then repeatedly revisualized. Such repeated revisualization, in and of itself, may serve to reduce emotional responsivity[7] and indicates to the patient that he controls his own thought processes, a universal theme throughout many types of psychotherapeutic techniques.

Sacerdote[46,47] reports a technique that he calls *induced dreams*. The patient is hypnotized and asked to dream. Sacerdote then uses free associative methods to unravel the meanings of the dreams. He attempts to interconnect a series of dreams so that each successive dream completes the understanding of a previously induced or spontaneous dream. He may also instruct a patient in a general way to dream about a current conflict or problem area. This active technique is used only with persons who are poor candidates for less directive forms of therapy.

Discussion of Inquiry and Suggestion

When the therapist inquires about or suggests increased use of image formation, he is indicating that he wishes something to happen. How the patient interprets this depends on the patient's relationship with the therapist. The patient may find multiple meanings in the intervention, using varied self-concepts and concepts of the therapist.[26,33] That is, the patient may simultaneously understand the therapist's intervention on different levels, according to the social, therapeutic, and transferential dimensions of the relationship. In what has been called the *therapeutic alliance* view of the patient-therapist relationship, the patient understands the therapist's inquiry or suggestion as one aspect of an agreement to explore and change psychopathology or immature development. In a *social alliance*, the patient understands the intervention as the opening gambit to an interesting conversation. As part of a *transference view*, the patient may regard the intervention as criticism that he was not communicating appropriately and needed correction, as a special gift to a needy child ("here, try this"), as an attempt at gaining control over his mind ("you will do as I say"), or as an exhibition by the therapist ("I am going to show off to you a powerful technique").

Image techniques, like any technical maneuver, are sometimes used by the therapist as if only a therapeutic alliance were organizing the patient's response to the therapist's intervention. These responses should be carefully observed to see how and to what degree social alliance or transference are also influencing the patient's view of the therapy situation.[26]

The therapist's efforts to increase the relative use of visualization may also be examined in terms of the direct regulation of thought by the patient. The theoretical models of image formation presented in Chapters 5 and 7 may now be used to analyze how therapy techniques operate to alter inhibitions.

The therapist does not intervene unless he thinks that the patient will benefit from thinking, feeling, and deciding something that he is unaware of or avoiding. In such techniques as suggesting a shift from the lexical to visual depiction of ideas and feelings, the therapist acts to counter inhibition used specifically, to ward off certain experiences, or habitually, as a personality characteristic.

In review of psychotherapy sessions, these actions often take two forms. One is to identify the inhibition by interpretive remarks; the other is to suggest alternative ways to regulate thinking and communication. Whether the therapist uses a more interpretive or directive approach depends upon his assessment of the state of the relationship, the climate of communication, and the propensity of the patient to make certain changes and not others. This can be understood more specifically by examining the cognitive sites of inhibition.

The five most frequent inhibitions of entry of information into the visual image system are illustrated in Figure 14-2 as follows:

1. Failure to attach word labels to images.
2. Avoidance of image associations to contents expressed in words.
3. Inattention to dim or fleeting image episodes.
4. Prevention of primary process or spontaneous flow types of image formation.
5. Nontranslation of enactive representations into imagery.

For the purpose of illustration, some densely worded interpretive and directive interventions are provided in Table 14-1.

What can be said about the differences between these techniques for the same type of inhibition? *Directive* interventions are reeducative. If the

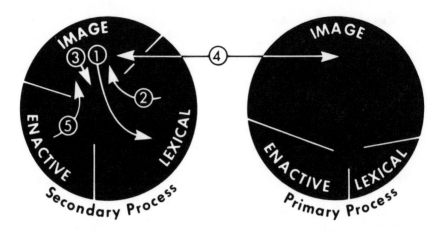

Fig. 14-2.   Illustration of sites where inhibition can affect flow of information.

assumption of a developmental lag and current deficiency in knowledge is indicated, that is, if the patient has not yet learned to make full use of various modes of thought, if inhibition has been in fact a longstanding limitation of cognitive style, then a simple directive statement may help the patient learn new ways of using thought processes.

Interpretive remarks are, of course, also covert suggestions. The patient hears such remarks with the implication that he ought to think about the focus of the interpretation and to try doing what he is told he is avoiding. But interpretive remarks give much more information and so require greater inference or knowledge on the part of the therapist. If this information is accurate and well timed, interpretations place the patient in a position of greater control. He can consciously choose to set aside the inhibitory processes activated by unconscious decisions. If he does not know how to process, however, he may be stymied unless the therapist adds more directive comments.

The transference potentials possible in intervention by direction or interpretation also influence the therapist in the choice of a technical style. Directive intervention may make some patients excessively dependent or passive, the directive acts of the therapist providing a nidus of reality for the elaboration of a transference in which the therapist is like a parent telling the patient what to do, a person he can hold responsible as he complies or stubbornly resists in an overt or covert manner. Interpretation can provide erroneous information which the patient may either

Table 14-1

Defensive Inhibitions and Related Interventions

Site of Inhibition	Interpretive Intervention	Directive Intervention
Images not associated with word meanings	"You do not let yourself describe those images you are having because you are afraid to think clearly about and tell me about those ideas."	"Describe your images to me in words." "Tell me what that image means."
Lexical representations not translated into images	"You do not let yourself think that idea visually because you are afraid of the feelings that might occur if you did."	"Let yourself think about that in pictures."
Vague images (pre-conscious) not intensified (conscious)	"You are afraid to let that fleeting image become really clear in your mind because you are afraid you will feel or act badly if you do."	"Try to hold onto those images and 'tune them up.'"
No cross-translation between secondary process and primary process images	"You are afraid to let yourself have daydreams because you are afraid you will lose control."	"Let yourself kind of dream about this right now."
Enactive representations not translated into images	"You are afraid to picture your present posture and facial expression because the self-image would shame you."	"Try to picture what you look like with that posture and expression on your face."

believe or use against the therapist. For example, if the therapist interprets a behavior as defensive when it is actually due to a lack of regulatory capacity, the incorrect interpretation will not help the patient to gain control over his thought process. Similarly, some patients may feel stymied by interpretations because they do not comprehend the covert suggestion to set aside their inhibitions and think more boldly.

In summary, any imagery technique should be considered in the context of the relationship between patient and therapist, and for its potential to effect individualized change in the patient's existing habits of controlling thought.

Drugs

Drugs have been used to alter substrates of thought and increase the relative use of image formation and primary process modes of organization. Sodium amytal has been used intravenously to reduce defenses and evoke the abreactive memory of previous traumatic experiences. These memories often emerge as visual images. Amytal was used in World War II to treat combat neurosis but has since been largely abandoned. Attention then focused on hallucinogenic drugs until their use was declared illegal.

Mescaline, peyote, and other hallucinogens have been used for centuries for ritualistic purposes. The emergence of vivid images, subjectively experienced as nonvolitional, naturally predisposed persons to consider the possibility of spiritual or transcendental causation to the images. Discovery of LSD rocketed the use of hallucinogens. While these drugs have many effects, including toxic ones, one is to change image formation. Some persons take such drugs in the hope of increasing image experiences and gaining insights. [12,38]

In view of the profound symbolic and transcendental quality of images and experiences while on hallucinogens, it is not surprising that these agents would be experimentally used for psychotherapeutic purposes. [1] The use of hallucinogens to produce images and feelings have followed two main techniques: the psychedelic and the psycholytic. [36]

In the *psychedelic technique*, a fairly high dose is given to produce a consciousness-expanding peak experience. The goal is self-understanding, rejuvenation, enhancement of self-esteem through a sense of greater relatedness to persons or to the cosmos, and hope for a path to some type of ultimate truth. Image formation is usually not directed in this technique, however, an effort is made to insure that the setting is warm, supportive, and nonhostile. This technique is sometimes used as experiential therapy in persons who are locked into self-destructive behavior patterns, in the hope that they will discover new meanings and ways of self-acceptance and change. The use of LSD in chronic severe alcoholism is one example. [2,23]

The aim of the *psycholytic technique* is not so much to expand consciousness as to break into repressed and compartmentalized memories and fantasies. [15] The dosage level of the hallucinogen is usually less, a therapist is present, and several sessions with or without the drugs are used. Repressed material often emerges in symbols that depict both the defensive and impulsive sides of a conflict. These symbols often take cosmic and primal forms, supernatural powers may appear to provide guidance, birth and death are imaginatively enacted. Because the train of image formation sometimes produces panicky states of mind, techniques for guiding images are used.

These techniques have been largely abandoned because the drugs are hazardous and results are unreliable. In terms of the psychologic utility of the experiences produced, the individual produces a flood of images containing elements of repressed ideas, feelings, memories, and fantasies, but for the procedure to be fully useful these images should be translated into word meanings. However, this is often impossible in the state of mind produced by the drug. The conflicts and resultant emotions cannot be worked through, new coping styles cannot be developed in the regressive state, and the new material may be rigidly compartmentalized or largely forgotten in subsequent drug-free states.

Directing the Contents of Images

Evocation of Images

Image evocation may be used as a diagnostic exploratory procedure. In such procedures certain themes may be suggested, much as in the visual stimuli provided in projective psychological testing. Themes to be visualized may include important persons, the self in various situations, or associations to certain emotional states. Various theorists have elaborated systems of evocation. Lazarus,[35] for example, has developed what he calls a "deserted island fantasy technique" where this setting is described and free imagery elaboration is solicited. Ahsen[4] has suggested a method for eliciting images about the relationship between oneself and one's parents. Shorr[48,49] provides a diverse repertoire of stimuli to evoke images in patients. To explore core interpersonal attitudes, for example, he may suggest that a patient image "taking a shower with his father." To explore attitudes about work or the future, he may suggest that the patient imagine "building a bridge across a gorge to the other side."

It is more typical of dynamic psychotherapy to suggest themes only when individually required, rather than as a routine technique. For example, suppose the patient has had a dream and does not report many associations. The therapist may ask him to attempt to reexperience the images of the dream and to associate to this experience. Or if the patient is talking abstractly of some dreaded situation, the therapist may ask him to visualize and describe some specific version of it. When the patient is talking of some abstract concept such as "venting aggression" or "being more self-confident," the therapist may ask him to imagine what that might be like. The concreteness of visual images helps to define abstractions and also propel the patient into some clear statement of his current concerns.[7] Similar techniques are used in cognitive-behavioral psychotherapies, as when the patient is asked either to visualize "the worst thing that can happen" in a future dreaded situation (Lazarus calls this a step-up technique) or to imagine successfully coping with a stressful event.[35]

Image Instruction

Ferenczi[17] wrote a paper in 1923 that he called "On Forced Fantasies." Patients who produced few fantasies were "forced" to recover emotional reactions to previous situations when the analyst insisted that they visualize the situations during the analytic hour. At first Ferenczi found his patients only rarely cooperative. In time, however, they became more courageous and fabricated experiences of almost hallucinatory distinctness. These are accompanied by unmistakable signs of anxiety, rage, or erotic excitement.

Although a patient may comply with the therapist's instructions and produce a volley of emotions and images, there may be a certain "transference expense." That is, as a result of complying with an instruction, the patient may expect a reward, feel he is submitting to a sadistic attack, feel humiliated, or try a new defense such as production of excessive material in order to avoid insight. The net effect may be rapid early progress in therapy, with transference complications limiting what can be accomplished in the long run.

Image instruction techniques, such as those to be described in the next section, may have the unspoken effect of encouraging the patient to gain control over image formation. They may motivate the patient to a maximum regulatory effort so that his thinking is less dominated by unbidden images and more occupied by the images suggested by the therapist. By telling the patient what to image, the therapist is also communicating that the patient can gain control of his own image formation and thus be free either to image or not image certain contents.

Beck[7] uses a variety of image formation tasks to gain information, pinpoint vagueness, or release emotion, and to teach patients to control their own thought processes. Some of his patients who complained of free-floating anxiety were having uncontrolled visual images of imminent danger. He found that by clapping his hands, for example, he could dispel the images in their minds. Patients could also learn to do this for themselves. Beck encouraged patients to form their unpleasant and unwanted images over and over again at will so that they would learn to control the image formation process and dispel unwanted images as soon as they formed. Furthermore, Beck found that repetition reduced the unpleasant emotions related to images. The emotions that emerged in the course of image formation were also discussed thoroughly to establish their relationship to other behaviors, attitudes, feelings, and memories.

Gestalt therapists, as one of their techniques, direct a patient to report a dream fragment or a fantasy image. First, the patient is asked to report the image in detail: like free associations, this often adds revealing information. As part of this detailed report, the therapist asks the patient to reexperience the image or dream "here and now." Next the patient is asked to speak or to act as if he were each aspect of the image content, again in the immediate present.[41] For example, if the dream fragment or fantasy was of a man shooting a horse, the patient would be instructed to speak as if he were the man: to say what he feels in that role as he experiences it now. Then he would be successively told to repeat the process while imagining himself to be the gun, the bullet, and the horse. For instance, while "being the bullet" he might speak of himself tearing into flesh. This directive technique forces the patient to speak clearly of the ideas and feelings expressed vaguely in the manifest image.

This type of image technique differs from the psychoanalytic use of free association. Gestalt therapists usually do not interpret: instead they act in such a way as to propel the patient toward clear expression of emotions and thoughts. When defensive maneuvers obstruct this goal, they push through or go around them. In contrast, the major activity of a dynamic therapist is interpretation of the defense, the threat, the warded-off contents, and their transactional significance.

Directed Imagery Techniques

In the directed daydream technique the therapist encourages a flow of images (as in the therapies suggested by Ferenczi, Jung, Kubie, and Sacerdote) and then suggests content material. As a story line is reported by the patient, the therapist suggests various maneuvers that the patient may use to change the image contents.

Hammer[21] and Gerard[18] further developed the guided daydream techniques of Jung,[28] Leuner,[36,37] Desoille,[16] and Assagioli.[5,6] Leuner bases an entire system of psychotherapy on what he calls GAI, for guided affective imagery (see also Kosbab[31] and Singer[50]). The patient reclines or sits comfortably, and relaxes his body. Deep breathing is used to deepen the relaxation and may also achieve an altered state of consciousness that increases the vividness and reduces the control over image formation.

Once the patient is suitably relaxed, the therapist suggests open-ended imaginary situations or symbolic themes. The patient fills in the details and continues the daydream, reporting his images as he goes along. Thus, the therapist may begin by suggesting that the patient visualize a door and step through it, or imagine himself in some setting such as a meadow, mountains, cave, forest, or bottom of the sea. The patient then describes what he encounters in his fantasy.

Most patients are afraid of some inner image, frightening memory, or external possibility. The "bad" parts of the self and "bad" parent images are often externalized and disguised. Thus, it is not surprising in the daydream during therapy that the patient imagines himself encountering something frightening such as a monster. Hammer[21] and Leuner[37] suggest five or six basic ways of guiding and managing the course of the ongoing "symbol-dramatic" events. The therapist may guide the patient with instructions to confront the symbol—to feed the monster, for example— or to reach a reconciliation with the symbol. The therapist may add ingredients to the imagery such as suggesting that the patient use magical fluids or engage the symbol so that exhaustion and killing take place. For example, a person may imagine himself confronting a huge snake. The therapist may say, "Try offering him a piece of candy," and the patient complies and subdues the snake through friendship. Leuner couples this technique with the more customary psychoanalytic methods of exploration and interpretation. He may ask patients to produce associations to their images or use guided imagery only at moments of resistance.

Hammer notes the danger of these techniques in the hands of inexperienced psychotherapists. He says that confrontation with monsters or symbols is a technique that may produce strong emotional outbursts, as when the train of images leads to episodes of death or violence. Leuner avoids using this technique in the treatment of very disturbed patients. In contrast, Biddle has described using such techniques not only individually with psychotic patients, but with large groups of such patients,[8,9] although systematic empirical research on positive and negative effects has not been reported.

As mentioned before, Ahsen[4] has developed an elaborate three-step system for directing images related to the patient's parents. First the patient experiences symptoms and is asked to form images related to the time of symptom onset. Age regression techniques from hypnosis may be used to bring the patient in imagination back to a time before the onset of the symptom. In the second step, themes that have emerged are elaborated with introduction of the suggestion that parents and other important early figures be included in the pictorializations. Finally, the therapist designs therapeutic images that the patient repeatedly forms in order to complete or correct the noxious images or fantasies connected with the need to form symptoms.

This type of guidance of image formation was sometimes used by "trip guides" in counseling persons during a drug-induced hallucinatory state. For example, a person on a "bad trip" may hallucinate that he is about to jump from a frightening height. On hearing such an image described, the trip guide may suggest that the person try flying safely. The feelings of intense fear may then change, with the permission and suggestion of the guide, to the ecstasy of flight.

Gerard[18] gives an example of how directed daydreaming may transform emotional states. A married woman in his care was frustrated and angry because her husband did not express warm feelings toward her. As she thought about divorcing him, she pictured a wooden heart. The therapist suggested that she imagine a door in the heart, open it, and report what she found on the other side. There she saw a wasteland of snow and ice, and a man bundled in a heavy overcoat which concealed his face. The therapist told her to dig into the ice and see what was underneath. She did so in fantasy and reported that she found green grass underneath the ice. Then, to her amazement, the ice receded, she found herself in a green meadow, and the man's face became that of her husband. Despite the warm sunshine, he seemed unable to remove his overcoat. The therapist encouraged the patient to help her husband. As she helped him take off the overcoat, he responded warmly. They embraced and decided to build a home on the spot. In the following session, the patient reported experiencing warm feelings toward her husband, who was responding in kind.

The therapist used the directed daydream technique to deliver a suggestion: Why not try harder to get through to your cold husband in a warm, positive way? Perhaps the image formation allowed the patient to rehearse the suggested change before actually implementing it. Many forms of image therapy are veiled modes of offering suggestions to patients.

Lazarus[34] reports a similar technique for transforming emotion in depressed patients. In one of his examples, a female patient was acutely depressed after being rejected by her boyfriend. Lazarus hypnotized the patient and suggested that she project herself into the future and imagine specific details about what she might be doing days and weeks later. Then he suggested images months into the future. At that point, he asked her to reflect back from her imagined future existence onto the "previous" (actually the current) incident. After arousal from the hypnotic state, she reported that she realized she was overreacting and that there were other things to do with herself. This treatment, according to Lazarus, completely overcame her depression. Lazarus concluded that "contemplation of future positive reinforcements may diminish depressive responses." Singer and Switzer[51] have suggested other methods of encouraging positive imagery to alter negative mood states.

Behavior Therapy

Systematic desensitization is one of the major techniques used by behavior therapists.[42] The procedure begins with a discussion of the patient's problems, and then the patient is taught to relax. When fully relaxed, the patient is told to imagine times from a hierarchy ranging from a very mild version of the phobic object or situation, for example, to extreme versions. Gradual steps are used so that the patient progressively learns to remain calm. Whenever anxiety is elicited, the therapist instructs the patient to stop the image formation, relaxation is deepened, and the same image is offered again. According to Wolpe's theory, the super-imposition of relaxation on the conditioned anxious response dissipates the anxiety by reciprocal inhibition.[5] As anxiety in response to the milder images on the hierarchy diminishes, more frightening images are suggested until the patient can tolerate, remaining relaxed, vivid visualizations of what he previously found anxiety provoking. For example, a patient with a cat phobia might first be asked to visualize a cat several hundred yards away. After suggesting this image, the therapist might remain silent, observing the patient's nonverbal responses. If the patient remained relaxed, the therapist might then suggest visualization of holding a toy cat. Eventually he would lead up to an image of fondling a real cat. Theoretically, and as some experiments demonstrate, there is a carry-over from image formation to reduction of anxiety on encountering the object in reality. Successful use of this technique, even in the treatment of LSD-induced flashbacks and a continued "bad trip," has been reported.[40]

What happens during the period of suggested image formation? Weitzman[54] asked patients this question after sessions of systematic desensitization. He found their thoughts were not restricted to the image given by the therapist, but that during the period of silence other images and associations occurred which digressed in content from the initial suggestion. Weitzman's findings suggest that the method of suggestion of usually anxiety-provoking images in a relaxed state may encourage the patient to review his problems conceptually, as in dynamic psycho-therapies. Brown[11] has observed Wolpe conducting systematic desensitization therapy, and he underscores the role of conceptual exploration as the patient describes and discusses his experiences with the therapist.

These observations suggest that desensitization procedures may involve a thinking through of emotionally threatening topics. The patient might have avoided conceptualization on his own because thinking about his problems was too unpleasant. With instruction, encouragement, and support from the therapist, however, the patient can begin to experience avoided ideas and emotions and feel more in control. This technique teaches the patient that he can start or stop images that previously were experienced as stemming from a lapse of control. He has these images when the therapist instructs him to have them, and presumably stops them when the therapist says to do so. The patient learns, under the protective umbrella of the relationship with the therapist, that he can contemplate forbidden or unpleasant topics.

Image formation can also be guided to contents that model or rehearse desirable but unfamiliar behaviors. An example of this process in behavior therapy is described by Cautela.[13] Sexually inhibited or homosexual patients may be encouraged to picture vividly, and with pleasure, particular courtship scenes such as kissing an attractive partner of the opposite sex.

Images can generate emotions, and these emotions can change conditioned responsivity. Kolvin[30] uses this principle in a form of *aversive training* in adolescent behavior disorders in which the patients are poorly communicative or intellectually dull. The therapist first discovers from the patient which images are most unpleasant to contemplate. Then the patient is instructed to conjure up such images in association with ideas the therapist wishes to render nonpleasurable. If the patient has a sexual perversion, he is instructed to visualize images related to the perversion while lying in a relaxed state with his eyes closed. When the therapist notes that the patient is becoming erotically aroused, he interrupts the fantasy with a suggestion to form the unpleasant image. For example, Kolvin reports a patient who assaulted women by suddenly slipping his hand up under their skirts. First the patient was told to picture a woman in a skirt. When the patient seemed to be aroused, he was suddenly told to visualize an unpleasant falling experience that he had previously revealed to be frightening. The juxtaposition of the unpleasant affect with the sexually arousing affect was believed to account for a reduction in the patient's perversion. Cautela and Wisocki[14] report the directive use of similar noxious images for adult patients.

Marks and Gelder[39] took this aversive imagery technique even further. Male patients with transvestism or fetishism were given electrical shocks as they imagined carrying out their deviant behavior. The authors report that the deviant images became indistinct and transient, lost their pleasurable quality, and ceased to be accompanied by penile erections.

Implosive or Flooding Therapy

Stampfl and Lewis[52] have advanced an implosive method of psychotherapy that is similar to behavior therapy in its reliance on learning theory, but which uses a different technique of instructed image formation related to what has recently been called *flooding* in behavior therapy. Instead of inducing a state of relaxation in the patient, the therapist uses images to create a situation of intense anxiety, hoping to implode symptom formation.

In brief, their theory holds that in phobias a painful experience has caused an association between certain ideas and feelings of anxiety. This conditioned association of anxiety to certain objects or situations does not yield to reality testing because the memory of the original painful experience has been repressed. The person has overgeneralized the painful experience, and current stimuli subliminally activate the anxiety without recall of the original events.

Stampfl and Lewis reason that bringing the traumatic events into consciousness may allow extinction of the conditioned anxiety when this anxiety is not reinforced by the contemporary experience. Thus, the goal of his therapy is reinstatement or symbolic reproduction of the cues to which the anxiety is conditioned. This reproduction is achieved by suggesting the anxiety-provoking images to the patient. As the patient experiences the images, he becomes very anxious, but the situation is not really anxiety provoking because no ill befalls the patient, the relationship is supportive, and the activity is fantasized rather than real. Thus, Stampfl and Lewis assert, the anxious response gradually diminishes or implodes.

Implosive therapy begins with diagnostic interviews during which the therapist forms an idea of what cues are avoided or anxiety provoking. In later sessions, the therapist tells the patient to image these cues as vividly as possible and adds his own lurid details to maximize the patient's anxiety. The therapist tries throughout the session to guess what the patient is avoiding and then direct him to imagine it. For example, the therapist may tell a person with rat phobia to image a rat touching him, running across his hand, biting him on the arm, piercing him viciously, devouring his eyes, and jumping down his mouth to destroy internal organs.[24] In accordance with their view of psychodynamics, Stampfl and

Lewis state that in a typical therapy they will touch upon most of the following categories of images: aggression, punishment, oral material (eating, biting, spitting, cannibalism, sucking), anal material, sexual material, rejection, bodily injury, loss of control, acceptance of conscience (scenes of confessing, being guilty, courtrooms, addressing God after death), and physical sensations.

Implosive therapy forcibly undermines the patient's defenses of conceptual avoidance: the patient visualizes vividly all that he has wished to avoid thinking about. Perhaps the experience is less anxiety provoking than the patient has feared, and perhaps it is less anxiety provoking to think the unthinkable in the presence of an authority figure who orders you to do it.

Discussion of Directive Image Techniques

The techniques just discussed share the common element of direction to visualize specific contents or themes. The rationale for these suggestions is provided by a theory of symptom formation and of symptom modification. At the present time, however, there has been insufficient research to indicate the comparative efficacy and/or safety of these techniques.

Singer[50] has reviewed the use of guided image formation in behavioral therapies in terms of how they may help in cognitive reorientation. He has suggested that the following change mechanisms may be facilitated by directive image formation approaches:

1. The patient can discriminate his ongoing fantasy processes more cleary.
2. He receives clues from the therapist to alternative ways of approaching situations.
3. He becomes aware of situations that he has avoided.
4. He is encouraged in a variety of fashions to engage in rehearsal of alternatives.
5. He is ultimately less afraid to approach these situations.

In following the instructions of the respected healer or authority figure, the patient thinks, in the form of images, of ideas and feelings that he previously prohibited himself from experiencing. The prohibition may have arisen by the internalization of real or imagined parental or social attitudes. Now a new powerful figure changes the censorship. Instead of being told not to think of sex or aggression, for example, the person is being told to think vividly of every aspect of sex and aggression. Instead of being forbidden to fantasize, the patient is instructed to fantasize with as much vividness as he can muster.

These procedures not only decondition the patient, they also highlight his current internal and external sources of stress and perhaps allow him to make new decisions about dilemmas and conflicts. By learning to turn his imagination on and off, the patient learns to clearly demarcate reality and fantasy. The relationship with the therapist bolsters his defense and self-esteem. Under this protective umbrella, he is encouraged to work through his conflicts and anxieties, even if these are not overtly labeled in the therapeutic transactions.

In the relationship with the therapist, the patient must also consider his image productions in a communicative network; he has to ask himself what another person thinks about his images. He wonders if the ideas expressed sound realistic or fantastic to the therapist, and if the therapist likes him better or less for having the images. Thus, the patient's internal image of the therapist begins to influence the patient's conceptual processes. The idealized image of the therapist, through identification, contributes to the patient's values. If mother said, "Don't ever think dirty thoughts," and the therapist says, "Think anything and tell me everything you think," the therapist's influence changes the dynamics of the patient by causing a shift in both the role-relationship models organizing his current state of mind and his enduring attitudes about what may be thought and communicated.

When the therapist intervenes to direct the sequence and contents of the patient's image formation, he is usually aiming toward revising habitual image sequences. The goal is often to reverse the emotional coloration of the patient's problematic state of mind. A good example is provided by Lazarus, a behaviorist who has expanded his orientation to develop a multimodal approach to formulating cases and conducting psychotherapy.[35]

Lazarus described his approach to a 32-year-old woman diagnosed as alcoholic. He broke down her problems into categories, according to preestablished classifications: behavior, affect, sensation imagery, cognition, interpersonal relationships, and biological conditions[35] (pp 211–212, 358). The patient's behavior and affect problems included excessive drinking when alone at home at night, avoiding confrontation with most people, speaking badly of herself to others, a repeated tic of her right shoulder, and screaming at her children. Lazarus' classification of sensation imagery is similar to enactive thinking as described in this book. The patient's problems in this category were troublesome physical sensations. Lazarus planned abdominal breathing exercises as a technique to reverse his patient's "butterflies in the stomach" and relaxation of her neck muscles for her complaint of pressure sensations at the back of her head. His classification of cognition is close to what I have called lexical representation. In this category the patient's problems involved irrational monologues about her worthlessness and numerous regrets. For these issues the proposed treatment interventions were, respectively, substituting rational for irrational ideas and elimination of categorical imperatives (by which Lazarus means removing enduring ideas about what one should, must, or ought to do).

These plans in the enactive and lexical modes are mentioned to illustrate the tactic taken by Lazarus of countering a problem with its opposite. The imagery aspect of his tactics in psychotherapy can now be considered in more detail.

Three imagery-related problems were listed by Lazarus for this case. The patient described vivid and presumably unbidden images of her parents fighting, of beatings by her father, and of being locked in a bedroom when she was a child. For each of these themes Lazarus proposed a directed imagery approach that used the principle of opposition.

For the pictures of her parents fighting, desensitization was used. That is, Lazarus had the patient visualize this theme in a graduated way during a session with him, as he attempted to help her remain in a relaxed rather than anxious state of mind. For the imagery about being beaten by her father, he guided her imagery toward retaliation, with the patient as aggressor. And for the theme of being locked in the bedroom, presumably with the patient experiencing anxiety verging on panic, he encouraged images of escape and of release of anger.

Discussion of this example from another theoretical orientation will close this chapter and the book. Some points made throughout this text also will be summarized in this way. As a psychodynamically oriented theorist and clinician, I tend to intervene with interpretations about image contents, while Lazarus uses more directive interventions. Lazarus might criticize my approach. This patient had a particular personality style, and directive approaches presumably were particularly suited to her mode of changing; interpretive approaches might have failed. I use the case only as a foil to illustrate another point of view.

There are areas of consensus. Both Lazarus and I would pay attention to multiple interactive ingredients of psychotherapeutic technique. We are in agreement that the kinds of shift in self-concept suggested by Lazarus' techniques might help the patient. Our major possible difference is in our views of the effect of the proposed interventions, especially in terms of their influence upon the relationship between therapist and patient.

/ The patient has recurrent intrusive images of her father beating her and locking her in the bedroom. I shall make some inferences based on the material Lazarus provided in this example, in the form of an answer to this question: If this were the current condition of the patient, how would directive imagery of the type suggested help or hinder working through her problems? My inference, closely linked to the material given, is that the woman has a vulnerable self-concept, leading to state of panic that she eases or avoids with alcohol.

What does Lazarus aim to do? It seems that he wants to alter her proclivity to this state of mind by shifting her weak and vulnerable self-concept in the direction of more activity, assertiveness, and strength. That is why he suggests an opposite kind of mental imagery, in which she imagines retaliating against her father, or being angry rather than terrified about being locked in a room. In other words, in order even to imagine retaliation or expression of anger, her representations have to be organized by a less helpless, more powerful self-concept.

From a psychodynamic perspective, one might formulate such a case in terms of various self-concepts that organized differing states of mind. For example, she might have not only a helpless, vulnerable self-concept in relation to a hostile attacker, but also one in which the roles are reversed. That is, in addition to having states of painful anxiety or panic, she may also have states in which she is enraged, perhaps seeing herself as unable to control hostile impulses. She may have problems both with a victim role and with the reciprocal aggressor role. The fear of loss of control over hostility, and of guilt over wishes to harm, may also cause anxiety. If this were so, directions to form retaliatory images might reduce fearfully vulnerable feelings, but also evoke fear and guilt over anger.

To this psychodynamic perspective on case formulation, let us add the assumption of dilemmas and complementarity. That is, the material presented by the patient is observed for opposites that may also be part of the patient's personality. If the patient is troubled by inferior self-concepts, she may also be troubled by grandiose ones. Telling her to imagine herself as strong may help her shift from an incompetent to a more competent self-concept. It may also help her shift to a grandiose self-concept, reinforce a therapeutic alliance, or fuel a transference reaction in which the therapist is regarded as admiring or himself idealized. If and when this sustainment of self-esteem fails, the patient may have a negative transference reaction in which the therapist is blamed for not doing enough.

The directive imagery approach may accomplish a shift in mood by redirecting self-concepts, in this instance from weak and passive to stronger and more assertive. It does so, however, in a complicated matrix.

Simply having the patient reverse the problematic self-concept may usefully teach increments in self-control but also invite a shift to other related, complementary problem constellations.

Let us suppose that Lazarus' case unfolded in the manner just indicated. It might turn out on exploration that the patient had problematic states of mind, colored by intense anxiety and followed by depression, and based on self-concepts of being misused and hated by her father. It might turn out that she was also vulnerable to and warding off states of mind of explosive rage in which she hated and wanted to harm her father. The oppositional technique of directing retaliatory images might either arouse this hate and guilt or make the patient resort to even more primitive defenses to avoid it and associated anxious guilt.

Once both the fear and rage states of mind and the relevant self-concepts, aims, and object concepts were clear, the therapist might encourage the patient to soften her extreme feelings of fear and rage. This might take the form of new imagery to the extent that the therapist would encourage a more realistic view of the patient's childhood memories or fantasies, especially as they colored her adult interpersonal relationships.

CONCLUSION

Image formation is one kind of thinking, a mode that is close to emotion. A psychotherapist listens for image experiences, but any exclusive focus on image formation is an unbalanced approach. Image techniques should be related to a larger, well-formulated plan for how a patient may change. This should include attention to how the therapist's intervention influences the patient's immediate train of thought and views of the relationship with the therapist.

REFERENCES

1. Aaronson B, Osmond H: Psychedelics. New York, Doubleday, 1970
2. Abramson HA (ed): International Conference on the Use of LSD in Psychotherapy and Alcoholism. Indianapolis, Bobbs-Merrill, 1967
3. Adler G: Methods of treatment in analytical psychology. In Wolman BB (ed): Psychoanalytic Techniques. New York, Basic, 1967
4. Ahsen A: Eidetic Parents Test and Analysis. New York, Brandon, 1972
5. Assagioli R: Dynamic Psychology and Psychosynthesis. New York, Psychosynthesis Research Found, 1959

6. ———: Psychosynthesis: A Manual of Principles and Techniques. New York, Hobbs and Dorman, 1965
7. Beck AT: Role of fantasies in psychotherapy and psychopathology. J Nerv Ment Dis 150:3, 1970
8. Biddle WE: Image therapy. Amer J Psychiat 126:408, 1969
9. ———: Images. Arch Gen Psychiat 9:464, 1963
10. Breuer J, Freud S: Studies on Hysteria. Stand Ed 2, 1955
11. Brown BM: Cognitive aspects of Wolpe's behavior therapy. Amer J Psychother 124:854, 1969
12. Buckman J: Theoretical aspects of LSD therapy. In Abramson HA (ed): International Conference on the Use of LSD in Psychotherapy and Alcoholism. Indianapolis, Bobbs-Merrill, 1967
13. Cautela JR: Reinforcement survey schedule. Psychol Rep 30:683, 1972
14. ———, Wisocki PA: Covert sensitization for the treatment of sexual deviations. Psychol Rec 21:37, 1971
15. Crocket R, Sandison RA, Walk A (eds): Hallucinogenic drugs and their psychotherapeutic use. In Proceedings of the Royal Medico-Psychological Association. London, Lewis, 1963
16. Desoille R: Exploration de l'affectivité subconsciente par la méthode du Reve Eveillé. Paris, D'Autry, 1938
17. Ferenczi S: Further Contributions to the Theory and Technique of Psychoanalysis. London, Hogarth, 1950
18. Gerard R: Symbolic visualization. A method of psychosynthesis. Top Probl Psychother 4:70, 1963
19. Glover E (ed): The Technique of Psychoanalysis. New York, International Univ Press, 1955
20. Greenson R: Empathy and its vicissitudes. Int J Psychoanal 41:418, 1960
21. Hammer M: The directed daydream technique. Psychother Theory Res Prac 4:173, 1967
22. Hobson RF: Imagination and amplification in psychotherapy. J Anal Psychol 16(1):79–105, 1971
23. Hoffer A, Osmond H: The Hallucinogens. New York: Academic Press, 1967
24. Hogan R, Kirchner J: Preliminary report of the extinction of learned fears via short-term implosive therapy. J Abnorm Psychol 72:106, 1967
25. Horowitz MJ: Stress Response Syndromes. New York, Aronson, 1976
26. ———: States of Mind. New York, Plenum, 1979
27. Jacobson E: Progressive Relaxation. Chicago, Univ Chicago Press, 1942
28. Jung CG: The Archetypes and the Collective Unconscious. New York, Pantheon, 1959
29. Knapp PH: Image, symbol, and person. Arch Gen Psychiat 21:392, 1969
30. Kolvin I: Aversive imagery treatment in adolescents. Behav Res Ther 5:245, 1967
31. Kosbab F: Imagery techniques in psychiatry. Arch Gen Psychiat 31:283, 1974
32. Kubie LS: The use of induced hypnagogic reveries in the recovery of repressed amnesic data. Bull Menninger Clin 7:172, 1943

33. Langs R: The Bipersonal Field. New York, Aronson, 1976
34. Lazarus A: Learning theory and the treatment of depression. Behav Res Ther 6:83, 1968
35. ——: The Practice of Multimodal Therapy. New York, McGraw-Hill, 1981
36. Leuner H: The present state of psycholytic therapy and its possibilities. In Abramson HA (ed): International Conference on the Use of LSD in Psychotherapy and Alcoholism. Indianapolis, Bobbs-Merrill, 1967
37. ——: Guided affective imagery (GAI). A method of intensive psychotherapy. Amer J Psychother 34:4, 1969
38. Lewin BD: The Image and the Past. New York, International Univ Press, 1968
39. Marks I, Gelder MG: Transvestism and fetishism: clinical and psychological changes during faradic aversion. Brit J Psychiat 113:711, 1967
40. Matefy RE: Behavior therapy to extinguish spontaneous recurrences of LSD effects. J Nerv Ment Dis 156:226, 1973
41. Perls FS: Dream seminars. In Fagan J, Sheperd IL (eds): Gestalt Therapy Now. Palo Alto, Calif, Science & Behavior, 1970
42. Rachman S: Systematic desensitization. Psychol Bull 67:93, 1967
43. Reyher J: Free imagery: an uncovering procedure. J Clin Psychol 19:454, 1963
44. ——: Self esteem and repression: two sources of anxiety in relation to psychopathology and the representation of meaning. In Freedman N (ed): Communicative Structures and Psychic Structures. New York, Plenum, 1976
45. Ross WD, Knapp FT: A technique for self analysis of counter transference. J Amer Psychoanal Assoc 10:643, 1962
46. Sacerdote P: Induced dreams. Amer J Clin Hypn 10:167, 1968
47. ——: Induced Dreams. New York, Vantage, 1967
48. Shorr JE: Psychotherapy through Imagery. New York, Intercontinental, 1974
49. ——: The use of task imagery as therapy. Psychother Theory Res Prac 12:207, 1975
50. Singer JL: Imagery and Daydreams: Methods in Psychotherapy and Behavior Modification. New York, Academic Press, 1974
51. ——, JL Switzer E: Mind Play. Englewood Cliffs, NJ, Prentice-Hall, 1980
52. Stampfl TG, Lewis DJ: Essentials of implosive therapy: a learning theory based on psychodynamic behavioral therapy. J Abnorm Psychol 72:496, 1967
53. Strosahl KD: Clinical Uses of Imagery: Experimental Foundations, Theoretical Misconceptions, and Research Issues. Psych Bull 89:422, 1981
54. Weitzman B: Behavior therapy and psychotherapy. Psychol Rev 72:300, 1967
55. Wolpe J: Psychotherapy by Reciprocal Inhibiton. Palo Alto, Calif, Stanford Univ Press, 1958

NAME INDEX

309

SUBJECT INDEX